T0108346

The House of the LORD

A Study of the Temple Scroll
Columns 29:3b–47:18

Publications of the Finnish Exegetical Society
Series Editor Antti Marjanen
Edited by Kirsi Valkama

Cover photograph by Kirsi Valkama

ISSN 0356-2786
ISBN 978-951-9217-48-2
ISBN 978-3-525-53989-7

Vammalan Kirjapaino Oy 2007

PUBLICATIONS OF THE FINNISH EXEGETICAL SOCITEY 93

The House of the LORD

A Study of the Temple Scroll Columns 29:3b–47:18

Magnus Riska

Finnish Exegetical Society, Helsinki
Vandenhoeck & Ruprecht, Göttingen
2007

Contents

3. Text and Translation of Columns 29:3b-47:18

4. A Comparison between the Scroll and Biblical Traditions

5. The Courtyards

6. The Results of the Study

Preface

It has been more than five years since I wrote the preface to my doctoral dissertation on Cols. 2–13:9 of the Temple Scroll. In this present study I have analysed Cols. 29:3b–47:18 which is the second large section of 11QT. Both sections relate to the temple and its furnishings.

Actually I did not plan to continue my involvement with this Scroll, but it seemed to be the right thing to do in response to a new opportunity to live in Israel. In August 2003 my family and I once more found ourselves in Jerusalem. This stay, however, was very different from our former one. After two months my wife Gunlög was diagnosed with cancer that was treated with surgery. After a brave fight she passed away on October 31st in 2004. May she rest in peace.

By God's grace I was able to finish this monograph in Finland. I am grateful to Professor Raija Sollamo, who supervised my research. Her feedback and supportive attitude have been of much assistance. I am also indebted for the comments and suggestions from the young Dead Sea Scrolls researchers at University of Helsinki.

From my time in Israel, I would firstly like to thank my friend Professor Elisha Qimron for his encouragement, which meant a lot to me. Especially as he is the world expert on the Temple Scroll, I have valued his advice highly. I am also very thankful to Professor Qimron for the loan of his high quality transparencies.

In this context I want to thank Miriam Berg, who at the beginning helped me to indicate the damaged Hebrew letters of the Scroll.

I would like to express my sincere gratitude towards the Finnish Exegetical Society for publishing this book and to the chairman of the Society, Professor Antti Marjanen, for insightful comments to improve the manuscript. Likewise, I am thankful to MSc Richard Croft for revising the English of my manuscript. All the remaining mistakes are due to my own negligence.

I am also very grateful to FLOM, my present employer, who has been a firm pillar of support. Furthermore, my thoughts go out to all those who have supported us and stood by our side during the process of finishing this work in the aftermath of the loss of my wife. During this period my parents Tor-Björn and Astrid were very important to me, as well as my new wife Gunilla, and my children Michelle, David and Daniel. They have indeed been a blessing and a reason for me to go on.

Helsinki, in June 2007

Magnus Riska

CHAPTER ONE

Introduction

1.1. The Present Study

In my first study of the Temple Scroll[1] I commented upon results – which were based on a limited amount of evidence – and made the final observation, that my conclusions were only valid for Cols. 2–13:9. The rest of the Scroll was left as a challenge for the future. This present study continues with this second section of 11QT: Cols. 29:3b–47:18. This section deals with the construction of the temple[2] and its furnishings. Between these two large sections, the Scroll deals with commands concerning various sacrifices and feasts (Cols. 14–28). From Col. 48 onwards the text is concerned with e.g. purity rules.

1.2. The Aims for the Study

As is well known, 11QT includes a lot of quotations from the Hebrew Bible, especially from the Torah.[3] The aims for this study will partly be the same as in my doctoral thesis. Thus we will try to reconstruct as much as possible of the biblical text that was quoted in 11QT.[4] This will be done by comparing the Temple Scroll to other textual witnesses. One of our aims is – if possible – to reconstruct parts of a biblical text-tradition in an earlier stage of development than 𝔐. Then, finally, to compare the results with the results of the analysis from the first study.

The method for the purpose of distinguishing between primary and secondary readings, is thoroughly presented in my doctoral thesis and

[1] Riska, 2001. *The Temple Scroll and the Biblical Text Traditions. A Study of Cols. 2-13:9*. Helsinki: Finnish Exegetical Society.

[2] The temple is also mentioned in other scrolls, e.g. in 1QpHab and in CD. In some of the cases when מקדש or עיר המקדש is mentioned, the issue is purity: i.e. the compound would be defiled if the law is not kept.

[3] In this study the word "Bible" is used in a broad sense, as several text-traditions were extant during the time BCE.

[4] I will use the term "author" or "writer" for the person behind 11QT.

will therefore appear here only in a footnote only.[5] Since one of the aims is to reveal the biblical texts that the author was using, we will from the outset be interested in quotations from the Bible.

Firstly, it is clear that there are citations in the Temple Scroll. Secondly, it is important to note that there are no introductory formulas for quotations for these citations, e.g. כאשר כתוב in the Damascus Document. The definition of a citation in this study is: 1) The general biblical connection is established. 2) The literal quotation in 11QT is used in the same context as in the Bible.[6] The length of the quotation is not of primary importance, even if it may sometimes be only a single word. This is possible in cases where the reconstruction is almost certain.

In addition to the quotations we will, furthermore, classify the textual material and make some observations in terms of the following groups: Biblical Paraphrase, Rewritten Bible, and Individual Composition. The analysis of all these four groups will continue in chapter four. The definition for a paraphrase in this study is the following: 1) The author keeps the original elements from the biblical text but reorganizes them.[7] 2) No new ideas are introduced. 3) The context needs to be the same as in the biblical text. In contrast with this, the definition for Re-

[5] One way to reconstruct an earlier stage of a possible text is to distinguish between the primary and secondary readings. A primary reading is understood as the original reading or as the more original reading of the readings we know from different textual sources. A secondary reading could either be a later reading than another it is compared to, it could be a less original reading, or even a less correct reading. Moreover, there may be times where the secondary reading seems to be "more correct" from the point of view of the reader. If that is the case, there is reason to believe that the secondary reading has been created from e.g. grammatical or contextual viewpoints. The method used in this study for differentiating those readings is based on the text-critical analysis in chapter two and will be presented in the beginning of chapter four.

[6] The context will be considered the same when the textual material about e.g. the lampstand in 11QT is compared to a biblical text from Exodus concerning the lampstand. In fact, the context for 11QT is the temple whereas the biblical background is related with the tabernacle. There are several cases, which will be defined as a Biblical Paraphrase. In these situations we note that the context of a paraphrase needs to be the same – or at least very close to – the Bible. Otherwise it would be strange to speak of a Biblical Paraphrase.

[7] When we suggest that an element or an idea is transferred from the Bible into the Scroll, this does not imply that the word that is used in the Scroll has to be literally the same as in the Bible. For example, a synonym may be used in the Scroll compared with a term in the biblical source. Since we are strict concerning a citation, we cannot therefore interpret this as a quotation, but as Biblical Paraphrase.

written Bible is: 1) New elements and 2) additional reasoning, which does not exist in the source text, is brought into it. 3) Quotations, which do not have the same context as the biblical text.[8] Lastly, the definition for Individual Composition is: the textual material is new with no obvious relation to the biblical text traditions.

1.3. The Methodology for the Text-critical Analysis

As the subject is to compare the Temple Scroll with the biblical text traditions, the use of different textual witnesses – mostly 𝔐, 𝔊 and ⅏[9] – will be extensive. Columns 29–47 are systematically analysed and the following aspects will be included:

1) A transcription of a line is presented. Yadin's suggestion is the one that I have initially displayed, because it has the most extensive commentary.
2) In the analysis the reconstructions of 11Q19 and 11Q20 by different scholars will be evaluated.
3) If a certain restoration cannot be accepted, another reconstruction that is based on the text-critical analysis will be suggested.
4) The biblical influence on the Temple Scroll has been established many years now. Therefore, there is nothing new about the biblical verses relating to 11QT. However, the relationship to the different biblical witnesses will be established, namely whether the Temple Scroll seems to stand closer to e.g. 𝔐 or 𝔊.

The possible differences between 𝔐 and the biblical texts from Qumran will also be recorded if there is enough textual material to enable a

[8] This is different from the study on Cols. 2-13:9: it is more logical to classify a reading as paraphrase if the context is the same as in the biblical text. Consequently, if the context is not the same concerning a quotation, the closest logical definition is understood as Rewritten Bible and not as Biblical Paraphrase.

[9] Comparison and comments concerning the Samaritan Pentateuch are based on the unvocalised text of ⅏. Readings in 𝔐 and ⅏ will be interpreted as identical even if one reading contains a *mater lectionis*-letter and the other does not, e.g. כול and כל. Concerning the comparative material, rabbinical literature is usually not referred to since the focal point in this study is directed towards the relation between the Temple Scroll and the biblical texts.

comparison. If there is no reference to a biblical Qumran-text, it means that the corresponding passage is not yet found in Qumran or that it is too short in order to help us towards a meaningful analysis.

A review of the reconstructions will be presented at the end of every subchapter of chapter two.[10] After each review there are notes on alternative readings. In this context I will not mention the scholars, with whom I agree in the summary.[11] In chapter three, we will have a summary of all the reconstructions followed by a translation.

1.4. Textual Editions in the Study

Since this study to a large extent pursues answers to text-critical questions, we will only deal with different textual editions in this section. There are three critical editions that incorporate 11Q19 as a whole: Yigael Yadin's *editio princeps*, which contains the plates (1977 vol. 3) and the transcriptions with reconstructions (1983 vol. 2). In addition, other scholars have also suggested several new readings. At present, the best critical edition is Elisha Qimron's (1996). In 1998 Florentino García Martínez and Eibert J.C. Tigchelaar published the helpful *Dead Sea Scrolls Study Edition*, which will also be employed in the present study.

11Q20 will obviously be discussed in this study. Its textual edition, the *editio maior*, is located in DJD XXIII and published by Florentino García Martínez *et alii* in 1998.

Other publications referred to in this study are: Ben Zion Wacholder's article from 1991 in HUCA 62, "The Fragmentary Remains of 11QTorah (Temple Scroll), 11QTorah^{b} and 11QTorah^{c} plus 4QparaTorah Integrated with 11QTorah^{a}"; Sidnie White's thorough study on 4Q365a from 1994, "4QTemple?" in DJD XIII and Wise's revised edition from 1990 of his dissertation, *A Critical Study of the Temple Scroll from Qumran Cave 11.*

---

[10] A summary of these reconstructions is also given before the translation in chapter three.

[11] This means that only scholars that I am in disagreement with are presented at the end of the chapter; otherwise it would be difficult to construct a conclusive picture. Those scholars with whom I am in agreement with are usually mentioned in the text-critical analysis.

1.5. The Manuscripts of the Study

The main body of the Temple Scroll is made up of two MSS, which are designated as 11Q19 and 11Q20. In addition to these texts, we have another MS which is somewhat problematic within this context: this manuscript, 4Q365a, comprises five fragments, of which Frg. 2 seems to have a close connection to the material in Cols. 29:3b–47:18 of 11QT. Lastly, there is 4Q524, which by Puech is claimed to be the oldest manuscript of the Temple Scroll.

1.5.1. 11Q19

The Scroll was in very poor condition when received and is comprised of 19 sheets, copied by two scribes.[12] Today 11 of the sheets have four columns each, while the others have three columns apart from the last sheet which only has one column, i.e. Col. 67.[13] The known length of the Temple Scroll today is 8.148 m and it is the longest scroll known so far.[14] However, as it had apparently included an introductory column, the original length was probably at least 8.75 m.[15] The Temple Scroll is written in Hebrew. Referring to the meticulous palaeographical studies by Avigad[16] and Cross,[17] Yadin notes that the handwritings of Scribes A and B are of Herodian type.

---

[12] Yadin calls them "Scribe A" and "Scribe B." Yadin 1983 vol. 1, 17. In addition to the two sheets, he mentions a fragment, Pl. 36*:2 on Rock. 43.975 in the context of Cols. 19-20. Yadin 1983 vol. 2, 80. This fragment is, however, identified as 11Q20 by García Martínez et al (Frg. 8a). DJD XXIII 1998, 358. Yadin also mentions a second fragment, which he calls Rock. 43.366 (40* 2), and is important concerning his dating of the Scroll. Yadin 1983 vol. 1, 20. This has become problematic as several scholars have expressed uncertainty as to whether this fragment belongs to 11QT at all. Vermes in Schürer 1986, 407; Wise 1990, 52; White 1994, 320.

[13] Yadin 1983 vol. 1, 11. Furthermore, the last column is empty. Yadin counts ten sheets with four columns. This is calculated by assuming that five columns are on the first sheet. The first column, however, has been lost and therefore there are now only four columns on this sheet.

[14] Compare with the Isaiah Scroll, which is 7.34 m. Yadin 1983 vol. 1, 10.

[15] Yadin 1983 vol. 1, 11.

[16] Avigad 1958, 56-87.

[17] Cross 1961, 133-202.

1.5.2. 11Q20

The texts of 11Q19 and 11Q20 are basically identical apart from orthographical variants.[18] 11Q20 comprises 63 fragments, of which 58 are photographed separately in the PAM series. Three fragments are found with the IAA photographs (Frgs. 4b, 7 and 42) while two (10g and 30b) were joined without being photographed.[19] The MS of 11Q20 will be discussed further in the analysis of Cols. 32, 37, 45, 46, and 47.

1.5.3. 11Q21

11Q21 is a possible witness to a third copy of the Temple Scroll. One of the fragments, that is Frg. 3 according to DJD XXIII,[20] is presented at the end of the analysis of Col. 47.

1.5.4. 4Q365a

This MS – found in cave 4 – consists of five fragments, which are written in the same script.[21] The most interesting fragment for this study is 4Q365 Frg. 2. Its identification has been problematic and still is. Yadin considered Frg. 3 together with Frg. 2 to be parts of the Temple Scroll.[22] This view has subsequently been questioned. On the other hand, Wise views both fragments to be part of a "proto-Temple Scroll."[23] The MS of 4Q365a will be discussed further in the analysis of Cols. 38, 41, and 42.

---

[18] Qimron 1996, 4.
[19] DJD XXIII, 357.
[20] DJD XXIII, 413, and plate XLVIII.
[21] White 1994, 319.
[22] Yadin 1977 vol. 3 Supplementary Plates, Pls. 40* 2, 38* 5.
[23] "A close study of fragment 3 points to the presence of interpolations in the present TS, deriving from sources other than D ('Deuteronomy Source') and the Temple Source." Wise 1990, 58.

1.5.5. 4Q524

As with the previous MS, this was also discovered in cave 4. Puech is so convinced that this manuscript belongs to the Temple Scroll that he calls it 4QRouleau de Temple.[24] His argument has a solid basis, because it is possible to find 22 of the 39 fragments to be parallel passages to 11Q19. In the context of this text, there is only one fragment that needs to be considered: this is Frg. 1 which is found on PAM 43.168. The fragment contains only two words partly and will be discussed further in the analysis of Col. 35.

It seems quite clear that 4Q524 have belonged to an old copy of the Temple Scroll. In comparison with the 4QQoh and 4Q504 – both dating to 175–125 BCE – Puech has with the help of palaeography pinpointed 4Q524 close to 4QProphets[a], which is dated to 150–125 BCE. He suggests a plausible dating for 4Q524 to 150–125 BCE which would give 200–150 BCE as a possible compositional date for the Temple Scroll.[25]

1.5.6. Transparencies

In the text-critical analysis some old transparencies[26] of very good quality have been used in order to decide on readings that have been extra ordinary difficult to transcribe.

[24] Puech 1998, 85.
[25] For the dating of the Temple Scroll, see Riska 2001, 26-28, 204.
[26] This material was kindly lent to me by Prof. Elisha Qimron.

CHAPTER TWO

A Text-critical Analysis of Columns 29:3b–47:18

2.1. Column 29

The upper part of this column is very difficult to read as nearly nothing has survived. Yadin defines these lines as 01–012 and reconstructs them with the help of Num 29:24 ff.[1] Qimron restores some words from line 010 onwards.[2] The influence from Num 29 is a reasonable possibility since the context seems to refer to offerings when the letters begin to be discernible, e.g.]ונסכ in line 1 and לעלוׄתׄ in line 3. Consequently Qimron and García Martínez agree with Yadin concerning the connection to the biblical context.

Since this study is limited to the temple, its constructions and its furnishings, the present analysis begins with line 29:3b and continues forward line by line. For the palaeographical evidence we will consult plates 44 and 14*.

(3)] ב֯בית א֯ש֯ר֯ א[שכין]
(4) שמי עליו [ ] עולות [דבר יום] ב֯יומו כׄתורת המשפט הזה
(5) תמיד מאת בני ישראל לבד מנדבותׄמה לכול אשר יקר֯יׄבו
(6) לכול נסכיהמה ו֯לׄכול מתׄנותמה אשר יבׄיאו לי לרצון לה[מה]

The restoration at the end of line 3 is quite certain. Qimron suggests [יום] עולׄתׄ [ויקריבו בו] שמי עליו at the beginning of line 4.[3] He notes, furthermore, that it seems possible to read עולׄתׄ on the original.[4] We agree

---

[1] מנחתם ונסכיהם לפרים לאילם ולכבשים במספרם כמשפט (Num 29:24). Yadin 1983 vol. 2, 125-127. Yadin 1983 vol. 2 is henceforth referred to as Yadin only. "The suggested restoration is not intended to render the missing text literally, and it is not unlikely that in places the word order differed." Yadin, 125.

[2] Qimron 1996, 44; García Martínez *et al* 1998, 1250. Qimron 1996 is henceforth referred to as Qimron only; García Martínez *et al* 1998 is henceforth referred to as García Martínez only.

[3] Qimron, 44.

[4] Qimron 1978a, 141.

with this since plate 14*:1 quite clearly allows for such a reading. Yadin's reconstruction, on the other hand, seems to rely on the end of Lev 23:37, להקריב אשה ליהוה עלה ומנחה זבח ונסכים דבר־יום ביומו. We note, moreover, influence from e.g. 1 Chr 23:31, במספר כמשפט עליהם תמיד לפני יהוה. In the middle of line 5 we see more influence from Lev 23, at the end of verse 38, ומלבד כל־נדבותיכם.[5]

At the beginning of line 6 Qimron transcribes לכול נדריהמה, which has a parallel in Lev 23:38, כל־נדריכם. We note, moreover, that the Scroll changes the biblical text into first person, אשׁר יביאו לי, *pro* third person in e.g. Lev 17:5, והביאום ליהוה. At the end of the same line we have אשׁר יביאו לי לרצון לה[מה], which may be an influence from Ex 28:38, תמיד לרצון להם לפני יהוה.[6] From this we can discern see the author's method of combining different passages of the Bible.[7]

(7) ורציתֿ֯י֯ם֯ ו֯ה֯י֯ו֯ לי לעם ואנוכי אהיה להם לעולם [ו]שכנתי
(8) אתמה לעולם ועד

There is no disagreement concerning the transcription of this passage. We may compare the beginning of line 7 with Ezek 43:27, ורציתי אתכם נאם אדוני יהוה.[8] Concerning the rest of the passage, there is a close parallel in e.g. Ex 29:45, ושכנתי בתוך בני ישראל והייתי להם לאלוהים. We may also compare lines 7–8 with Ezek 37:23, והיו־לי לעם ואני אהיה להם לאלהים, even though the context of this verse is not as close as in the former example.[9] The lines 7–8 are interpreted as Biblical Paraphrase.

(8) ואקדשה [את מ]ק֯דשי בכבודי אשר אשכין
(9) עליו את כבודי עד יום הברכה אשׁר אברא אני את מק֯דשי
(10) להכינו לי כול ה֯ימים כברית אשר כרתי ע֯ם יעק֯וב בבית אל

Yadin notes that the closest biblical parallel to line 8 is Ex 29:43-45, which is in the context of the tabernacle, ונקדש בכבדי.[10] Smr agrees with 𝔐 but 𝔊 has a slightly different reading, καὶ ἁγιασθήσομαι ἐν δόξῃ μου with the verb in future passive first person singular,

---

[5] Yadin, 128.
[6] Yadin, 128.
[7] Yadin, 127.
[8] Yadin, 129.
[9] Exodus 29 refers to sacrifices and Ezekiel 37 relates to deliverance.
[10] Yadin, 129.

translated as “I will be sanctified in my glory.” This is an interesting textual tradition as 11QT has אקדשה, which is cohortative first person singular and could be translated with “I will sanctify.”

There seems to be quite a close relationship here between 11QT and the biblical text-traditions. This is from two points of view: 1. As one looks at 𝔐 and ࠌ, the subject is not mentioned but may easily be imagined. That is אהל־מועד. If the subject is included in the sentence it could look like the following: ונקדש אהל־מועד בכבדי. This is a text which is not very far from what is written in line 8. 2. The second point is the usage of first person singular in both 11QT and 𝔊. We need, however, to conclude that 11QT does not quote the Bible in line 8. On the other hand this passage could be categorised as Rewritten Bible. The writer seems to take in a new element that is not included in the biblical text traditions.[11]

On lines 8–9 we read אשר אשכין (9) עליו את כבודי. The closest biblical text is, as Yadin writes, Ex 24:16, וישכן כבוד־יהוה על־הר סיני.[12]

In the middle of line 9 Yadin reads עד יום הברכה.[13] Qimron disagrees with him and prefers the reading of עד יום הבריה. García Martínez goes with Qimron.[14] According to the computerised Microfiche-edition,[15] in photo SHR 5029 NB, the fourth letter in the word הברכה / הבריה may be a *yod.* The top of this letter seems, however, to be quite broad for a *yod*, which is unusual for this script. On the other hand, the absolute top of the letter seems not to be bent up as a *caph* usually is in this script.

The broadness of the top alone cannot support the reading by Yadin. Additionally, SHR 5029 NB reveals something that cannot be detected on plate 44:[16] there is a clearly distinguishable

---

[11] Yadin also mentions 2 Chr 7:16, which is a text that relates to the temple of Solomon, ועתה בחרתי והקדשתי את־הבית הזה. Yadin, 129. This passage is clearly not as close to 11QT as the text mentioned above.

[12] Yadin, 129. Concerning similar sequences in 11QT, compare with lines 29:3–4, בבית אשר א[שכין] (4) שמי עליו and lines 45: 11-12, לוא יבוא אל כול עיר (12) המקדש אשר אשכין שמי בה.

[13] He compares this passages with e.g. 1QM 2:9, לשלום וברכה כבוד ושמחה ואורך ימים. Yadin, 129.

[14] Qimron writes in a footnote, that Yadin has admitted that Qimron's reading of הבריה is also possible. Qimron, 44; García Martínez, 1250.

[15] Brill’s computer edition of the Dead Sea Scrolls.

[16] Yadin 1977a, plate 44.

line[17] that begins at the lower end of this letter and continues to the left moving slightly downwards. If one compares with the *caph* in כברית in line 10 this lower line is very similar to both letters.

These palaeographical comments do not really help us to determine the most probable reading. Before arriving to a conclusion, we have to consider the comparison that Qimron makes with 4QpsJb 1:7, עד יום הבריאה.[18] Since this is an extant expression in DSS literature and the following context is אשר אברא אני את מקדשי, it seems that Qimron's reading הבריה is the better alternative.

Lines 9–10 read אברא אני את מקׄדשי (10) להכינו לי, which according to Yadin refers to Ex 15:17, מקדש אדני כוננו ידיך.[19] This seems to be Biblical Paraphrase since lines 29:9-10 include the rephrase of contents from Exodus. Concerning the rest of line 10 כברית אשר כרתי עׄם יעקוב בבית אל there is an allusion to Gen 28:19 and to Lev 26:42.[20]

Summary of Col. 29:3b–10

(3)] בׄבית אשר֯ א[שכין]
(4) שמי עליו [ויקריבו בו] עולׄת [יום] בׄיומו כתורת המשפט הזה
(5) תמיד מאת בני ישראל לבד מנדבותׄמה לכול אשר יקריׄבו
(6) לכול נדריהמה ו֯לׄכול מתׄנותמה אשר יבׄיאו לי לרצון לה[מה]
(7) ורציׄת֯י֯ם֯ ו֯ה֯י֯ו֯ לי לעם ואנוכי אהיה להם לׄעולם [ו]שכנתי
(8) אתמה לעולם ועד ואקדשה [את מ]קׄדשי בכבודי אשר אשכׄין
(9) עליו את כבודי עד יום הבריה אשר אברא אני את מקׄדׄשי
(10) להכינו לי כול הׄימים כברית אשר כרתי עׄם יעקׄוב בבית אל

Notes on Readings

4: [ויקריבו בו] עולׄת [יום] – Yadin has [דבר יום] עׄולות [ ].
6: לכול נדריהמה – Yadin transcribes לכול נסכיהמה. **9**: הבריה – Yadin reads הברכה but admits that Qimron's reading הבריה is possible.

---

[17] This line is clearly of a lighter colour than the other letters. It looks like something was written and then later erased. Another possibility is that this line is a trace from another column.

[18] DJD XIII, 143. The dropping of gutturals – *alef* in this case – is not a unique phenomenon in 11QT. We have examples of that in line 45:4 הרישון *pro* הראישון, line 57:12 נשיי *pro* נשיאי, and line 66:9 רויה *pro* ראויה. Yadin 1983 vol. 1, 32.

[19] Yadin, 129.

[20] Yadin, 129. ויקרא את־שם־המקום ההוא בית־אל and וזכרתי את־בריתי יעקוב, respectively.

2.2. Column 30

The condition of this column was so poor, that some of it could only be detected only with the help of infrared photographs from the back of Col. 31.[1] According to Yadin, the section missing at the beginning of Col. 30 is a continuation of the end of Col. 29. The content here is the command to build the temple.[2]

(1)] [ואקדש (?)] [
(2)] [
(3)] [עשות ועשי]תה [
(4) למעלות מס̊] [בבית אשר תבנה] [י/ו
(5) עלי ◦]

Yadin and García Martínez restore only one word on line 1 as Qimron notes תי[right before this word.[3] According to the infrared photograph, plate 15*:2,[4] this could certainly be a possible reading. This could perhaps be the ending of a verb in first person perfect singular. Since ואקדש] is similar to Col. 29:8, one reasonable possibility would be ושכנתי from the line before, i.e. Col. 29:7. Concerning line 2, Yadin leaves it empty.[5] Qimron transcribes two letters, מל, which are clearly discerned on plate 15*:2.[6]

On the next line Yadin reads two words close to the end, עשות[ועשי]תה. With this reading he suggests a preceding context like that in e.g. Lev 8:5, זה הדבר אשר־צוה יהוה לעשות. Yadin then tentatively sug-

---

[1] Yadin 1977a, plate 45 and Yadin 1977b, plate 15*.

[2] Yadin, 130. Wacholder begins the column with an additional line, that is 01. This reconstruction is built around the fragment plate 40*:6, ע[ל מכונה̊] to ובניתי] (01) את העיר הקדש על מכונה̊ [. Another interpretation into the beginning of this same line 01 are letters הרז[ ] from plate 40*:8, which seem to be a single word. Wacholder 1991, 29. These are, however, such uncertain reconstructions that we will not add it to the summary at the end of this subchapter. It seems that Wacholder would consider these two readings as alternatives to each other, even if he does not mention that specifically.

[3] Yadin, 130 and García Martínez, 1250; Qimron, 45.

[4] Yadin 1977b, plate 15*.

[5] "No letter is left that can be read with certitude." Yadin, 130.

[6] Qimron, 45.

gests as a possibility, ושמרתה כל אשר צויתיכה ל]עשות.[7] Qimron has discerned two additional words earlier on the same line, i.e. ◦◦ מׄעל[ ]מסבהׄ.[8] From that García Martínez restores מׄעל]ות[מסבה.[9] At the end of line 3, Yadin suggests ועשׄי]תה בית[as he argues that it would suite the context better of the beginning of line 4, למעלות. This is a reasonable suggestion since the expression בית מעלות is found in Col. 42:7.[10] Yadin continues the line with מסׄ]בה.[11] García Martínez does not restore anything after the *mem* as Qimron disagrees with Yadin and restores משׄ]ני צדי השע[רׄיׄם אׄשׄרׄ.[12] This is a possible reading according to the old transparencies, and only Qimron has used them before.[13]

At the end of line 4 we have בבית אשר תבנה. Yadin compares it with 1 Chr 17:4, as a kind of inverted comparison, since David is forbidden to build the temple, לא אתה תבנה־לי הבית לשבת.[14]

At the end of the line Qimron restores]להיות שמ[י.[15] According to the Study Edition, García Martínez seems to discern שמי without problems while Yadin in addition also suggests]יעל[ו as an alternative to שמי.[16]

---

[7] Yadin, 130. Since עשה is such a common verb, this passage cannot be interpreted as a quotation.

[8] Qimron, 45. These two words are very difficult to discern.

[9] García Martínez, 1250. The word מְסִבָּה does not appear in the Hebrew Bible as such. In Ezek 41:7, however, we have וְנָסְבָה which is commented upon in the critical apparatus of BHS: based on the 𝕿-reading, מְסִבְּתָא, the apparatus suggests the reading הַמְּסִבָּה, that is a spiral staircase. In 1 Kgs 6:8 לולים seems to have the same meaning. According to the Dead Sea Scrolls Concordance there are only three certain appearances of this word and all of them are found in 11QT: Cols. 30:5, 31:8 and 42:8 (מסבות). מסבה appears later on line 5.

[10] Yadin, 130-131.

[11] Yadin mentions מס]ביב as another theoretical possibility similar to the passage in line 10 according to his restoration. However, he seems to prefer מס]בה due to contextual reasons. Yadin, 131.

[12] Qimron, 45.

[13] These transparencies are also used by the present writer. I will later refer to them as "the old transparencies."

[14] Yadin, 131.

[15] Qimron, 45.

[16] García Martínez, 1250; Yadin, 131.

(5) עלי [ועשי]תׄה את מסבה צפון להיכל בית מרובע
(6) מׄפנה אלׄ פׄנהׄ עשרים באמה לעומת ארבע פנותיו ורחׄוק מקיר
(7) [ה]היכלׄ שבׄעׄ אמׄות במערב צפונו

At the beginning of line 5, Yadin notes that עלי may be connected to Col. 31:6 ובעלית or 31:7 לעלית.[17] Qimron and García Martínez read עליו. Since the column is reconstructed with the help of mirror-writing on the back of Col. 31, letters that do not belong to the beginning of Col. 30:5 make it difficult to choose between the two readings. Due to contextual reasons עליו is preferred here.

After this there seems to be a *vacat* after which Yadin restores ועשי]תׄה את מסבה. He admits, however, that this is problematic with Hebrew grammar.[18] Qimron has a better grammatical alternative with וע]שׄ̊יׄ̊תׄה [בי]תׄ מסבה. García Martínez agrees with Qimron concerning this reconstruction.[19] Line 5 ends with the expression בית מרובע, of which מרובע is a biblical term from only Ezekiel.[20]

On line 6 the preposition לעומת seems to make a comparison to the measurements in the Bible. Yadin mentions, for example, Ex 38:18, ועשרים אמה ארך וקומה ברחב חמש אמות לעמת קלעי החצר.[21] Since לעמת means "corresponding to" or "exactly as" the allusion to the biblical style may be recognised. At the end of the same line Yadin reads ורחׄוק and compares the reading with Col. 31:11-12, ועשרים (11) אמה ר̊ח̊ו̊ק̊ מׄהׄמׄזׄבׄחׄ.[22] Qimron and García Martínez agree with using רחוק.[23] However, the traces on plate 15*:2 are very unclear especially at this spot due to a disturbing horizontal line that goes across the manuscript at this point.

Qimron and García Martínez agree with Yadin concerning the first half of line 7.[24]

---

[17] Yadin, 131.

[18] "Apparently to be read את המסבה." Yadin, 131. On plate 15* the former word is quite similar to את. In a footnote, Qimron notes this and similarly suggests that the את could belong to הזואת in Col. 31:8. He basis his argument on the original manuscript. Qimron, 45.

[19] García Martínez, 1250.

[20] Yadin, 131. E.g. Ezek 45:2, יהיה מזה אל־קדש חמש מאות בחמש מאות מרובע סביב.

[21] Yadin, 131.

[22] Yadin, 131.

[23] Qimron, 45; García Martínez, 1250.

[24] Yadin, 132; Qimron, 45; García Martínez, 1250.

(7) ועשיׄתׄה רוחב קׄירׄוׄ ארבע

(8) אמות]] כׄהׄיכל ותוכו מׄמׄקצוע אׄל֯ מקצוע

(9) שתים עשׄר[ה באמה] ועמוד בתוך באמצעו מרובע רוחבׄוׄ ארבע

(10) אׄמות ל֯כ֯ו֯ל֯ רׄוחותיו[ ]ת אשר מסביבׄ עולה מעלות א[

In the second half of line 7 and at the beginning of line 8 we are given information concerning the thickness of the wall of בית המסבה, that is the stair house. Into the *lacuna* in line 8, Yadin suggests as an approximate reconstruction, [וגבוהו ארבעים אמה (?)] היכל.[25] Qimron restores עולה ישר מהׄ[פרור הז]ה and compares the line with line 35:10, ועשיתה מקום למערב ההיכל סביב פׄרור עמודים עומדים.[26] Both reconstructions are viable but due to the expression כהיכל, that is "like a temple", it seems that Yadin has a better alternative in this case. The word תוכו in the second part of the line reveals that the dimensions mentioned relate to the inside of the building.

Yadin argues that the words ועמוד בתוך in the middle of line 9 are found on plate 16*:1.[27] This is actually an expression that can also be found in the Bible, Judg 16:29, וילפת שמשון את־שני **עמודי התוך** אשר הבית נכון עליהם.[28] There is no disagreement concerning the transcription of this line.

Concerning ל֯כ֯ו֯ל֯ רׄוחותיו there is no biblical parallel, although Cols. 31:10 and 36:5, both include the same expression.[29] After this Yadin restores tentatively [כמדת הזאו]ת אשר מסביבׄ עולה but Qimron and García Martínez read ורוחב המסבה עולה.[30] There is no difficulty to discern עולה on plate 45. However, there is difficulty with discerning ורוחב המסבה. These two words are quite clearly readable on the old transparencies. The letters are discernable behind the letters Yadin has read, slightly above them but in a less dark colour. Furthermore, since the description of the stair house continues in line 31, it is also logical

---

[25] Yadin, 132.

[26] Concerning the mid-part of Col. 30:8, הז]ה], Qimron also gives another option, that is מד]ה]. Qimron, 45. García Martínez follows Qimron apart from that the former does not restore anything inside the *lacuna*. García Martínez, 1250.

[27] Yadin, 132. This is a photograph of mirror-writing on the back of Col. 32 that is printed in reverse. Indeed, the two words are quite clearly discerned on the line next to the lowest one.

[28] Yadin, 132.

[29] Col. 38:13-14 has the feminine suffix, that is לכול (14) רוחותיה. Yadin, 133.

[30] Yadin, 133; García Martínez, 1250. Qimron comments עולה in a footnote: "Apparently a phonetic variant of העולה, 'the ascending (stair-case).'" Qimron, 45.

that מסבה is mentioned on line 10. At the end of the line Qimron and García Martínez transcribe אׄרׄבׄעׄ [א]מׄות. This reading is difficult to discern from plate 15*.[31]

Summary of Col. 30

(1)] ושכנ]תי ואקדש[[
(2)] [
(3)]]עשות ועשי֯[תה בית[
(4) למעלות משׄ[ני צדי השע]ר֯י֯ם אׄשׄר בבית אשר תבנה [להיות שמ]י
(5) עליׄו֯ *vacat?* [וע]שׄיׄתׄה [בי]תׄ מסבה צפון להיכל֯ בית מרובע
(6) מׄפנה אל֯ פׄנׄהׄ עשרים באמה לעומת ארבע פנותיו ורחׄוׄק מקירׄ
(7) [ה]היכל שבׄעׄ אׄמׄוׄתׄ בׄמערב צפונו ועשׄיׄתׄה רוחב קׄיׄרׄוׄ ארבע
(8) אמות [וגבוהו ארבעים אמה] כׄהׄיכל ותוכו מׄמׄקצוע אׄל֯ מקצוע
(9) שתים עשר[ה באמה] ועמוד בתוךׄ באמצעו מרובע רוחבוׄ ארבע
(10) אׄמׄוׄתׄ לׄכׄו֯ל֯ רׄוחותיו ורוחב המסבה עולה מעלות א[

Notes on Readings

1:]ושכנ]ת ואקדש Yadin and García Martínez read]ואקדש[. Qimron transcribes]תי ואקדש[. **2:** Qimron transcribes ◦מל◦◦ close to the end of the line. **3:** עשות ועשי֯[תה בית] – Qimron reads]ועשות ועשי֯[תה and discerns]מׄעל◦◦מסבהׄ[earlier on the line. García Martínez reconstructs close to Yadin ל]עשות עשי[תה. **4:** למעלות משׄ[ני צדי השע]ר֯י֯ם אׄשׄר – Yadin reads]למעלות מס֯ | תבנה [להיות שמ]י – Instead of שמ]י Yadin suggests [יעל]ו as another alternative. **5:** עליו֯ – Yadin reads עלי֯ | וע]שׄי֯תׄה [בי]תׄ מסבה – Yadin transcribes ועשי]תׄה את מסבה. **6:** ורחׄוׄק – Qimron and García Martínez read ר֯חׄו֯ק. **8:** אמות [וגבוהו ארבעים אמה] – Qimron restores אמות עולה ישר מהׄ[פרור הז]ה / מד]ה. **10:** רׄוחותיו ורוחב המסבה – Yadin reads]רׄוחותיו]ת אשר מסביׄב | מעלות א[– Qimron and García Martínez have מעלות אׄרׄבׄעׄ [א]מׄות.

[31] Qimron, 45; García Martínez, 1250.

2.3. Column 31

In contrast to the two former columns, the lines 6–13 of Col. 31 have been preserved quite well on plate 46. It is moreover possible to discern the ends of lines 1–5 from the same photograph. According to Yadin, it is clear that this column continues to discuss the stair house.[1]

(1)] ת[
(2)] השער [
(3)] ה . . . . [
(4)] הכוהן המשנה[
(5) אׄלׄ בׄיׄתׄ] הכוהן הג]דׄול

On the first line only a *taw* has been preserved. At the end of line 2 we can clearly read the word השער. Yadin only discerns a *he* here. Qimron transcribes *nun sophit* followed by המשיחה and restores alternatively שמ]ןׄ המשׂיׄחה. Another option would be [הכוה]ןׄ המשׂיׄחׄ if thc *he* at the end of line 3 is dislocated.[2] Both expressions are derived from the root משח and are found in the DSS literature.[3] It is difficult to choose between them on palaeographical grounds. Further, García Martínez reads שמ]ן המשיחה.[4]

In this grammatical form הכוהן המשנה is *hapax legomenon* in DSS. The "deputy priest" is, however, found – as Yadin[5] points out – in 1QM 2:2, הכוהנים יסרוכו אחר כוהן הראש ומשנהו. At the beginning of line 5 Yadin alone reads, albeit tentatively, אׄלׄ בׄיׄתׄ.[6] At the end Yadin, Qimron and García Martínez agree concerning the reconstruction הכוהן הג]דׄול.[7] At the end of the line there is a *vacat*.

---

[1] Yadin, 133.

[2] Qimron argues that the *chet* is superimposed on another letter, "perhaps *mem*; therefore the final *he* may belong to another word terminating מה, in which case one might alternatively read [הכוה]ןׄ המשׂיׄחׄ." Qimron, 46. It does not, however, have to be מה that belongs to another *locus* but only the possible *mem*.

[3] הכוהן המישח in 4Q375 1i9 and 4Q376 1i1; שמן משיחת כהונתם בדם in 1QM IX, 8 and שמן המשיחה in 4Q3751i9.

[4] García Martínez, 1250.

[5] Yadin, 134.

[6] Yadin, 134. The traces in the manuscript are nearly impossible to discern.

[7] The context is possibly related to the entrances for the high priest and deputy priest. Yadin, 134; Qimron, 46; García Martínez, 1250.

(6) ובעלית הב[ית הזה תעשה שע]ר̇ פתוח לג̇ג ה̇היכל וד֯ר֯ך֯ עשוי
(7) ב̇שער הזה {א} לפת̇ח̇] גג(?) ה]ה̇יכל אשר יהיו באי̇ם בו לעלית ההיכל
(8) [כו]ל̇ בית המסבה הזואת צפו זהב קירותיו ושע̇ר̇יו וגגו מבית
(9) [ומ]בחוץ ועמודו ומעלותיו ועשה ככול אשר אנוכי מדבר אליכה

Yadin restores the *lacuna* at the beginning of line 6 with הב[ית הזה תעשה שע]ר̇[8] supported by Qimron and García Martínez.[9] According to Yadin, וד֯ר֯ך֯ at the end of the line is not a certain reading. On plate 46 it is, however, possible to read it accompanied with some degree of uncertainty. The last word on line 6, עשוי, is a biblical term. It is quite frequently used in Ezekiel. On the other hand, it is never found together with דרך.

At the beginning of line 7, an *alef* seems to have been written and then erased. Concerning the restoration after this *alef* Qimron disagrees with Yadin's suggestion above and reads לפר̇ו̇ר [ה]ה̇י̇כל based on an early transparency.[10]

The restoration at the beginning of line 8, [כו]ל̇ בית המסבה, is certain here. Yadin notes that צפו זהב is regular phraseology for building the temple in 1 Kgs 6.[11] This particular expression does not, however, exist in the Bible. On the other hand, we have ויצף and ויצפהו several times in the Bible.[12] At the end of line 8 Yadin reads מבית (9) [ומ]בחוץ. Qimron transcribes מב̇י̇ת (9) [ו]מ̇חוץ.[13] According to plate 46 it is possible to discern a part of a line to the right of *chet* as the base for a *beit*. On the other hand, the stroke is little too long and, secondly, it is doubtful whether an extra letter would fit into the beginning of line 9.

At the end of line 9 we have ועשה ככול אשר אנוכי מדבר אליכה. Yadin compares it with Ezek 44:5, את כל־אשר אני מדבר אתך.[14] Since these two passages do not have the same context, we cannot define it as

---

[8] Yadin, 135. Qimron and García Martínez agree with him. Qimron, 46; Garcia Martínez, 1250.
[9] Qimron, 46; García Martínez, 1250.
[10] Qimron, 46. According to plate 46 this is, indeed, unclear. Yadin adds that the scribe appears first to have written אל פתח and then struck out the *alef.* Yadin, 135.
[11] Yadin, 135.
[12] 1 Kgs 6:21 etc.
[13] Qimron, 46.
[14] Yadin, 135.

a quotation.[15] Lines 8 and 9 may, however, be understood as Rewritten Bible.

(10) וׄעשיתה בית לכיור נגב מזרׄח מרובע לכול רוׄחותיו אחת ועשרים
(11) אמה רׄ֯ח֯ו֯ק֯ מׄהׄמׄזׄבׄח חמשים אמה ורחב ה[ק]יׄר שׄלושׄ אמות וגבה
א
(12) [ע]שׄריׄם מׄה[ ] ושערים עשו לה מהמזרח ומהצפון
ו
(13) ומהמערב ורחב השׄעׄרים ארבע אמות וגובהמה שׄבׄע

There are no disagreements concerning transcription on line 10. It is worthwhile to mention, however, that García Martínez has restored 11Q20 8:9–12 with the help of lines 31:10–13.[16] This is certainly a possible solution, even though only a small amount of letters that have survived on Frg. 14. The כיור is mentioned in Ex 30:18, ועשית כיור נחשת וכנו נחשת לרחצה ונתת אתו בין־אהל מועד ובין המזבח and the ים in 1 Kgs 7:39, ואת־הים נתן מכתף הבית הימנית קדמה ממול נגב. These two biblical verses mention the laver and the sea, respectively, and 11QT speaks about the house of laver. It is interesting that 1 Kgs and line 10 use the same specification of the *locus*, which is south-east. In conclusion there seems to be some biblical influence in this line. Additionally, there is a new element – בית לכיור – introduced in relation to the biblical texts at the beginning of the line. Therefore, this is understood as Rewritten Bible.

At the end of line 11 García Martínez agrees with Yadin concerning וגבה.[17] Alternatively Qimron reads וגבהׄו.[18] We prefer the former reading due to palaeographical reasons.

There is a hole in the MS which covers the beginning of line 12. However, Yadin notes that the scribe first wrote מה and then afterwards he added an *alef* above the *he*.[19] Further down the line the preposition לְ with feminine suffix is used and is unusual in Hebrew. Yadin suggests

---

[15] The context of line 9 is the construction of the stair house while Ezek 44 speaks about the abominations in the temple and the call to repentance. Concerning the issue of context, see chapter one, footnote 6.

[16] 11Q20 Frg. 14 (lines 8:9–12) (9) [מרובע לכול רוחותיו אחת ועשרים אמה רחוק מהמזבח חמש[ים] (10) אמה ורחב הקיר שלוש אמות וגבהו עשרים אמה *vacat* [*vacat*] (11) *vacat*] שערים]עשו לה (12) [מהמזרח מהצפון ומהמערב רוחב השערים ארבע אמות וגובהמה]שבע. García Martínez, 1298.

[17] García Martínez, 1298.

[18] Qimron, 46.

[19] Yadin, 136.

that it could be an aramaism whereas Qimron cautiously interprets it as לו.[20] There seems to be a similar phenomenon on line 13 concerning a *waw* above a *resh*. Qimron reads רׄ֗חב, which seems to be a good alternative according to the old transparencies. However, due to grammatical reasons Qimron's suggestion is better.[21] After the possible *vacat* on line 12, Yadin transcribes ושערים [only. Qimron restores ושלוש]ה שערים from contextual support from line 33:10.[22] This is a very reasonable suggestion. However, with Yadin's reading ושערים [, it is easier to discern a *he* than a *waw* in front of שערים on plate 46. This supports the reconstruction by Qimron.

Summary of Col. 31

(1)] [◦ת
(2)] [◦ השער
(3)] הכוה]ן המשׄיׄחׄ[23]
(4)]הכוהן המשנה
(5)] הכוהן הג]דוׄל *vacat*
(6) ובעלית הב[ית הזה תעשה שע]רׄ פתוח לׄגג ההׄיכל ודׄרׄךׄ עשוי
(7) בׄשׄער הזה {א}לפרׄוׄר [ה]הׄיׄכל אשר יהיו באיםׄ בו לעלית ההיכל
(8) [כו]לׄ בית המסבה הזואת צפו זהב קירותיו ושׄעׄרׄיׄוׄ וגגו מביׄת
(9) [ומ]חוץ ועמודו ומעלותיו ועשה ככול אשר אנוכי מדבר אליכה
(10) וׄעשיתה בית לכיור נגב מזרׄחׄ מרובע לכול רוחׄותיו אחת ועשרים
(11) אמה רׄ̊חׄ̊וׄ̊קׄ מׄהׄמׄזׄבׄחׄ חמשים אמה ורחב ה[ק]יׄרׄ שׄלוש אׄמות וגבה
(12) [ע]שׄרׄיׄםׄ אׄמׄהׄ[שלוש]הׄ שׄעׄרים עשו לה מהמזרח ומהצפון
(13) ומהמערב רׄ֗חב השערים ארבע אמות וגובהמה שׄבׄעׄ

Notes on Readings

3: הכוה]ן המשׄיׄחׄ – Yadin discerns *he* only, at the end of the line. **5:** Yadin discerns א̊לׄ̊ ב̊י̊ת̊ at the beginning of the line. **7:** {א}לפרׄוׄר [ה]הׄיׄכׄל – Yadin reads {א} לפׄתׄחׄ] גג(?) ה[הׄיכל. **8:** מביׄת (9) [ומ]חוץ – Yadin has

---

[20] Yadin, 136; Qimron, 46.
[21] Qimron, 46.
[22] Qimron, 46. García Martínez agrees with this reconstruction. García Martínez, 1252. Line 33:10 mentions two directions, מצפונו ודרומו while there are three directions in line 31:12.
[23] Another possible reading is שמ]ן המשׄיׄחׄהׄ.

מבית (9) [ומ]בחוץ. **11:** וגבה – Qimron reads וגבהוׄ. **12:** שלוש]הׄ שׁעׄרים – Yadin reads וׄשׁעׄרים [. **13:** רׄיחב – Yadin reads וׄר{ו}חב.

2.4. Column 32

This column has several missing parts on plate 47. Fortunately, we find an additional textual witness on plate 17*. This has a photograph of mirror-writing on the back of Col. 33 and printed in reverse. The main textual bulk that is legible begins in the middle of line 6. According to Yadin, the missing top of the column may have included a description of either the upper chamber, the house of the laver or the laver itself.[1] From the beginning of line 10 onwards we seem to have a parallel text, that is 11Q20.[2]

[ ] שלוש אמוֹת [ ] (1)
[ ]..........[ ] (2)
[ ].....[ ] (3)
[ ]...............[ ] (4)
[ ]עש.....ה..[ ] (5)

On the first line there are only two legible words, which are שלוש אמוֹת. No letters have survived on line 2. On line 3 Qimron and García Martínez read a recurrence of שׁלוֹשׁ.[3] The same scholars read four letters]יהמה[on line 4.[4] This seems to be the an of a word with a plural-ending and a suffix. The traces are unclear, but it is still possible to discern these letters or parts of them.

On the next line Yadin transcribes three letters only, that is *he* and]עש. The latter he suggests could be restored as ו]עש[יתה or]עש[רה.[5] Alternatively Qimron, supported by García Martínez, restores this passage]מׄה למׄזבח עש[.[6]

---

[1] Yadin, 137.

[2] When we get to line 10, the different textual witnesses will be discussed.

[3] Qimron, 47; García Martínez, 1252. This is indeed very difficult to verify palaeographically.

[4] Qimron, 47; García Martínez, 1252.

[5] Yadin, 137.

[6] Qimron, 47; García Martínez, 1252.

(6)]]א֯ש֯מ֯ת֯ם֯ לכפר על העםׄ ובעלות[ם]
(7)]] לכ . . . . ם ולהקטיר על המזבח
(8) העו[לה] . . . . . . ו֯ע֯ש֯י֯[ת]הׄ (?) בקיר הבית
(9) הזה בת[ים (?) פני]מה ובת֯ו֯כ֯ימהׄ [ ] ר֯ו֯ח֯ב֯ [ב]אמה וגובהמה
(10) מן הארץ ארבע אמ[ות]

Instead of Yadin's א֯ש֯מ֯ת֯ם֯, Qimron reads אשמׄם in the middle of line 6. Qimron's reading is supported by García Martínez.[7] At the end of the line, García Martínez agrees with Yadin concerning ובעלות[ם].[8] Qimron reads ובעלות which also seems to be a good solution.

According to plate 17* the margin on line 6 may come already after *mem.* It does not have to, however, because the lines 10 and 12 seem to be the longest lines of the survived column. They are still the longest ones even if Yadin's longer solution would be preferred.[9] Qimron continues at the beginning of line 7 with the restoration הכוהנים].[10] In Josh 4:18 we have a similar expression, that is **ויהי בעלות הכהנים** נשאי ארון ברית־יהוה מתוך הירדן.[11]

Concerning the reconstruction of the mid-part of line 7, Qimron and García Martínez do not support Yadin's restoration of לכ[והני]ם. Yadin's restoration is based on a possible solution according to plate 17*. There is well preserved old transparency, which shows this reading to be impossible. Therefore, Qimron reads למנ]חת[ם instead, supported by García Martínez. This reading has solid palaeographical support and is therefore to be preferred.[12] At the end of the line, Qimron does not read a *waw* as Yadin and García Martínez do.[13]

According to plate 17*, there is a weak before להקטיר, which Yadin reads as a *waw*. This is not an impossible reading according to

---

[7] Qimron, 47; García Martínez, 1252. The manuscript is very unclear at this location. According to Qimron this reading is, however, most probable.

[8] Yadin also suggests another reconstruction, that is ובהעלותם. Yadin, 138; García Martínez, 1252.

[9] Qimron argues that Yadin's reading ובעלות[ם] is less likely even if Qimron does not give any reasons to support his own restoration.

[10] Qimron, 47.

[11] This is the *Qere*-reading of BHS. The *Ketiv*-reading mainly reads כעלות *pro* בעלות. Moreover, we learn from the critical apparatus of BHS, that there are also some oriental versions of 𝔐 that read בעלות.

[12] Qimron, 47; García Martínez, 1252. As a matter of fact García Martínez writes למנ]הת[ם, which must have been a misprint.

[13] Qimron, 47; García Martínez, 1252.

the photographs. On the other hand the *waw* hangs too low in relation to the other consonants. Therefore, we assume that the letter does not belong to this line but has been moved from another location.

The restoration at the beginning of line 8 העו]לה is beyond doubt, because it suites the preceding המזבח very well. This gives us the expression "the burnt offering." Later, on the first half of the same line, Qimron transcribes רות[, which can be verified from the old transparency. The end of the line is agreed – בקיר הבית (9) הזה – but in other parts of the line, however, there are some alternative interpretations: Yadin suggests ו֯ע֯ש֯י֯]ת[ה, even though he admits that this is an uncertain reading.[14] Qimron does not suggest a word here but transcribes *taw* twice.[15] ו֯ע֯ש֯י֯]ת[ה seems to be a possible suggestion.

Line 9 is very distorted in the manuscript. This can be seen by different transcriptions. Yadin suggests בת]ים (?) פני]מה ובת֯ו֯כ֯י֯מ֯ה.[16] Qimron, supported by García Martínez, transcribes בת֯[ ]א֯ מה לאמה ומ֯צ֯[ ] מן.[17] Qimron's transcription is a good solution according to the palaeographical evidence. At the end of the line, there is no disagreement concerning אמה]. וגובהמה Immediately before this expression, however, Yadin tentatively suggests ר֯ו֯ח֯ב֯ on the basis of contextual reasons.[18] Qimron does not transcribe anything. At the beginning of line 10, the restoration is clear: מן הארץ ארבע אמ]ות].

(10) **מצופות זהב אשר֯** יהיו מניחים [ש]ם֯ עליהמה
(11) את בגדיהמ֯ה אשר יהי[ו באי]ם֯ [בה]ם למעלה מ֯על ל֯בית ה֯מ[ ]
(12) ב֯ב֯ואם ל֯שר֯ת בקודש

In the middle of line 10 *taw* and זהב are visible clearly visible. Yadin restores the letters in bold font with the help of PAM 42.178. The two

[14] Yadin argues that his reading is supported by the context. He also compares this passage with line 31:10, ו֯ע֯שיתה בית לכיור, and with 32:12, [ו]עשיתה ת֯ב֯ל֯ה. Yadin, 138. Contextually this seems to be one possibility. It does not, however, fit with the letters that Qimron sees "quite clearly."

[15] "Some of the letters are quite clear, but I was not able to determine a suitable reading." Qimron, 47.

[16] Yadin, 138.

[17] Qimron, 47; García Martínez, 1252.

[18] Yadin, 138.

joined fragments are shown on plate 38*:3.[19] These fragments have later been identified as belonging to 11Q20. The transcription is below together with a limited part of the reconstruction of 11Q20 Col. 9, Frgs. 15, 16:[20]

(1)]מצופות זהב אש[ר יהיו
(2) למע]לה מע֯[ל]לב֯ית֯[ה
(3) מזבח]ה֯[עולה
(4) יהיו ה]מים נש[פכים
(5) כול א]ד֯ם[כי

Qimron and García Martínez do not read שם close to end of line 10 of 11Q19. Yadin does.[21] According to plate 17* there are indeed traces of one possible letter between מניחים and עליהמה. Under these traces, however, there are at least three minimal spots on a horizontal line reaching down to the next line. It seems, therefore, plausible that the darker spots together with these traces do not belong to this line. Moreover, the letters of a hypothetical שם need to be closer to each other for them to have originally been written on this line together.

There seems to be biblical influence on lines 10–12: אש֯ר יהיו מניחים עליהמה (11) את בגדיהמ֯ה אשר יהי[ו באי]ם֯ [בה]ם למעלה מ֯על ל֯בית ה֯מ[ ] (12) בב֯ואם לשרת בקודש, from Ezek 42:14, ושם יניחו בגדיהם

[19] Yadin, 138. Wacholder supports this reading and identifies the fragments as Fragment 24 and 25. Wacholder 1991, 29. The joining of these fragments has also been noted by García Martínez in his preliminary publication of 11Q20. García Martínez 1992, 379. In this publication García Martínez did not yet, however, combine these two fragments of PAM 42.178 with one fragment on 44.008. This he skilfully does later. When Qimron restores Col. 32, he mentions two fragments – evidently PAM 42.178 – of 11Q20, which are fragments 11 and 38. Qimron, 47. The reason for this seems to be that Yadin uses the code 38*:3 for these two fragments in the *Temple Scroll, vol. 3, Supplementary Plates* and that García Martínez in his preliminary publication (1992) labels the same fragments "Fragment 11." In his *editio maior* of 11Q20 García Martínez identifies the two fragments on PAM 42.178 (also on PAM 43.978) as 15a and 15b. DJD XXIII, plate XLIV.

[20] DJD XXIII, 386. García Martínez has completed the reconstruction of Frgs. 15 and 16 with the help of 11Q19 lines 32:10–15 in his edition of 11Q20. The reconstruction is not repeated above since it is very similar to the text, which is analysed in this subchapter. We have added some of the restored words so that it would be easier to read the fragments in their context. Wacholder identifies one of the fragments, that is Frg. 15 c in DJD XXIII, as 11QT[b] 34. He interpolates it tentatively into lines 7 and 9 instead in Col. 46. See analysis of Col. 46.

[21] Qimron, 47; García Martínez, 1252.

אשר־ישרתו בהן.[22] The end of line 10 and the beginning of line 12 could be interpreted as Biblical Paraphrase. The additional information on line 11, however, makes this interpretation difficult because the line also gives us some new details. These are not extant in the biblical source. We, therefore, need to interpret this as Rewritten Bible.

In the mid-part of line 11 Qimron and García Martínez disagree with Yadin's reading of באי]ם֯ [בה]ם, and they suggest באים א֯ל֯[יה]ם.[23] According to the palaeographic evidence on plate 17*, there does not seem to be enough space for the longer reading.[24] Due to this reason we prefer Yadin's reconstruction, באי]ם֯ [בה]ם. For the rest of the line García Martínez supports Yadin's transcription.[25] At the end of line 11 Yadin tentatively restores ה̇מ]וקד[.[26] This reading seems to be quite speculative and so we do not support it.

Further, for the end of line 11, 11Q20 line 9:2 provides us with additional palaeographic evidence, למע]לה מע֯]ל]לב֯י̇ת[.[27] Qimron disagrees with the reconstructions and reads למעלה מ֯על בי̇ת ה̇כ֯י֯ו]ר̇[.[28] He reads בית *pro* לבית and seems to interpret the *yod* on Frg. 15b[29] as belonging to הכיו]ר[. This solution has difficulties because there is not enough space for it.

At the beginning of line 12 we read ב̇בואם ל̇שר̇ת בקודש. This can be compared with Ex 28:43, והיו על־אהרן ועל־בניו בבאם אל־אהל מועד או בגשתם אל־המזבח לשרת בקדש. A comparison shows us that they have very similar contexts. That is, the priests ministering at the sanctuary. We will not consider this to be a quotation since the beginning part of

---

22 It seems that Yadin is influenced by ושם in Ezek 42:14 as he reads [ש]ם֯ at the end of line 10. Primarily our reconstruction needs, however, to be based on palaeography. Due to this and the reasons described above, we will not include this reading in the summary of Col. 32. Concerning בהן in Ezek 42:14: this is one of the few exceptions in the Hebrew Bible when בגד is recognized as a feminine form. In the middle of line 11 Yadin restores יהי]ו באי]ם֯ [בה]ם. If the last letter here had been a *nun* the relation to Ezek 42:14 would have been very close. Moreover we note that the root of שרת included in Ezek 42:14 also appears at the beginning of line 12. See also the analysis of that line.

23 Qimron, 47; García Martínez, 1252.

24 There is simply not enough space for באים אליהם after יהיו.

25 García Martínez, 1252.

26 Yadin, 139.

27 DJD XXIII, plate XLIV. Wacholder reads line 2 to [ל]מעלה [ב֯י̇ת]ו]. Wacholder 1992, 29.

28 Qimron, 47. The traces on plate 17* are indeed very unclear on this location.

29 PAM 43.978 in DJD XXIII, plate XLIV.

line 12 is shorter. However, as the same words appear in Ex 28:43, it may be a formula or a part of a formula that was used in similar contexts.[30]

(12) [ו]עשיתה תע֯ל֯ה֯ סביבׄ לכיור אצלׄ ביׄתו֯ ו֯התעלׄ[ה]
(13) ה֯ולכתׄ [מבית] הכיור ל֯מחלה יׄורׄדת [ופוש]טת אל תוך הארץׄ א֯שׄר
(14) יהיו המים נשפכים ו֯הולכים א֯ליה ואובדים בתוך הׄארץ ולוא
(15) יהיה נוגעים בהׄמׄה כול אדם כי מדם ה֯עולה מתערב במה

The mid-part of line 12 has similarities with 1 Kgs 18:32, ויעש תעלה כבית סאתים זרע סביב למזבח. At the end of line 12 Qimron, supported by García Martínez, reads מׄזׄבׄח ה֯ע֯ו֯ל֯ה֯.[31] It is not easy to give a priority to either Yadin's or Qimron's reading on the basis of palaeographical evidence, since the MS is hard to read at the end of the line. We note that Qimron's reading is closely connected with the 1 Kgs 18. Nonetheless, we cannot count this as a Biblical Paraphrase, because the end of the line is a reconstruction. On the other hand, we note that Qimron has used line 3 from 11Q20 Col. 9[32] in his restoration, which makes his solution more plausible.

At the beginning of line 13 Qimron, followed by García Martínez, reads ל֯[ת]חתׄ *pro* [מבית] by Yadin. Plate 17* has dark stains caused by a hole in the manuscript on plate 47 at this spot. There is also a slight disagreement concerning Yadin's reading of ל֯מחלה for the same line. In contrast, Qimron does not seem to have problems to transcribe the word ומחלה.[33] In his textual analysis Yadin calls this a probable reading.[34]

Towards the end of line 13 Qimron and García Martínez read יורדת ל֯מ֯טה *pro* Yadin's יׄורׄדת [ופוש]טת. The photograph on plate 17* seems is in favour Qimron and García Martínez.

---

[30] Cf. Ex 30:20, בבאם אל־אהל מועד ירחצו־מים ולא ימתו או בגשתם אל־המזבח לשרת להקטיר אשה ליהוה.

[31] Qimron, 47; García Martínez, 1252.

[32] מזבח]ה֯[עולה. Even though line 3 also is a restoration we consider this to be a good solution.

[33] Qimron, 47. On plate 17* there are traces of a letter before the spot that Qimron seems to interpret as a *waw*. It seems that these dark spots are parts of the *lamed* that Yadin transcribes.

[34] Yadin, 139. It is, therefore, strange that Yadin does not change his own reading ל֯מחלה. It is possible, that Yadin's reconstruction [מבית] earlier on the line is connected to his reading of למחלה, and so he has not removed the *lamed*.

For the beginning of line 14, line 4 from 11Q20, Col. 9 – יהיו ה]מים נש[פכים – clearly overlaps the reading on line 14. This is quite well discernable on plate 47.

At the end of line 14 we have the expression בתוך הארץ, which is found only once in the Bible, that is Ezek 21:37, דמך יהיה בתוך הארץ. The context is similar because both texts speak about something which is lost. On the other hand, the substance is different – water for line 14 and blood for Ezekiel – and therefore is not a quotation.

In the middle of line 15, line 5 of 11Q20, Col. 9 – כול א]דם[כי – is similar. The expression כול אדם is recorded five times in the Bible,[35] but only once in a negative sentence, that is וכל־אדם לא־יהיה באהל מועד בבאו לכפר בקדש עד־צאתו (Lev 16:17). We note that line 15 does not have the same context as in the Bible. The context in line 15 is the prohibition to touch the water and in the Bible it is who is allowed to be present in the tabernacle.

Summary of Col. 32

(1) [ ] שלוש אמות [ ]
(2) [ ] . . . . [ ]
(3) [ ]שלוש[ ]
(4) [ ]יהמה[ ]
(5) [ ]מה למזבח עש[ ]
(6) [ ]אשמם לכפר על העם ובעלות
(7) [ ] למנ[חת]ם להקטיר על המזבח
(8) העו[לה]רות . . . . ועשי[ת]ה (?) בקיר הבית
(9) הזה בת[ ] אמה לאמה ומצ[ ] מן [ ] אמה וגובהמה
(10) מן הארץ ארבע אמ[ות] מצופות זהב אשר יהיו מניחים עליהמה
(11) את בגדיהמה אשר יהי[ו באי]ם [בה]ם למעלה מעל לבית ה[
(12) בבואם לשרת בקודש [ו]עשיתה תעלה סביב לכיור אצל מזבח העולה
(13) הולכת [ ] הכיור ומחלה יורדת למטה אל תוך הארץ אשר
(14) יהיו המים נשפכים והולכים אליה ואובדים בתוך הארץ ולוא
(15) יהיה נוגעים בהמה כול אדם כי מדם העולה מתערב במה

[35] Lev 16:17, Jer 10:14, 51:17, Job 36:25, 37:7.

Notes on Readings

5:]מׄה לׄמׄזבח עש[– Yadin suggests ו[עש]יתה or alternatively [עש]רה. **6:**]אׄשׄמם – Yadin reads]אׄש֯מ֯ת֯ם֯. **7:** Qimron restores [הכוהנים] at the beginning of the line | לׄמׄנ[חת]ם להקׄטיר – Yadin reads לכ[והני]ם ולהקׄטיר. **8:** ו֯ע֯ש֯י֯[ת]הׄ – Qimron transcribes ◦◦◦◦◦◦◦◦ ת ת ◦◦◦◦. **9:** בׄת[ ]אׄמה לאמה ומׄצׄ[ ]מן[ ]אׄמׄה וגובהמה – Yadin reads בׄת[ים פני]מה ובׄת֯ו֯כ֯י֯מ֯ה֯ [ ] ר֯ו֯ח֯ב֯ [ב]אמה וגובהמה (?). **10:** יהיו מניחים עליהמה – Yadin reads יהיו מניחים [ש]םׄ עליהמה. **11:** למעלה מׄעל לׄביׄתׄ הׄ[– Yadin restores the end of the line to מׄעל לׄביׄתׄ הׄמ[וקד] as Qimron reads למעלה מׄעל ביׄתׄ הׄכ֯י֯ו֯[ר]. **12:** אצׄל מׄזבׄח הׄע֯ו֯ל֯הׄ – Yadin reads ביׄתו וׄהתעלׄ[ה]. **13:** הׄולכׄתׄ[ ] – Yadin reads הׄולכׄתׄ [בית] כיור whereas Qimron has הׄולכׄתׄ לׄ[ת]חׄתׄ כיור | וׄמחלה יורדת לׄמׄטׄהׄ – Yadin reads לׄמחלה יורדת [ופוש]טת.

2.5. Column 33

This is the best preserved column so far. In addition to plate 48, plates 18* and 19* can also be consulted. Plate 18* represents the mirror-writing from the back of Col. 34. Plate 19* is a photograph of the column when it first had been opened.[1]

(1)]]ים באים [[
(2)]]ובעת אשׁ[ר [
(3)]]מם ואתׄ[[
(4)]]אשׁׄר עליהמה ומנׄ[חים [
(5)]] . . . ביׄ[ת] הכיור ומ◦◦שׁׄ◦◦ם [ ] לכיו[ר [

There is not enough textual material on these first lines to make meaningful restoration. On line 1 Qimron reads]יׄם באים, which is a correct transcription,[2] since the *yod* is quite clear on plate 19*. García Martínez supports Yadin with his shorter transcription.[3] On line 2 we have a temporal expression, ובעת. This makes it possible to reconstruct the first word on line 3 to be יומם, i.e. "daily." This reading is partly supported by Qimron and García Martínez, who both transcribe a part of this word as]ומם.[4] The adverb יומם is quite common in the DSS literature. These are 24 occurrences with some of them having been restored. However, there is one in this Scroll, i.e. 11QT 57:10. So this is in addition to the possible present one we are discerning.[5]

There is no disagreement concerning line 4. In the middle of line 5 Qimron, supported by García Martínez, does not transcribe a *shin* as Yadin does and instead reads ומ[ ]ם.[6] Qimron's transcription is preferred here, because the *shin* is very difficult to discern. In the second half of the line Yadin locates a *vacat*, supported by García Martínez.[7] The MS is very unclear on all three plates at the end of line

---

[1] Yadin 1977b, plate 19*.
[2] Qimron, 48.
[3] García Martínez, 1252.
[4] Qimron, 48; García Martínez, 1252. Indeed, the *waw* is a possible reading according to traces on plate 19*.
[5] 11Q19, lines 57:9-10, והיו עמו (10) יומם ולילה. If the present restoration is correct, we then have two cases of יומם in 11QT.
[6] Qimron, 48; García Martínez, 1252.
[7] Yadin, 141; García Martinez, 1252.

5. From plate 48 Qimron's transcription seems to have the stronger support.

(6) [ ]ם אליה֯מ֯ה֯ (?) ו֯ה֯יוצאים מ֯המה אל[ ]
(7) י֯ה֯י֯ו֯ מקדשים את֯ עמ֯י בבגדי ה֯קודש אש֯ר [ ]
(8) ועשיתמה בית֯ למזר֯ח בית ה[כ]יו[ר] כמדת [בית הכי]ור

At the beginning of line 6 Yadin presents an approximate restoration with והבאי]ם] and אל [החצר התיכונה ולוא] par the end of the same line. He is probably right in suggesting an influence from Ezek 44.[8] The first half of the line is very unclear on plate 48 but plate 18* gives us a little more palaeographical evidence.

The difficulties to reconstruct line 6 become evident because of disagreeing suggestions. Qimron, supported by García Martínez, restores the beginning as [יהיו באי]ם֯.[9] This reconstruction follows the pattern of the beginning of line 7. Line 7 probably[10] begins with י֯ה֯י֯ו֯ מקדשי֯ם and is a solution to prefer.

In the middle of line 6, Qimron's reading – אל הכיו֯ר ויוצאים ב֯המה – seems to have stronger support from plate 18*, with one exception.[11] The two dots beside each other after the possible *waw*, which are in a position of about 3 mm from the base for the line, suggest a *he* before יוצאים. This is the way Yadin transcribes.

Concerning the next word, García Martínez[12] supports Yadin's reconstruction of מ֯המה. Both Yadin and Qimron note that the first letter in this word is uncertain. Yadin's choice of the shortened form of the preposition מן seems to be preferable because there is a line immediately before המה. This line begins very closely to the base line and

---

[8] Yadin, 141. The temple in the vision of Ezekiel has two courts only: the inner and the outer court. The temple of 11QT, on the other hand, has a third court which is called החצר התיכונה, "the middle court."

[9] Qimron, 48; García Martínez, 1252.

[10] Some of the letters are damaged.

[11] Qimron, 48. As a matter of fact Yadin admits to his uncertain reading, since he writes a question-mark after his transcription of אליה֯מ֯ה֯. Yadin actually reads the same word – עליהמה – similar to line 4. On line 6 it is, however, difficult to interpret the little dark circle after the damaged but certain *lamed*. Qimron seems to have understood the dark traces as belonging to another location. This is the preferred solution.

[12] García Martínez otherwise supports Qimron with אל הכיור ויוצאים. García Martínez, 1252.

goes diagonally upwards to the right. This would normally be interpreted as a part of a *mem*. On the other hand, we would expect a singular form after יוצאים, that is e.g. ממנו, if the text refers to "going out of the laver (הכיור)." Therefore, it seems even more probable, that the pronoun המה is related to the clothes, which are mentioned indirectly on line 4, עליהמה, and directly on line 7, בגדי קודש. Therefore in conclusion we prefer בהמה.[13]

On line 7 Yadin suggests אתׄ עמׄיׄ, supported by García Martínez, whereas Qimron reads אתׄ הׄשׄער.[14] Yadin seems to rely on Ezek 44:19,[15] ולא־יקדשו את־העם בבגדיהם, concerning his restoration while Qimron is certain of his transcription, albeit the letters are unclear. The palaeographical evidence on plate 18* seems to favour Yadin's reconstruction. For the end of the line Yadin restores tentatively [המה משרתים בהמה].[16] Qimron reconstructs the end as [ישרתו בהמה], which is supported by García Martínez.[17] The shorter alternative seems to be more probable, since the line possibly begins with an imperfect, that is יהיו].[18]

Line 8 seems to begin with a *vacat*. There is no disagreement concerning the restoration on this line.[19]

(9) [ו]ר[ח]וק קירוׄ מק[י]רׄו שבע אמות ו[כ]ול בנינוׄ ומׄקרותיו כׄביתׄ הׄכיור
(10) וׄשנים שערים לוׄ מצפונו ומדרומו זה נוכח זה כמדת שערׄ[י] ביתׄ
(11) הכיור וכול הבית הזה כולו קירו עשויׄ חלונׄים פנימה אטומים
(12) שתי אמות רוחבמה בׄשתי אמות וגובהׄמׄהׄ ארבע אמות

At the beginning of line 9 Qimron does not restore a *waw* and is supported by García Martínez.[20] According to the palaeographical evidence on plate 19* the transcription is generally difficult here. At the

---

[13] If this is a correct transcription the diagonal line seems to have been attached here from another location. We need to remember that plate 18* is a photograph taken of mirror-writing on the back of Col. 34.
[14] García Martínez, 1252; Qimron, 48.
[15] ולא־יקדשו את־העם בבגדיהם.
[16] Yadin, 141.
[17] Qimron, 48; García Martínez, 1252.
[18] יהיו is a reconstruction. On the other hand, this reconstruction is endorsed by Yadin. He also reads active participle, at the end of the line, משרתים.
[19] Yadin notes that the only biblical book that contains כמדת is Ezek 40:21-22, כמדת השער. Yadin, 142.
[20] Qimron, 48; García Martínez, 1252.

very beginning of the line, one can see traces of letters, possibly אל, which do not seem to belong to this line at all.[21] The first visible letter is partly similar with a *chet*. However, this may not be a *chet* because the left vertical stroke is short and does not reach up to the horizontal stroke belonging to a *chet*. Yadin's transcription of two letters – *waw* and *resh* – are a very cramped solution, because there is not enough space for two letters. Due to this reason we prefer Qimron's reading.

In the middle of line 9 Qimron does not transcribe the word completely, but reads ∘∘וֹל.[22] Yadin's reading ו̇[כ]ול is possible considering the available space and in addition it seems to be an intelligible solution. Yadin notes that the following word, בנינו, is only found in Ezek.[23] In the context of 11QT the word "structure" is a possible translation.

The expression זה נוכח זה on line 10 is found in the Bible in 1 Kgs 20:29, ויחנו אלה נכח אלה.[24] At the end of the line Qimron prefers not to reconstruct שער into a plural form, although he notes that Yadin's reading is "equally possible."[25] On the old transparency there is a tiny trace of dark colour after the *resh*. In our opinion it is not impossible to be read as a part of a *yod*. It is more probable that this dark dot – which is pale indeed – would be a part of the left edge of horizontal line belonging to the *resh*.[26]

At the end of line 11 we have the expression חלונים פנימה אטומים. Similar expressions are found in 1 Kgs 6:4, חלוני שקופים אטמים and Ezek 40:16, וחלנות אטמות אל־התאים ואל אליהמה לפנימה לשער סביב סביב וכן לאלמות. From these passages we may draw the conclusions that חלונים אטומים[27] is in fact a biblical expression. In 𝔊 וחלנות אטמות is

---

[21] There is no disagreement concerning this observation.

[22] Qimron, 48.

[23] Ezek 40:5; 41:12, 15; 42:1, 5, 10. Yadin, 142. In the biblical context it may be translated with "building" and not necessarily with "wall" as Yadin has suggested.

[24] Yadin calls it "a classical biblical expression." Yadin, 142. On the other hand it does not appear literally in the Bible and so cannot be understood as a biblical quotation.

[25] Qimron, 48. Yadin's transcription שער̇[י] is supported by García Martínez. García Martínez, 1252.

[26] It is moreover possible to discern a *taw* in front of the word בית, a little below the base line and slightly touching the left corner of *beit*. It seems probable, however, that *taw* is dislocated and does not belong to this line.

[27] חלונים is found with both masculine and feminine endings in Ezekiel. However, feminine form does not seem to be extant in DSS, although we cannot be totally convinced about that since חלונים is a result of two reconstructions. Only once it is found without reconstruction, which is this case.

translated with καὶ θυρίδες κρυπταὶ which is an expected version for "blocked windows."[28] There is no disagreement concerning the transcriptions of lines 11 and 12.

וׄת
(13) מדולתים בתים לכלי המזבח למׄזורקים ולקשׄוא ולׄמׄחתות
(14) ולכוננות הכסף אשר יהיו מעלׄים במׄה את הקרבים ואת
(15) הׄרגלים על המזבח ובבלותמה לקטׄיר

At the beginning of line 13 we have a *hapax legomenon* מדולתים, because this seems to be the only known occurrence of the word. The DSS Concordance suggests "to be opened" as a translation. A more natural solution for this is Yadin's "have doors" or García Martínez "with doors."[29] The word בתים seems here to refer to the חלונים אטומים. The rest of the line seems to have quite close parallels – although not quotations – to Ex 27:3, Ex 38:3 and Num 4:14.[30] Concerning the letters above the end of line 13, the scribe seems to have added them after he wrote the word in singular.[31] Therefore line 13 is understood as Rewritten Bible, because the line contains new elements.

At the beginning of line 14 Qimron has suggested ולכוננות. This seems to refer to some kind of a bowl. This transcription can indeed be discerned on plate 18*.[32] In the middle of line 15 there is a *vacat* after which a new subject begins.

---

[28] Actually we do not have real windows here but a niche or – with modern terms – some kind of a "cupboard," which is used as a storage-room for the utensils of the altar. This "blocked window" is drawn by Yadin and presented in fig. 11. Yadin 1983 vol. 1, 227.

[29] Yadin, 143; García Martínez, 1252.

[30] ועשיתה סירתיו לדשנו ויעיו ומזרקתיו ומזלגתיו ומחתתיו (Ex 27:3); ויעש את־כל־כלי המזבח את־הסירת ואת־היעים ואת־המזרקת ואת־המזלגת ואת־המחתת (Ex 38:3); ונתנו עליו את־כל־כליו אשר ישרתו עליו בהם את־המחתת את־המזלגת ואת־היעים ואת־המזרקת כל כלי המזבח (Num 4:14).

[31] Qimron does not read *waw* above the line but only a *taw*. Qimron, 48. The manuscript is very unclear at this location.

[32] Qimron notes that the word is not found in Hebrew sources and adds: "יש לה מקבילות בארמית, בערבית ובאכדית: בארמית הבבלית באה המלה בצורה 'כנונ' והיא מעין קערה או מחתה, שמביאים בה גחלים להתחמם. בערבית אתה מוצא كنون באותה משמעות, ובאכדית: kinūnu." Qimron 1982, 133.

Summary of Col. 33

(1)]]י̊ים באים [
(2)]] ובעת אשׄ[ר
(3)] י]ו̊מׄם ואת̊ׄ[
(4)]]אשׄר̊ עליהמה ומני̊[חים
(5)]]בׄיׄ[ת] הׄכׄיׄוׄרׄ ומׄ[ ]םׄ לׄכיו[ר
(6) [יהיו באי]םׄ אלׄ הכׄיׄוׄרׄ ו̊ה̊יוצאים ב̊המה אל [החצר התיכונה ולוא]
(7) י̊ה̊י̊ו̊ מקדשים את עמׄיׄ בׄבגדיׄ הׄקוׄדׄש אשׄרׄ [ישרתו בהמה]
(8) *vacat* ועשיתמה ביתׄ למזרׄח בית ה[כ]יו[ר] כמדת [בית הכי]ור
(9) ר[ח]וק קירוׄ מק[י]רׄו שבע אמות וׄ[כ]ולׄ בנינוׄ ומׄקרותיו כׄבׄיׄתׄ הׄכׄיוׄרׄ
(10) וׄשנים שערים לוׄ מצפונו ומדרומו זה נוכח זׄה כמדת שׄעׄרׄ ביתׄ
(11) הכיור וכול הבית הזה כולו קירו עשויׄ חלונים פנימה אטומים
(12) שתי אמות רוחבמה בׄשתי אמות וגובהׄמהׄ ארבע אמות
(13) מדולתׄים בתים לכליׄ המזבח למׄזרקים ולקשׄוׄאׄ[ת̊] ולמׄחׄתות
(14) ולכוננות הכסף אשר יהיו מעלׄים במׄה את הקרבים ואת
(15) ה̊רׄגלים על המזבח *vacat* ובכלותמה לקטׄירׄ

Notes on Readings

1:]י̊ים באים[– Yadin and García Martínez read]ים באים[. **3:** י]ו̊מׄם ואת̊ׄ[– Yadin reads]מׄם ואת̊ׄ[as Qimron and García Martínez have]ומם ואת̊ׄ[. **5:**]בׄיׄ[ת] הׄכׄיׄוׄרׄ ומׄ[ ]םׄ לׄכיו[ר – Yadin interprets this as בׄיׄ[ת] הׄכׄיׄוׄרׄ | אלׄ הכׄיׄוׄרׄ, García Martínez transcribes בׄיׄ[ת] הׄכיו ומ[ ] וׄמׄ◦◦ש̊◦◦םׄ [ ] לׄכיור. **6:** [יהיו באי]םׄ – Yadin tentatively [והבאי]ם | [ ]םׄ לׄכיו[ר. Qimron has אל ו̊ה̊יוצאים ב̊המה (?) אליהמה, Yadin reads ו̊ה̊יוצאים ב̊המה – ו̊ה̊יוצאים ב̊המה whereas García Martínez transcribes אל הכיור ויוצאים ב̊המה הכׄיׄוׄרׄ ויוצאים ב̊המה מהמה. **7:** את עמׄיׄ – Qimron transcribes את הׄשׄער | [ישרתו בהמה] אשׄרׄ – Yadin has [משרתים בהמה] אשׄרׄ. **9:** ר[ח]וק – Yadin reads [ו]ר[ח]וק | וׄ[כ]ולׄ – Qimron has ◦◦ו̊לׄ. **10:** שׄעׄרׄ – Yadin reconstructs שׄעׄרׄ[י].
13: ולקשׄוׄאׄ[ת̊] – Yadin reads ולקשׄוׄאׄ[ות].

2.6 Column 34

This column is missing a part of its text in the upper left corner due to a tear in the manuscript. In spite of this, a large amount of the text has survived. Plate 49, together with plates 20* and 21* which represent infra-red photographs of mirror-writing from the back of Col. 35 increase the certainty of the transcription.[1]

(1)]]נ̊י̊ם̊(?) בלוח נחו]שת [
(2)]]. . . ובין העמוד לע]מוד [
(3)]]אׄשר בין הׄעמודים [[

At the beginning of line 1 Qimron reads מצו]פׄים *pro* Yadin's]נ̊י̊ם̊. Qimron provides evidence for this transcription by arguing that the letters פׄים can be found on plate 19*. This is indeed the case.[2] This seems to be a probable solution. The expression לוח נחושת is not found in the Bible and so it could be categorized as Individual Composition. Concerning lines 2 and 3 there is no disagreement about the transcription and reconstruction.

(4)]] . . . ים אל בין(?) הגׄלׄג]לים [
(5)]]ים וסוגרים את הגלגלים ואׄ[[
(6) ואוסרים אתׄ רׄאׄשי הׄפרים אל הטבעות ו[ ] בׄטבעות
(7) אחר יהיו טובחׄים אותמה ויהיו כונסים א[ת הדם] במזרקות
(8) וזׄורקים אותׄוׄ עׄל יסוד המזבח סביב ופותחים

At the beginning of line 4 Qimron restores [ומביאים את, which seems to be a good suggestion. In comparison with Yadin, Qimron transcribes slightly differently: הׄפרים אל תוך הגׄלׄג]לים.[3] From the photo on microfiche, SHR 5034, we will deal with two details: the *he* that Qimron has suggested at the beginning of the line and the difference between *nun sophit* and *caph sophit* in בין / תוך. Firstly, there are some traces that could possibly be a *he*. Secondly, it is hard to tell the difference

[1] Yadin, 143.
[2] Qimron, 49. These three letters – פים – may have been stuck slightly to the upper right of the letters י̊ם באים on line 1 on plate 19*. Yadin agrees about the *yod* in the middle but claims that the preceding letters could be neither *nun*, *yod* nor *caph*. Yadin, 144.
[3] Qimron, 49.

between the transcription of *nun* and *caph*. For a *nun*, the vertical stroke downwards is a little too long. On the other hand we would expect the traces of the horizontal stroke of the *caph* to be longer. This is, however, a possible interpretation if the vertical line was bent slightly to the right before its attachment with the horizontal stroke. In conclusion we can say that the *caph* therefore has more palaeographical support.[4]

At the beginning of line 5 Yadin suggests [ופותח]ים as a possible restoration. At the end of the line he reads וא֯[חר.[5] Alternatively Qimron is able to discern [הגל]גלים at the beginning of line 5. Again we consult SHR 5034 that shows us that the *gimel* is very uncertain. The computerized photo reveals, however, a quite clear *lamed*.[6] Due to this evidence we agree with Qimron's solution for the beginning of line 5.

For the beginning of line 6 plate 49 is very unclear. On the other hand, ואוסרים is quite clearly discerned from plate 21*. On the same line Qimron transcribes ק֯ר֯ני *pro* Yadin's ר֯א֯שי.[7] According to the palaeographical evidence, *qof* is an unclear but possible transcription. *Nun* and *yod* are quite possible. In the light of the palaeographical evidence ק֯ר֯ני is therefore the better alternative.

At the end of line 7 Qimron restores את֯ [כול הדם] במזרקות.[8] This reconstruction seems to be a good solution considering the length of the tear which is shown on plate 21*. Therefore, for the same reason Yadin's solution of א[ת הדם] is too short.[9] There is no disagreement concerning the transcription of line 8 up to the *vacat*. In addition, Yadin has noted that the first half of this line has the same content as Lev 1:5, וזרקו את־הדם על־המזבח סביב.[10]

---

[4] The other letters possible are תוך. These are also uncertain. On the other hand we get support for this alternative from the context.

[5] Concerning his reconstruction at the beginning of line 5, Yadin refers to the lines 8–9 ופותחים (9) את הגלגלים. Yadin, 145.

[6] Qimron, 49.

[7] Qimron, 49; Yadin adds that Qimron's reading is "very doubtful." Yadin, 145.

[8] Qimron, 49.

[9] Yadin, 145. García Martínez prefers Yadin's transcription. García Martínez, 1252, 1254.

[10] Yadin, 145.

(8) ופותחים
(9) את הגלגלים ו֯פ֯ו֯שטים את עורות הפרים מעל לבשרמה ומנתחים
(10) אותמה לנתחיהמה ומולחים את הנתחים במלחׄ ומרחצים את
(11) הקרבים ואת הכרעים ומולחים בׄמׄלח ומקטירים אותמה על
(12) האש אשר על המזבח פר ופר ונתחיו אצלוׄ ומנׄחת סולתו עליו

For line 9, the transcription of ו֯פ֯ו֯שטים seems to be difficult, since at least three different solutions have been offered. It has to be admitted that the first part of this word is very unclear. Qimron reads ו֯מ֯פשיטים whereas García Martínez transcribes [ומ]פושטים.[11] The palaeographical evidence on plate 21* – which is the photograph where we can see the most of the word – the situation is as follows: ופושטים is difficult because the letter after the possible *pe* is a broad letter and not a narrow one such as a *waw*. Another problem with this reading is the remains before the *tet*.

Yadin seems to interpret the traces as part of a *shin*, which could be possible. Qimron transcribes the line as a *yod* and this is the more likely solution. Further, there is enough space for García Martínez' reading [ומ]פושטים, which is not an impossible reconstruction from a palaeographic point of view. It is, however, grammatically difficult.[12] Yadin points out, that ופושטים would be the best alternative for this context.[13] Therefore the best solution palaeographically and as we cannot build our transcription mainly on context, we agree with Qimron's *hiphil*-form of ומפשיטים.

At the end of line 9, Yadin reads a *lamed* in לבשרמה, but that does not exist in the manuscript. When we compare plates 49 and 21* closely together, it becomes obvious that the *lamed* belongs to the end of the preceding word מעל.

---

11 Qimron, 49; García Martínez, 1254.

12 מפושטים is *pual* and should generally be translated with a passive. This does not make any sense in this context.

13 Yadin noted that *qal* would be more suitable than *hiphil*, since the subject here is the hide and not the sacrifice. Yadin, 146. It is, however, possible that the author wanted to keep the *hiphil*-form, since line 9 quite clearly is related to Lev 1:6. 𝔐 reads the verb in singular, והפשיט, and ࠔ has the verb in plural, הפשיטו, like 𝔊 with ἐκδείραντες. Moreover, Yadin's restoration – ופושטים – reflects the mentioned 𝔊-reading, as both are participle-forms: active participle and aorist participle, respectively. In any event, we will not continue this discussion, since ופושטים is a reconstructed form and therefore uncertain.

At the end of line 9 we read מנתחים. Yadin has noted there is a difference in the biblical sources concerning this.[14] 𝔐 has singular in Lev 1:6, ונתח אתה לנתחיה, while ɯ and 𝔊 read the verb in plural, ונתחו and μελιοῦσιν, respectively. At the beginning of line 10 the structure אותמה לנתחיהמה is also in plural. One possibility is that the author wished to be consistent and therefore changed all the words and not only the verb into plural.

On lines 10–11 there are no disagreements concerning the transcription, since the manuscript is quite clear. These lines are, however, interesting enough since we have a biblical parallel in Lev 1:8-9, וערכו בני אהרן הכהנים את הנתחים את־הראש ואת הפדר על־העצים אשר **על־האש אשר על־המזבח:** (9) וקרבו וכרעיו ירחץ במים והקטיר הכהן את־הכל המזבחה עלה אשה ריח־ניחוח לה'. Moreover, Lev 2:13 reads וכל־קרבן מנחתך במלח תמלח.

Firstly, it seems clear that we have Biblical Paraphrase, that is on line 10, influenced by Lev 2:13. The end of line 10 and line 11 are influenced by Lev 1:9. Secondly, we have an expression at the end of line 11 and at the beginning of line 12, which seems to be a biblical quotation, על (12) האש אשר על המזבח. This quote is in bold at the end of Lev 1:8 in the passage above. ɯ agrees with 𝔐 literally on this text. In 𝔊 (BA) we find, however, a subtle difference represented by ἐπὶ τοῦ πυρὸς τὰ ὄντα ἐπὶ τοῦ θυσιαστηρίου. In addition there is a minuscule manuscript, 376, which reads του *pro* τὰ ὄντα. This reading seems to be equivalent to the readings in 11Q19, 𝔐, and ɯ.[15]

If we consider the context of the passage in the Scroll with the context of the biblical sources, we notice that they are the same – to burn the sacrifice on the altar – and therefore this part of Col. 34 will be considered as a quotation on the basis of our study's definition.

[14] Yadin, 146.

[15] The analysis of this passage will be continued in chapter four.

(13) ויין נסכו אצלו ומ֯מנו עליו והקטירו֯ הכוהנים בני אהרון את הכול
(14) על המזבח אשה ריח ניחוח לפני יהוה
(15) ועשיתה שלשלות יורדות מן מקרת שני עשר העמודים

On the first half of line 13 García Martínez reads ושמנו *pro* ומ֯מנו.[16] From the following והקטירו֯ on the same line to the end of line 14 the author has been strongly influenced by Lev 1:9. The plural of the verb and subject והקטירו הכוהנים may come from a tradition close to 𝔊, that reads καὶ ἐπιθήσουσιν οἱ ἱερεῖς.[17]

Comparison the end of line 13, with 𝔐, ⅏ and 𝔊, we find את הכול in 𝔐 but no את in ⅏ and 𝔊 has τὰ πάντα. From here to the end of line 14 the text is close to a biblical quotation. The only differences are that in 𝔐 has המזבח *pro* על המזבח and ליהוה *pro* לפני יהוה. Also, 𝔊 reads here ἐπὶ τὸ θυσιαστήριον· καρπωμά ἐστιν, θυσία, ὀσμὴ εὐωδίας τῷ κυρίῳ. Therefore, 𝔊 seems closer to 11Q19 than 𝔐 and ⅏.

We remember והקטירו in plural and note that the Hebrew *Vorlage* behind the passage in Greek could have been equivalent to the Scroll here.[18] Therefore, we conclude that 𝔊 seems to agree with 11Q19 concerning this passage. In addition 𝔐 and ⅏ represent textual traditions, which differ from the Scroll. There is a *vacat* at the end of line 14.

Also, there are no disagreements concerning the transcription of line 15. Further, a new topic begins in line 15 begins here: the construction of some kind of ceiling structure, and this continues into Col. 35

[16] García Martínez, 1254. It seems that also Yadin transcribed ושמנו before, because he writes that he accepts Qimron's reading ומ֯מנו instead of ושׁמנו. Yadin, 146. If we take a closer look at plate 21* it is quite clear that two *mems* can be discerned together. This makes ושמנו an impossible reading.

[17] The equivalence between *hiphil* of קטר and ἐπιτιθέναι is not based on the lexical translation. There are times – as in Lev 1:9 – when the context seems to give them a very similar meaning.

[18] The only difference is that this passage does not include οἱ υἱοὶ Ααρων.

Summary of Col. 34

(1)] מצו]פים בלוח נחו[שת
(2)]]ובין העמוד לע[מוד
(3)]]אׄשר בין הׄעמׄודים[
(4) [ומביאים את] הׄפׄרים אל תׄוׄךׄ הגׄלׄג[לים
(5) [הגלג]לים וסוגרים את הגלגלים ואׄ[
(6) ואוסרים אׄת קׄרׄנׄי הׄפׄרים אל הטבעות ו[ ]בׄטבעות
(7) אחר יהיו טׄובׄחׄים אותמה ויהיו כונסים אׄ[ת כול הדם] במזרקות
(8) וׄזורקים אותׄוׄ עׄל יסוׄד המזבח סביב *vacat* ופותחים
(9) את הגלגלים וׄמׄפׄשׄיטים את עורות הפרים מעל בשרמה ומנתחים
(10) אותמה לנתחיהמה וׄמולחים את הנתחים במלׄחׄ ומרחצים את
(11) הקרבים ואת הכרעים ומולחים בׄמׄלח ומקטירים אותמה על
(12) האש אשר על המזבח פר ופר ונתחיו אצלׄוׄ ומנׄחׄת סולתו עליו
(13) ויין נסכו אצלו וׄמׄמׄנו עליו והקטירׄוׄ הכוהנים בני אהרון את הכול
(14) על המזבח אשה ריח ניחוח לפני יהוה *vacat*
(15) ועשיתה שלשלות יורדות מן מקרת שני עשר העמודים

Notes on Readings

1: מצו]פים – Yadin reads נׄיׄםׄ]. **4:** [ומביאים את] הׄפׄרים אל תׄוׄךׄ – Yadin reads (?)ים אל בין . . .]. **5:** [הגלג]לים – Yadin tentatively [ופותח]ים. **6:** קׄרׄנׄי – Yadin transcribes רׄאׄשׄי. **7:** אׄ[ת כול הדם] – Yadin restores א[ת הדם]. **9:** וׄמׄפׄשׄיטים – Yadin reads וׄפׄוׄשׄטים whereas García Martínez has [ומ]פושטים | בשרמה – Yadin transcribes לבשרמה. **13:** וׄמׄמׄנו – García Martínez reads ושמנו.

2.7. Column 35

The text for Col. 35 is found on the plates 50, 22*, and 23*. The writing is not very clear on plate 50 but the infra-red photographs of the mirror-writing on the back of Col. 36 are very helpful for the restoration. Close to a fifth of the total text in the top of the column is not extant due to a great tear in the column.[1]

(1)] קוד]ש̇ הקודשי̇[ם [
(2)]] ◦ כול איש אשר לוא̇[[
(3)]]א כול איש א̇שר לוא̊[ק]ו̊דש
(4)]]ה מ . . . . ה

The beginning of line 1 is restored with [אל קוד]ש̇, which is a probable solution.[2] From line 2 and forward there are a series of prohibitions that continue into line 8. Yadin has pointed out that we have biblical passages that begin in a similar way, e.g. in Lev 21:18, כי כל־איש אשר־בו מום לא יקרב and Lev 22:3, אל־הקדשים כל־איש אשר־יקרב מכל־זרעכם.[3] Qimron restores the first word on line 2 as [או]ת̊ה.[4] It is possible to read the *he* clearly but the tear in the manuscript prevents us from verifying the *taw*.[5]

Qimron suggests, furthermore, a restoration of parts from the end of line 2 to the beginning of line 4 based on Ex 30:22-33, which gives a solution of משחת קודש] (3) [תהי]ה̇ כול איש אשר לוא̇ . . . [הק]ו̊דש (4) [ימש]ח̇. For comparison, Ex 30:31 reads ואל־בני ישראל תדבר לאמר שמן משחת־קדש יהיה זה לי לדרתיכם.[6] The first impression concerning כול איש אשר לוא̇ at the beginning of line 2 is, that we may have a quotation from Leviticus, e.g. Lev 21:21, but in this verse we read about the burnt offering. This means that we do not have the same context and thus it

---

[1] Yadin 1977a, plate 50.

[2] Qimron, 50; García Martínez, 1254. In addition to this reading Yadin also has another alternative, this is [כי קוד]ש̇. Yadin, 148.

[3] In addition to these verses, 1QM lines 7:5-6 use the same words at the beginning. The War Scroll teaches who may go into battle on יום הנקם and who may not go: וכול (6) איש אשר לוא יהיה טהור ממקורו ביום המלחמה לוא ירד אתם. Yadin, 148.

[4] Qimron, 50.

[5] García Martínez reads no more than the *he* at the beginning of line 2. García Martínez, 1254.

[6] Qimron, 50.

cannot be a Biblical Quotation according to our definition. It is instead interpreted as Rewritten Bible.[7] Lev 22:3 may be closer to the context of 11QT, since the Scroll tells us about the holiness and purity of the temple.

Lev 22 has a similar content with the prohibition for the unclean not to approach the holy. Since these lines suffer from a lack of restoration, we cannot know the exact context of lines 2 and 3. Consequently we also understand line 3 as Rewritten Bible.

If we consider the context later in the column, we note that line 8 refers to the sanctification of the altar. It is, therefore, reasonable to propose that the holy oil for anointing was in the picture in the previous lines. However, it seems a little difficult to include the oil into the list of the prohibitions. Therefore, I agree with Yadin and do not present a fuller restoration for the lines 2–4a. At the beginning of line 3 Yadin reads an *alef pro* Qimron's *he*. The traces on the existing plates are very unclear at this location. At the end of the same line Yadin and García Martínez read ק]ו֯דש *pro* Qimron's הק]ו֯דׄש.[8]

Concerning the first discernible letter at the beginning of line 4, Qimron reads *chet pro* Yadin's *he*. These two letters can sometimes be very similar in the Scroll's handwriting. One difference between *chet* and *he* is in the way the horizontal stroke is drawn: it should usually not pass the left vertical line but continue downwards with a sharp turn of 90 degrees. If we look very closely on plate 23* at the letter at the beginning of line 4, the horizontal stroke slightly passes the left vertical line. Due to this observation, I tend to read a *he* like Yadin.[9]

At the beginning of line 4 Qimron, supported by García Martínez, reads ממנה, which is a reasonable restoration of this unclear passage.[10]

---

[7] The imminent context of line 2 is, however, a bit unclear due to the need for further restoration of the line.

[8] Yadin, 148; García Martínez, 1254. We need to remember that Qimron's determined article *he* can be derived from the fact that he uses Ex 30 for his restoration.

[9] García Martínez also supports Yadin's reading of a *he*. García Martínez, 1254.

[10] Qimron, 50; García Martínez, 1254. Even if the reading of ממנה is reasonable, it can be noted that the word takes more space than usual for so few letters. If we take a closer look at plate 23*, one can see a vertical stroke above the first *mem* in ממנה. This seems, however, to be traces from another location.

(4) וכוׄל [ ]הוא אין
(5) הׄואׄ כ֯ו֯ה֯ן֯ יׄ[ו]מת וכול איׄשׁ֯ א֯שׁר֯(?) [הוא כו]ה֯ן אשר יבוא
(6) א֯ ∘∘∘∘ והוא אין הׄואׄ לׄבושׁ בגׄ[די הקודש אשר בה]מ֯ה֯ מלא את
(7) יׄדיו גם המה יומתו ולוא יחׄל[לו את מק]ד֯ש אלוהׄיהמה לשאת
(8) עׄוון אשמה למות

There is no disagreement concerning the transcription of וכוׄל at the beginning of line 4. After that Yadin does not restore anything while Qimron reconstructs the line as וכוׄל [איש מבני ישראל אשר יביא אותה ו]הוא אין.[11] This reading is constructed based on the model of the end of line 5 and the beginning of line 6, which means that it is partly depending on the transcription of the last word at the end of line 5. This may be either יביא or יבוא – a fact that also is noted by Qimron. According to plate 23* the down stroke of the third letter is quite long: the down stroke actually continues downwards in a lighter colour. On an old transparency of this column, it is possible to discern that the colour gets darker at the lowest parts of this vertical line. This darker spot is located as low as the base line of the preceding *beit*. In the light of these observations we prefer the transcription of יבוא, which tentatively is also supported by Yadin.

Since יבוא seems to be the better solution palaeographically, it is impossible to begin line 6 with אותה. It is, however, possible to read איתם from the old transparency. This actual reading is suggested by Yadin.[12]

According to Puech, 4Q524 is the oldest known copy of the Temple Scroll.[13] In his reconstruction of Frg. 1, which possibly is a parallel to Col. 35, he tentatively suggests the following reading for line 4, וכול [איש אשר יקרב אל המזבח(?) ו]הוא.[14] This restoration seems to be based on the context of Lev 21 and 22 mentioned above. However, it seems quite clear that this solution is too short taking only 23 spaces, whereas Qimron's reconstruction with 30 spaces fits well on this line.

---

[11] Qimron, 50.
[12] Yadin, 149.
[13] Puech 1998, 86.
[14] Puech 1998, 90. Contextually this is not a bad solution at all, since the altar is mentioned also on line 8.

In the light of the comments above we prefer, therefore, to restore the mid part of line 4 as follows: וכול̊ [איש מבני ישראל אשר יבוא איתם.

At the beginning of line 5 there are no disagreements concerning the transcription. After איש Qimron suggests מ̇ה̇[כוהנים בני אהרו]ן אשר יביא/יבוא (6) אותה, which is not an impossible solution.[15] At the end of line 5 and at the beginning of line 6 García Martínez suggests יבוא (6) אותה, which is a strange combination.[16] It seems that we have only two alternatives here: 1) יביא אותה or 2) יבוא איתם.

The problem with line 6 is focused at the end of the restoration. Qimron suggests הקודש או אשר] ל̊ו̊א̊ מלא את (7) ידיו.[17] It is very difficult to give priority on palaeographical grounds. Concerning line 7, we have a parallel of two words in 4Q542 Frg. 1:2, המ]ה יומת[ו].[18] This parallel does not help us much; although it seems to help Puech in the opposite direction, since he uses 11Q19 for the restoration of 4Q542.

After these two words, line 7 contains a passage that is very similar to Lev 21:12, ולא יחלל את מקדש אלהיו and Lev 22:16, והשיאו אותם עון אשמה באכלם את־קדשיהם. Yadin notes this.[19] At the end of the line we have מק]דש אלוהיהמה. Firstly, this passage cannot be interpreted as a Biblical Quotation, since the context is not the same.[20] Moreover, Leviticus has the verb in singular whereas the verb in the Scroll – due to its context – needs to be restored in plural.[21]

The אלוהיהמה at the end of thc line has a textual parallel in a 𝔊-manuscript belonging to the *f*-group, that is 53*-129 which reads τοῦ θεοῦ *αὐτῶν* *pro* τοῦ θεοῦ *αὐτοῦ* in B. It could be assumed that the plural of *αὐτῶν* is caused by a verb in plural. This is, however, not the case since 53*-129 of 𝔊 seems to read βεβηλώσει.[22] Due to the dif-

---

[15] Qimron, 50. As have been noted above, we prefer the restoration יבוא איתם.

[16] García Martínez, 1254.

[17] Qimron, 50.

[18] Puech 1998, 90. It seems clear that this indeed is another copy of the Temple Scroll, since the fragments of 4Q542 contain several short passages that equal the text of 11Q19.

[19] Yadin, 149. He notes that the beginning of the sentence is like 𝔊 to Lev 21:13. This seems to be inaccurate to some extent, since 𝔊 here agrees with 𝔐.

[20] The acting subject in Leviticus is the high priest and in 11QT it seems to be any man among the priests.

[21] The preceding words are המה יומתו.

[22] The footnote apparatus of 𝔊 does not give us an alternative reading for βεβηλώσει.

ference in context, we therefore understand אלוהיהמה as Rewritten Bible and not as a Biblical Quotation.

(8) וקדשת{מ}ה את ס֯[בי]ב למזבח ולהיכל ולכיור
(9) ולפ֯רו֯ר והיה קודש קודשים לעולם ועד

There is no disagreement concerning the transcription on lines 8 and 9. We can note a scribal mistake in the word וקדשת{מ}ה as the scribe at first wrote a *mem* and erased it afterwards. The rest of the passage is close to Ex 30:29, וקדשת אתם והיו קדש קדשים and 40:10, וקדשת את־המזבח והיה המזבח קדש קדשים.[23]

(10) ועשיתה מקום למערב ההיכל סביב פ֯רור עמודים עומדים
(11) לחטאת ולאשם מובדלים זה מזה לחטאת כוהנים ולשעירים
(12) ולחטאות העם ולאשמותמה ולוא יהיו מערבים כולו אלה
(13) באלה כי מובדלים יהיו מקומותמה זה מזה למען לוא
(14) ישוגו הכוהנים בכול חטאת העם ובכול אלו אשמות לשאת
(15) חטא אשמה והעוף על המזבח יעשה התורים

On these six lines there is only one disagreement concerning the transcription, which is found on the second half of line 14, that is אלו. Qimron reads אלי – more exactly אֵילֵי – and argues that it is very unlikely that אלו could be interpreted as a pronoun. As a result we get the expression אילי אשמות, "rams of the guilt-offering."[24]

Yadin notes that Ezek 46:19b-20a uses מקום in a similar manner as line 10, והנה־שם מקום בירכתם ימה (20) ויאמר אלי זה המקום אשר יבשלו־שם הכהנים את־אשם ואת־החטאת.[25] The use of both מקום and the two words for the offering, אשם and חטאת, shows that there is a biblical influence behind line 10.

---

[23] Yadin, 150. Yadin mentions several texts but only these two passages from Exodus have a similar context of sanctification of the vessels belonging to the altar. In addition, Lev 8:11 also includes sanctification but uses anointing oil, which is not mentioned in our context.

[24] We suggest reading the whole and convincing discussion by Qimron in Tarbiz 51, 136-137. It has to be pointed out that the letter *yod / waw* on plate 50 is long. On the other hand we agree with Qimron that the difference between these two letters is decided according to the context.

[25] Yadin, 150.

Moreover, it is very interesting that the Scroll has למערב as Ezek reads ימה. The *masorah* in 𝔐 suggests a *Qere*-reading of בירכתים. In this context, however, 11Q19 shows us that the *Ketiv*-reading of ימה is possibly the correct one.

After the *vacat* on line 15 a new subject begins concerning sacrificing birds. This is in agreement with Lev 1:14, ואם מן־העוף עלה קרבנו ליהוה והקריב מן־התרים או מן־בני היונה את־קרבנו.[26]

Summary of Col. 35

(1) [אל קוד]ש̇ הקודשי̇[ם
(2) [   ]ה כול איש אשר לוא̊[
(3) [   ]◦ כול איש א̇שר לוא̊[ק]ו̊דש
(4) [   ]ה ממ̊נה וכו̊ל [איש מבני ישראל אשר יבוא איתם ו]הוא אין
(5) ה̇וא̇ כ̊ו̊ה̊ן̊ י̊[ו]מת וכול אי̊ש̊ מ̇ה̇[כוהנים בני אהרו]ן אשר יבוא
(6) אי̇תם והוא אי̇ן ה̇ו̇א̇ ל̇בוש בג̊[די הקודש   ] מלא את
(7) י̇דיו גם המה יומתו ולוא יח̇ל̇[לו את מק]ד̊ש אלוה̇י̇המה לשאת
(8) ע̇וון אשמה למות וקדשת{מ}ה את ס̇[בי]ב למזבח ולהיכל ולכי̇ו̇ר
(9) ו̇ל̇פ̇רו̇ר והיה קודש קודשים לעולם ועד *vacat*
(10) ועשיתה מקום למערב ההיכל סביב פ̇רור עמודים עומדים
(11) לחטאת ולאשם מובדלים זה מזה לחטאת כוהנים ולשעירים
(12) ולחטאות העם ולאשמותמה ולוא יהיו מערבים כולו אלה
(13) באלה כי מובדלים יהיו מקומותמה זה מזה למען לוא
(14) ישוגו הכוהנים בכול חטאת העם ובכול אלי אשמות לשאת
(15) חטא אשמה *vacat* והעוף על המזבח יעשה התורים

Notes on Readings

1: [אל קוד]ש̇ – Yadin has [קוד]ש̇. **2:** [   ]ה כול איש אשר – Yadin reads ◦ כול איש אשר as Qimron has [או]ת̊ה כול איש אשר. **3–4:** ◦ כול איש א̇שר לוא̊[. . . ק]ו̊דש (4) [   ]ה ממ̊נה – Qimron reads (3) [משחת קודש תהי]ה̇ כול איש אשר לוא̇ . . . [הק]ו̊דש (4) [ימש]ח̇ ממנה. **4:** וכו̊ל [איש מבני ישראל אשר יבוא איתם ו]הוא אין – Yadin and García Martínez read וכו̊ל [. . .]הוא אין. **5:** וכול אי̊ש̊ מ̇ה̇[כוהנים בני אהרו]ן – Yadin has וכול אי̊ש̊ א̊ש̊ר̊(?) [הוא . . . כו]ה̊ן. **6:** איתם – Yadin transcribes | א̊ ◦◦◦◦. בג̊[די הקודש   ] – Yadin reads בג̊[די הקודש אשר בה]מ̊ה̊ as Qimron has [הקודש או אשר] לו̊א̊. **14:** אלי – Yadin reads אלו.

---

[26] Yadin, 151.

2.8. Column 36

There is a tear at the right top of this column. The text, that has survived, is clear and relatively easy to transcribe. We get additional textual support from plate 24*, which is a photograph of mirror-writing from the back of Col. 37.

(1) [ ]א[ ]
(2) [ ]שׁע֯רים ו֯מ֯א֯ה֯ [ ]
(3) [ ] מן המׄקצוׄע֯[ ]
(4) [עד פנ]תׄ הׄשׄע֯[ר עשרים ומאה באמה

On the first line only an *alef* is discernible, that is an *alef*. Concerning the first word on line 2, שׁע֯רים, both Qimron and García Martínez agree with Yadin.[1] The last word is very unclear, and Yadin is the only one that suggests a transcription, of ו֯מ֯א֯ה֯.[2] From plate 24* the transcription of מן המׄקצוׄע֯ on line 3 is clear. Qimron, however, discerns a damaged but certain *lamed* before these two words.[3] Even if the traces are clear, they are not very similar to the vertical down stroke of a *lamed*, since it slightly turns to the right on plate 24*.

There is no disagreement concerning the reconstruction of the first half of line 4. Yadin's suggestion is based on lines 12–13, עשרים ומאה באמה (13).[4]

(4) ו]השער רחב אר֯ב֯ע֯י֯ם֯
(5) [באמה] לׄכול רוח ורׄוׄחׄ [כמדה הזואת] וׄ[רו]חׄב קיׄ[רו] שׄבׄע אמׄוׄתׄ
(6) [וגוב]הׄו֯ חמש [וארבעים באמה עד מק]רת גׄגׄ[ו ורוח]בׄ תׄ[איו] שׄשׄ
(7) וׄעׄשׄרׄיׄםׄ באמה מׄמׄקצוע אל מקצוע

At the end of line 4 there is no disagreement concerning the restoration, which is based both on plate 51 and 24*. At the beginning of line 5 Qimron restores אמׄהׄ *pro* [באמה] by Yadin and García Martínez.[5] It

[1] Qimron, 51; García Martínez, 1254.
[2] Yadin, 152.
[3] Qimron, 51. Yadin tentatively suggests restorations at the end of the line, מן המקצוע [הראשון or מן המקצוע [למזרח צפון. Yadin, 153. These restorations are, however, very uncertain.
[4] Yadin, 155.
[5] Yadin, 153; García Martínez, 1254.

seems that אמה is to be preferred – otherwise the letters would be unnaturally cramped together.[6] Before the mid part of the line, Qimron claims that the correct reading – which seems to be more likely – is רוחותׄיו *pro* Yadin's רוח ורׄוׄחׄ.[7] Concerning the restoration of זואת *pro* Qimron's זאת, the shorter reading is better because of the amount of space available.[8]

The transcription and restoration of line 6 include some problems. One problematical locus is באמה / אמה in the middle of the line. Here we a have a similar phenomenon as at the beginning of line 5 and again the shorter reading אמה is preferred due to space-reasons.[9]

Another uncertainty is found at the end of the line. According to Qimron there are two alternatives [תׄ[איו or [תׄו֯[יו.[10] Indeed, it is a bit difficult to read the second letter as an *alef* but it is not an impossible reading palaeographically. The *alef* reading makes more sense in this context.

There is no disagreement concerning the first half of line 7.

(7) והש[ע]רׄיׄםׄ הבאיםׄ בׄמׄה
(8) והׄ[יו]צאים במה רוחב השער ארבע [עש]רׄה באמה וגובהמׄהׄ
(9) שמונה וׄ[ע]שׄרים באמה מן הס{◦}ךׄ עד הׄמשקוף

There is no disagreement concerning the transcription and reconstructions of these lines. Yadin noted that there is a similar expression in e.g. Jer 7:2 and 17:20, הבאים בשערים האלה.[11] The context, however, is different in Jeremia, i.e. the passages exhort the readers to come and

---

[6] Furthermore, Qimron seems to be certain concerning the first letter, which according to his transcription is an *alef*. Qimron, 51. This is, however, impossible to verify palaeographically from the plates 51 and 24*.

[7] Yadin argues that he has based his restoration on the observation that the same expression, רוח ורוח, is found in line 40:8. Yadin, 153. Qimron notes that רוחותׄיו "is clearly extant on an old transparency and on the original." Qimron, 51.

[8] Otherwise אמות would extend further than the end of line 4.

[9] Qimron is the only one that reads the shorter אמה. Moreover, Qimron notes that the traces at מ[קׄרת barely fits a *qof*. Qimron, 51.

[10] Qimron, 51. As a matter of fact a more correct way of putting the brackets for the first alternative would be [תׄא֯[יו, since there are some clear traces after the *taw* according to plate 51.

[11] Yadin, 154.

listen to the word of God. Therefore we cannot interpret this as Biblical Paraphrase.[12]

In the middle of line 8 we have the measure of ארבע [עש]רֹה, which seems to be a fairly certain reconstruction. As Yadin has noted, this width of the gate is also found in the Septuagint version of Ezek 40:48, τὸ εὖρος τοῦ θυρώματος πηχῶν δέκα τεσσάρων. [13] We cannot, however, speak about a variant here in terms of a Biblical Quotation, because the context is not the same: 11Q19 speaks about one of the gates of the inner court and the context of 𝔊 is the width of the gate that leads to the vestibule entrance of the temple. Therefore, this is can be understood as Rewritten Bible.

In the middle of line 9, it seems likely that the scribe wrote a letter after *samech,* which was afterwards erased.[14]

(9) וגובה
(10) המקרֹה מֹן המשקוף ארבע עשרה באמה ומקורה כיור
(11) ארז מֹצֹופֹהֹ זהב טהור ודלתותיו מצופות זהב טוב

At the end of line 9 a new sentence begins about the height of the roof. There is no disagreement concerning the transcription of these lines. At the end of line 10 we note the occurrence of כיור again. This word also appears in line 5:7 with the same meaning.[15] The expressions of זהב טהור,[16] and זהב טוב,[17] are quite common in the Bible. However, as these are not in the same context as in the Scroll, we cannot interpret these as a Biblical Quotations.

---

[12] Even if the context would be the same, we could not include it in the analysis, since it is a reconstruction.

[13] Yadin, 155. 𝔐 does not read this measurement at all but goes on and seems to combine the width of the שער with the the width of the כתפות, that is שלוש אמות. The word כתפות is, however, only mentioned in 𝔊, ἐπωμίδες.

[14] Yadin, 155. Qimron restores the deleted letter to an *alef.* Qimron, 51.

[15] In my doctoral dissertation I translated כיור with “platform.” Riska 2001, 141. The word is also found in line 3:15 with another meaning, that is “a basin.”

[16] E.g. Ex 25:11, וצפית אתו זהב טהור. The context here is different, since Exodus deals with the ark.

[17] E.g. 2 Chr 3:8, ויחפהו זהב טוב. The context here is another with קדש הקדשים.

(12) וׄמפנת השער עד המקצוע השני לחצר עשרים
(13) ומאה באמׄה וככה תהיה מדת כול השערים האלה אשר
(14) לחצר הפׄנׄימית והשערים באים פנימה אל תוך החצר[18]

There are no disagreements concerning the transcription of the last lines of this column. In the middle of line 13 the scribe wrote מת, and later a *dalet* was added above the letters.[19]

Summary of Col. 36

(1) [ ]א[
(2) [ ]שׄעׄרים [
(3) [ ]◦ מן המׄקצוׄעׄ[
(4) [עד פנ]ׄת הׄשעׄ[ר עשרים ומאה באמה ו]השער רחב ארׄבׄעׄיׄםׄ
(5) אמׄהׄ לׄכול רוחותׄיׄוׄ [כמדה הזאת] ו[רו]חׄב קי[רו] שׄבׄע אמׄוׄתׄ
(6) [וגוב]הׄוׄ חמש [וארבעים אמה עד מק]רת גג[ו ורוח]ב בׄאׄ[יו] שׄש
(7) וׄעׄשׄרׄיׄםׄ בׄאמה מׄמקצוע אל מקצוע והש[ע]רׄיׄםׄ הבאׄיׄםׄ בׄמׄה
(8) וׄהׄ[יו]צאים במה רוחב השער ארבע [עש]רׄה באמה וגובהמׄהׄ
(9) שמונה ו[ע]שרים באמה מן הס{◦}ף עד הׄמשקוף וגובה
(10) המקרׄה מׄן המשקוף ארבע עשרה באמה ומקורה כיור
(11) ארז מׄצופׄהׄ זהב טהור ודלתותיו מצופות זהב טוב *vacat*
(12) *vacat* וׄמפנת השער עד המקצוע השני לחצר עשרים
(13) ומאה באמׄה וככה תהיה מדת כול השערים האלה אשר
(14) לחצר הפׄנׄימית והשערים באים פנימה אל תוך החצר

Notes on Readings

2: [ ]שׄעׄרים – Yadin restores [ ]שׄעׄרים וׄמׄאׄה. **3:** [ ]◦ מן המׄקצוׄעׄ – Qimron transcribes [ ]לׄ מן המׄקצוׄעׄ. **5:** אמׄהׄ – Yadin and García Martínez restore [באמה] | רוחותׄיׄוׄ – Yadin reads רוח ורׄוׄחׄ | [כמדה הזאת] – Yadin and García Martínez restore [כמדה הזואת]. **6:** תׄאׄ[יו] – Yadin, Qimron and García Martínez read תׄ[איו]. **9:** הס{◦}ףׄ – Qimron reads הס([א])ףׄ. **13:** מדת – *dalet* is written above the letters מת in the MS: מדת.

[18] Yadin restores tentatively [x אמות ויוצאים מקיר החצר y אמות] as a continuation of the sentence on line 14. Yadin, 156.

2.9. Column 37

This column is found on plates 52 and 25*. However, there is an additional witness on plate 38*:4. This fragment is included in the microfiche edition of the Dead Sea Scrolls on PAM 43.978[1] and is presented by García Martínez as belonging to 11Q20 Col. 10.[2] It will be presented as we get closer to the location of its interpolation, on line 9.[3]

A large part of the upper half of Col. 37 has not survived. It seems probable that Col. 37 continues the description of the inner court gates.[4]

(1) [ ] . . . . [ ]
(2) [ ]חׄדש מׄהׄגנות(?) לכוׄל הש[ ]
(3) [ ]ה בׄין . . . [ ]
(4) [החצר] הׄפנימית לׄעזרת ה[מז]בׄחׄ אׄשרׄ . . . .[ ]
(5) [א]תׄ זבׄחי שלמי בני ישראל . . . . . ולכ[והנים]
(6) [ ] עש[ ] פׄנׄות(?) הפרור הׄתחתון עׄשׄוׄיׄםׄ . . .
(7) וׄ[מב]שׄלות אׄצׄל [ה]שׄ[ע]רים מׄשני [עברי] הׄשער

Yadin does not transcribe a single letter on line 1. Qimron notes a line above this line and defines it as line 01,[5] in which he is able to transcribe a *mem*. This is actually discernable on plate 25*:2.[6] On line 1 Qimron transcribes *nun sophit* right below the *mem*. Before *nun sophit* there are clear traces, which may not belong to this column. It would – however – not be impossible to interpret them as two *yods*, that is one right after the other, which would give us the reading יין.

On line 2 Qimron agrees with Yadin's transcription but adds the word [יין before חׄדש. If this reconstruction is correct, my suggestion of

[1] Another location is PAM 44.010, which is, however, quite a dark photograph, however.
[2] García Martínez presents this as Frg. 17 in his edition of 11Q20. DJD XXIII, 387.
[3] The interpolation of this fragment is made on lines 37:9-38:01.
[4] Yadin, 157.
[5] Qimron, 52. There is actually no reason not to define line 01 as line 1. It seems, nevertheless, that Qimron makes the comparison with other editions easier and, therefore, follows the line-numbering of Yadin.
[6] The same traces are less clear on plate 25*:1.

יין on the former line would gain some support.[7] At the end of the line Qimron suggests the likely reconstruction of לכול הש]נה.[8]

On the next line Yadin discerns one word, בין. Before that he reads a *he*, which could tentatively be restored to תבנ]ה. This restoration is supported by Qimron who reads ופרור ת]בנה.[9] At the end of line 3 Yadin suggests אר]בעת, which is also supported by Qimron.[10]

At the beginning of line 4 Qimron has added קיר in front of החצר.[11] When we study plate 25*:2 closely, it becomes clear that neither Yadin nor Qimron reconstructs the text according to the photograph. Also, לעזרת – which is the most clearly seen word on plate 25* line 4 – should be closer to the end of the line. This is possible to check with the manuscript with תבנה on line 3. The *lamed* on line 4 should be located right below *beit* on line 3. The consequence of this comment is that there is more space on line 4, which Qimron's longer reading more probable than Yadin's shorter one. At the end of line 4 Qimron restores יהיו אוכלים] or alternatively יהיו זובחים].[12]

Again Qimron presents a longer reading than Yadin's and begins line 5 with שמה את זבחי.[13] We have noted above that a longer reading is welcome at the beginning of line 5, therefore, this suggestion is a possible alternative. Yadin compares this line with e.g. Lev 7:34, ואת שוק התרומה לקחתי מאת בני־ישראל מזבחי שלמיהם ואתן אתם לאהרן הכהן ולבניו לחק־עולם מאת בני ישראל. He seems to base his restoration from the end of the line in this biblical passage, because Yadin reads ולכ]והנים.[14] We interpret this passage as Rewritten Bible. Qimron reads בני ישראל ול[עו]לה מהפרור at the end of line 5. It is very difficult to discern even parts of the last word on the manuscript. Concerning ול[עו]לה, Qimron also gives another alternative, that is ול[מע]לה.[15]

---

[7] It is hardly possible that the two *yods* would have moved one line up to the present location.

[8] Qimron, 52.

[9] Qimron, 52. The reconstruction is possible. תבנה is actually not very unclear on plate 25*.

[10] Yadin, 157; Qimron, 52.

[11] This is done according to the "model" on line 9: קיר החצר החיצון. Qimron, 52.

[12] Either reading is possible but it is difficult to choose between them. Qimron compares the reading with שלמיהמה אשר יהיו זובחים on line 11.

[13] Qimron, 52.

[14] Yadin, 158.

[15] Qimron, 52.

At the beginning of line 6 Qimron transcribes the letters עש.[16] At the end of the line he adds the word ז֯ה֯ב֯.[17] At the beginning of line 7, Qimron doubts Yadin's reading ו֯[מב]ש֯לות and prefers ה֯מ֯עֿלות instead.[18] He continues and restores ה֯שֿערים [קירות], which is also supported by García Martínez.[19]

We will now take a closer look at the fragment from 11Q20,[20] since its interpolation begins on line 9 and continues to line 38:01. When the text-critical analysis is done, we see that 11Q20 Col. 10 overlaps with the end of Col. 37 so frequently that it is beyond doubt that this fragment belongs to another copy of the Temple Scroll. Below 11Q20 lines 10:1–6 are presented:

(1)]]ה֯פנימי אצל ק֯[י]ר֯ ה֯ח֯צר ה֯[חיצון]
(2)] ולב]כורים ולמעשרות *vacat* [
(3)] יתע]ר֯בו זבחי שלמי בני יש֯[ראל]
(4)] *vac*[*at* [*vac*]*at*
(5)] לה]מה[מ]קום לכירים אשר יהיו מב[שלים]
(6)] במקצ]ו֯ע המזרחי צפונה ואת ∘∘ [ ]

Nearly at the beginning of line 5 of 11Q20 Col. 10 it can be seen very clearly on the MS that the letters קום were inserted as a correction by the copyist. The reconstruction [מ]קום is very likely.

Yadin reads line 6 as [המקצו]ע המזרחי צ֯פ֯ו֯נ֯י֯ יואכל֯ו֯.[21] According to Frg. 17 on plate XLIV[22] García Martínez' reading of צפונה above is

[16] On the other hand Qimron also notes that the letters עש could belong to the word עשוים at the end of the line. Qimron, 52.

[17] Qimron, 52. This word is very difficult to discern from the manuscript.

[18] Qimron notes that the first three letters, that is המע, are extant on an old infra-red photograph in the margin and only tentatively relocated here. Qimron, 52. Also García Martínez reads המעלות. García Martínez, 1256.

[19] Qimron, 52; García Martínez, 1256. This is a possible solution.

[20] DJD XXIII, 387. This passage is restored with the help of Col. 37. The reconstruction will not be presented here, but later in Col. 37 as the text-critical analysis moves forward.

[21] Yadin is the only one that reads *he* at the beginning of [המקצו]ע. Yadin, 154. Further on we will see how 11Q19 is restored with the help of this fragment and to discern if the more natural solution would be [במקצו]ע.

[22] DJD XXIII.

probable.[23] Moreover, Yadin's transcription of יואכלׄוׄ is problematic with a closer look at the manuscript. If the first letter would be interpreted as a *yod*, it makes the transcription of the preceding letter extremely difficult, since that letter has a clear vertical stroke that likely belongs to a *he*. Thus, we prefer the reading צפונה.

At the end of line 6 Wacholder and Qimron prefer to read ואכׄלׄ[ו. From plate 38*:4, it seems that García Martínez' comment concerning the *lamed* is correct: it is likely that the stroke that is interpreted as the upper arm of *lamed* is indeed not ink but dark stains in the manuscript.[24] Therefore we would prefer the reading of ואת, because it is a better alternative palaeographically. After this, we will now return to the text-critical analysis of 11Q19.

(8) עׄ[ש]יתמה בחׄ[צר פ]נימה בׄ[י]תׄ מ[ו]שבות לכוהׄנׄים ושולחנות
(9) לׄפׄנׄי המושבות בפרור הפנׄימי אצל קיר הׄחצׄר החיצון
(10) מקומות עשוים לכוהנים לז[ב]חׄיהמה ולבכוׄרים ולמעשרות
(11) ולזבחי שלמיהמׄה אשר יהיו זובחיםׄ ולוׄאׄ [י]תערבו זבחׄיׄ
(12) שלמי בני ישראל בזבחי הכׄוהׄנים *vacat*

There is no disagreement concerning the transcription and reconstruction of these lines. The underlined passages above show the common text between 11Q19 and the fragment of 11Q20.[25]

In the middle of line 8 we have the probable restoration of בׄ[י]תׄ מ[ו]שבות. As Yadin notes, Lev 25:29 has a similar expression, ואיש כי־ימכר בית־מושב עיר חומה.[26] The context is, however, clearly different in the Scroll. The second half of line 12 is *vacat*.

---

[23] It seems that Yadin interpreted the *he* at the end of the word as one *yod* for the end of צפוני and as a second *yod* for the beginning of the next word (יואכלו). This suggestion can hardly be correct.
[24] DJD XXIII, 388.
[25] The common material will also be underlined as we analyze the rest of the lines belonging to Col. 37.
[26] Yadin, 158.

(13) ובארבעת מקצועות הׄחצר עׄשׄית[ה] להמהׄ מקׄוׄם לכׄירים
(14) אשר יהיו מבשלים שמה אׄתׄ זבחיהמה [ו]את הׄחׄאטות

(01)] במקצ]וׄע המזרחי צפונה ואתׄ

At the beginning of line 13 we have a similar expression as in Ezek 46:22, בארבעת מקצעות החצר. We do not interpret it as a quotation since the context is different.[27] Instead we understand it as Rewritten Bible. In the middle of the same line Qimron transcribes [ל]עשׄות *pro* Yadin's עׄשׄית[ה].[28] As noted before the difference between *yod* and *waw* is often very little. The last word, כירים, represents a specific kind of a stove and is *hapax legomenon* in the Bible.

In the first part of line 14 Wacholder transcribes rather strangely מבשיל even if plate 52 shows a very distinct מבשלים.[29] At the end of line 14 Qimron transcribes את *pro* Yadin's [ו]את.[30] Concerning the space available Qimron's shorter reading seems to be more likely.[31] For the last word on the same line Qimron has two alternative readings: the one suggested by Yadin or the singular form, הׄחׄאטת.[32]

It is likely that line 01 belongs to Col 38.[33] The subject is not changed and since its restoration lies heavily on line 6 of 11Q20 Col. 10 we will analyze it in this present context. Wacholder reads [יבשלו במקצוׄע המזרחי צׄפׄונׄהׄ ואכלוׄ אותו הכוהנים והכירים].[34] Qimron reads similarly at the beginning, [יבשלו במקצ]וׄע המזרחי צפונהׄ ואכׄלׄ[ו].[35]

[27] The Scroll speaks of the angles for the inner court as Ezekiel speaks of the angles of the outer court. Yadin, 159.

[28] Wacholder supports Yadin's עׄשׄית[ה]. Wacholder 1991, 31. García Martínez reads as Qimron, that is [ל]עשות. García Martínez, 1256.

[29] Wacholder 1991, 31.

[30] Qimron, 52. Wacholder and García Martínez read [ו]את as Yadin. Wacholder 1991, 31; García Martínez, 1256.

[31] We note, however, that this is a strange grammatical construction.

[32] Qimron, 52.

[33] Line 01 is written one line below the expected location in order to show more clearly that it may belong to the next column. In the summary of the restorations in chapter three, line 01 is located at the beginning of Col. 38. The location of the text in comparison with the rest of the lines in Cols. 37 and 38 is not possible to determine.

[34] Wacholder 1991, 31. He has restored this reading with the help of his transcription and reconstruction of line 6 of 11Q20 Col. 10 which is underlined above. The reading of line 01 is possible but speculative.

[35] Qimron, 53.

Summary of Col. 37

(01) [ ]°°°מ°°°°

(1) [ ]°°° ° יין ה °°°°°

(2) [יין] חדש מהגנות לכול השנה [

(3) [ת]בנה בין [אר]בעת [

(4) [קיר החצר] הפנימית לעזרת ה[מז]בח אשר [יהיו אוכלים / זובחים

(5) [שמה א]ת זבחי שלמי בני ישראל ול[ ]לה [

(6) °°° עש [ ] פנות(?) הפרור התחתון עשוים [

(7) המעלות אצל [קירות ה]ש[ע]רים משני [עברי] השער *vacat*

(8) וע[ש]יתמה בח[צר פ]נימה ב[י]ת מ[ו]שבות לכוהנים ושולחנות

(9) לפני המושבות בפרור הפנימי אצל קיר החצר החיצון

(10) מקומות עשוים לכוהנים לז[ב]חיהמה ולבכורים ולמעשרות

(11) ולזבחי שלמיהמה אשר יהיו זובחים ולוא [י]תערבו זבחי

(12) שלמי בני ישראל בזבחי הכוהנים *vacat*

(13) ובארבעת מקצועות החצר עשית[ה][36] להמה מקום לכירים

(14) אשר יהיו מבשלים שמה את זבחיהמה את החאטות[37]

Col. 38:

(01) [במקצוע המזרחי צפונה ואת]

Notes on Readings

01–1: Yadin does not read anything on these two lines. **1:** Qimron transcribes °°° ן ה °°°°°. **2:** יין] חדש – Yadin transcribes]חדש. **3:** ת]בנה – Qimron restores ופרור ת]בנה. **4:** [קיר החצר] – Yadin restores only [החצר] | אשר [יהיו אוכלים / זובחים – Yadin has אשר. **5:** [שמה א]ת – Yadin has א]ת | ול[ ]לה [– Yadin reads ולכ]והנים . . . . . Qimron restores ול[עו]לה מהפרור or alternatively ול[עו]לה מהפרור. **6:** עשוים [– Qimron restores עשוים זהב. **7:** המעלות אצל [קירות ה]ש[ע]רים – Yadin reads ו[מב]שלות אצל [ה]ש[ע]רים. **14:** מבשלים – Wacholder transcribes מבשיל | את החאטות / החאטת – Yadin, Wacholder and García Martínez reads [ו]את החאטות.

[36] Another alternative is [ל]עשות.

[37] Another alternative is החאטת.

Col. 38

01: [במקצוׄע המזרחי צפונהׄ ואתׄ] – Yadin reads [המקצו]ע המזרחי צׄפׄוׄנׄיׄ
יׄואכלוׄ, Wacholder has [יבשלו במקצוׄע המזרחי צׄפׄוׄנׄהׄ ואכלוׄ אותו הכוהנים
והכירים], as Qimron reads [יבשלו במקצ]וׄע המזרחי צפונהׄ ואכׄלׄ[ו].

2.10. Column 38

The following two columns are badly preserved. Col. 38 is found on plates 53, and 26*. The photograph 38*:5 includes textual material from two different columns. It is the column on the right, which concerns us for this column. This fragment is found among a group that is called 4Q365a.[1] It seems to include words, which we also find in 11Q19. Since its possible influence[2] begins on line 4 the fragment of 4Q365a Frg. 2 Col. i will be presented before the analysis of that line.

The first three lines of Col. 38 belong to the material that are the most difficult to restore for this column.[3]

(1)] [יׄהׄיׄו אוכלׄיׄםׄ] [

(2)] [. . .] [שיתמה . . .] [

(3)] [יהׄיו אוכלים ושוׄתׄיׄםׄ] [

The first transcribed word on line 1 was possibly preceded by שמה, as on line 10.[4] Only one word is preserved on line 2. Qimron, who is supported by García Martínez, restores it to רא]שיתמה.[5] There are no disagreements concerning the third line.

We will now take a closer look at Frg. 2 Col. i:

---

[1] This fragment is presented in the *editio maior* of 4Q365a by Sidnie White in DJD XIII, 323-324. Wacholder's analysis, which was carried out three years earlier, will also be commented upon. His analysis of the text is, however, quite problematic.

[2] See subchapter 1.5 The Manuscripts of the Study.

[3] Line 38:01 is analyzed at the end of the previous column, since the content of the line is closely tied up with the end of Col. 37. Wacholder restores tentatively five additional lines, which are 02-06. They are based on two fragments that in García Martínez' edition of 11Q20 are Frgs. 31a and 31b and moreover classified as "Unidentified Fragments". DJD XXIII, 403. Since there is no evidence for Wacholder's restoration, the lines 01–06 will be presented in this footnote with the material from the fragments underlined: (01) [יבשלו במקצוׄע המזרחי צׄפוׄנׄהׄ ואכלו אותו הכוהנים (02) [והכירים] יהיו נחושת ברור ...] (03) [... ממסד עד טׄפחים זהב טהור...] (04) [... והשלחנות אשר יהיו מניחים שׄם עליהם את שלמיהמה] (05) [...] (06) [ומנחתׄמה חׄלבי זבחימה ...]. Wacholder 1991, 32. In his transcription of the fragments 31a and 31b, García Martínez defines the line numbers slightly different due to interlinear writing. Moreover, García Martínez transcribes יׄם *pro* Wacholder's שׄם on line 04 and ∘שׄ∘[תׄמה on line 06 *pro* ומנחתׄמה]. See a thorough discussion and transcription of fragments 31a and 31b in DJD XXIII, 403.

[4] Another possibility is ככה as in line 43:5, ככה יהיו אוכלים. Yadin, 161.

[5] Qimron, 54; García Martínez, 1256.

(1)]◦ם לדגן וליצהר
(2)]◦[ ]בני ישראל וביום הבכורים
(3)]מה[ ]ה̊ת̊אנים והרמונים
(4)]ה מנחת הקורבנים הב̇אה עליה
(5) מנח]ת̇ ה̊קנאות ולימין השער הזה
(6)]◦ וה̇יו אוכלי̇ם̇ את◦חטאות
(7) [*vacat*
(8) בא]מ̊ה ו̊א̊ורד לרוח
(9) א]ו̊רד לכול רוחותיה
(10) ב̇ין תו לתו שלוש אמ̇ות̇ וחצי

In the middle of line 2, Wacholder reads שני [*pro* בני [. The photograph on PAM 43.366 clearly shows a *beit.* On line 3, Yadin and Wacholder transcribe ה]ענבים *pro* Qimron and White's ה̊ת̊אנים].[6] On the next line Yadin transcribes הקורבנות היאה עליה whereas Wacholder has הקורבנ{{ים}}ות הב̇אה עליה.[7] We agree with White that the final *mem* is clear in the manuscript. Moreover we read הב̇אה together with Qimron.

At the beginning of line 5 Wacholder restores ומנח]ת̊ *pro* Yadin's מנח]ת̇.[8] At the beginning of line 6 Yadin and Wacholder read יהיו *pro* וה̇יו. At the end of the same line Yadin, followed by Wacholder, transcribes התבואות *pro* ◦חטאות, of which the latter fits better into the context. Lastly, Wacholder restores ואו]ר̊ך *pro* א]ו̊רך at the beginning of line 9.

As we return to the analysis, we will compare the fragment of 4Q365a with 11Q19. Below we continue the text-critical analysis of Col. 38:

(4) ו̇י̇ואכל̇] [. . . . לדגן לתירוש ול]יצהר [
(5) . . . .] [
(6) א̊ו̊כ̊ל̊י̊ם̊ א̊צ̊ל שער המערב [[
(7)]]כ̊ו̊ל̊ עץ אשר י̊ב̊ו̊א̊ ל . . .] [
(8)]] ע̊ליה לבונה ול. . . . . .] [
(9) ו̊לימ̇[ין ה]שער הזה . . . .] [
(10) . . . . . . שמה יה̇יו אוכלים [ ] העוף ולתורים ולבני היונה̇] [

---

[6] Yadin, 162; Wacholder 1991, 32; Qimron 1987, 33. It is difficult to give priority based on palaeographical reasons.

[7] Yadin, 161; Wacholder 1991, 32.

[8] Wacholder 1991, 32; Yadin, 161.

At the beginning of line 4 the word]ויואכל is very difficult to discern.[9] After this, Yadin suggests the reading ובימי הבכורים] לדגן לתירוש ול[יצהר.[10] We note that the order is different in 4Q365a line 1, לדגן וליצהר. We support Qimron, who claims that there is not enough space for ויואכל at the beginning of this line.[11]

On line 5 Qimron is able to restore רׄיׄשׄיׄתׄ on the first half. After that he finishes the first half with אׄלׄ ל∘∘∘.[12] At the end of the line Yadin suggests the interpolation of line 2 from 4Q365a, that is בני] ישראל וביום הבכורים]. Qimron adds לפרי at the end of this line and continues with יביאו לשׄמׄאׄל] (6).[13] Yadin begins line 6 in a different way, that is אׄוׄכׄלׄיׄםׄ אׄצׄל. The manuscript is unclear at this location due to dark stains. In his restoration of the second half of the line, Qimron has skillfully interpolated line 3 from 4Q365a with the result of את כול] פרי ארצמה את התׄאׄנׄים.[14]

Wacholder and Qimron agree with each other on line 7 apart from the beginning of the line, where Wacholder restores [והתאנים ופרי] העׄץ and Qimron has והרמונים ו]העׄץ]. Yadin transcribes less and reads ...כׄוׄלׄ עץ אשר יׄהׄוׄאׄ ל[, whereas Qimron and Wacholder read אשר יׄאׄכׄל after העץ.[15] The paleographical evidence is unclear and the restoration is difficult on the first half of the column. Qimron continues with the restoration of the second half of line 7, with ו]לימין השער הזהׄ מנחת הבׄאה] עׄליה] (8) [הקורבנות. This agrees with Yadin – except הבאה, where Yadin reads היאה.[16] Yadin suggests an interpolation of line 4 from Frg. 2.[17]

Qimron continues the reconstruction of the line with לבונה ולשׄמׄאול

---

[9] In addition to Yadin, Wacholder also restores this word. Wacholder 1991, 33.

[10] The interpolated material from 4Q365 is underlined in the following passage.

[11] Qimron, 54.

[12] Qimron, 54.

[13] Qimron, 54. Wacholder does not read לפרי at the end of line 5. Wacholder 1991, 33.

[14] Qimron, 54. Wacholder restores אׄוׄכׄלׄיׄםׄ אׄצׄל שער המערב [מן הדגן החדש ומהיין והעׄנבים והרמונים]. Wacholder 1991, 33. His reading, that is to keep והרמונים on line 6, seems to be too long.

[15] Qimron 1987, 33. In his *editio maior* of 11Q19 from 1996, Qimron notes a comparison with Tobit 1:7b, ומעשר הדגן התירוש והיצהר והרמונים והתאנים ושאר פרי העץ ... **יאכל** אותם בירושלים בכל־שנה ושנה. Qimron, 54. יאכל needs to be interpreted as third person passive singular.

[16] Qimron is probably right as he notes that היאה "hardly fits the traces". Qimron, 54.

[17] Qimron, 54; Yadin, 162.

ולימ[ין ה]שער הזה (9) [ות הקנאות] מנחת האשמ[ות הקנאות]...

ש[ער הצ]פון מנחת האשמ[ות הקנאות] (9) ולימ[ין ה]שער הזה.[18] He continues with a likely suggestion for the rest of the line, כול ה מנחה ושעיר[י ה]חטאת אשר יקריבו בני (10) [י]שראל.[19] The rest of line 10 is less problematic and includes an interpolation of line 6 of Frg. 2, שמה יהיו אוכלים [את ח]טאות העוף ולתורים ולבני היונה.[20]

(12) ועשיתה [ח]צר שנית סב[י]ב ל[חצר הפנ]ימית רחוב מאה באמה
(13) ואורך לרוח הקדם שמונים וארבע מאות באמה וככה רוחב ואורך לכול
(14) רוחותיה לנגב ולים ולצ צפון ורוחב קירה [אר]בע אמות וגובה שמונ[ה]
(15) ועשרים באמה ותאים עשוים לקיר מחוץ ובין התאו לתאו שלוש

Instead of Yadin's סב[י]ב ל[חצר, Qimron reads סובבת את החצר in the middle of line 12.[21] Plate 26*:4 shows that there seems to be a trace of an upper, vertical stroke of a *lamed*. It seems likely, however, that this *lamed* belongs to the word זבולון on line 39:13. Moreover, we note that the words סובבת את fit better palaeographically with the other traces. There is no disagreement concerning the transcription and restoration of the rest of the lines.

On the first half of line 14, ולצ is written. After that the scribe wrote צפון. It is likely that his intention was to write לצפון, according to the directions that are mentioned before this. Concerning the interpolations of Frg. 2: line 8 fits into the end of line 38:12 and into the beginning of 13; line 9 fits into the end of line 38:13 and into the beginning of 14; line 10 fits into the end of line 38:15.[22]

---

[18] The end of line 8 is problematic. It could also have been restored as האשמ]ות ומנחת הקנאות]. On the other hand this would make the line too long. Qimron, 54. Wacholder reads differently until the end of the line, לבונה ול[וא ימוש ממנה לבונה רק ממנחת הקנאות]. Wacholder 1991, 33. The photograph on plate 53:2 shows a quite clear *lamed* at the end of the line on the fragment. This fits in with ולשמאול, which was suggested by Qimron. Wacholder does not read *lamed* but restores in a way that suits less good the manuscript. Lines 8-9 include an interpolation of line 5 of Frg. 2.

[19] Qimron, 54.

[20] Qimron, 54. Wacholder reads התבואות *pro* חטאות. Wacholder 1991, 33. He seems to transcribe this word with the help of Frg. 2, which is interpolated. It should be noted that *beit* and *tet* are not easy to distinguish from each other on plate XXXIII in DJD XIII. *Tet* seems, however, to be the likely reading.

[21] Qimron, 54.

[22] There is, however, a minor difference: Frg. 2, line 10 reads תו לתו *pro* התאו לתאו as in Col 38:15. This is shown through the underlined letters of line 38:15.

Qimron continues to reconstruct the text that follows by using material from line 10 of Frg. 2, אמות וחצי.[23] It is possible to identify this line as 39:01.

Summary of Col. 38

(1)] [יה֯יו אוכלי֯ם֯]
(2)] [. . [רא]שיתמה . .]
(3)]]יה֯יו אוכלים ושות֯י֯ם֯ [
(4) [ובימי הבכורים] לדגן לתירוש ול֯[יצהר
(5) . . . . [בני ישראל וביום הבכורים לפרי]
(6) . . . . . .ל֯. . .ל שער המערב [את כול פרי ארצמה את הת֯א֯נים]
(7) . . . . . . .ה֯עץ אשר י֯אכ֯ל ו[לימין השער הזה֯ מנחת הקורבנות]
(8) [הב֯אה] ע֯ליה לבונה ולשמ֯אול ש֯[ער הצ]פון מנ֯חת ה֯אשמ[ות ה֯קנאות]
(9) ו֯לימ֯[ין ה]שער הזה כול ה֯מנחה֯ וש֯ע֯יר֯[י ה]חטאת אשר יקריבו ב֯נ֯י֯
(10) [י]שראל֯ ש֯מה יהיו אוכלים [את ח]ט֯א֯ות֯ העוף֯ ולתורים ולבנ֯י היונה֯
(11) *vacat*
(12) ועשית֯ה֯ [ח]צר שנ֯ית סובבת א֯ת הח[צר הפנ]ימית רחוב מאה באמה֯
(13) ואורך לר֯וח הקדם שמונים וארב֯ע מ֯אות באמה֯ ו֯כ֯כה֯ רוחב ואורך לכול
(14) רוחותיה֯ ל֯נג֯ב ולים ולצ֯ צפון ו֯רוחב קירה֯ [אר]ב֯ע אמ֯ות וגובה שמו֯נ֯[ה]
(15) ועשר֯ים באמה ותאים עשוים לקיר מחוץ ובין התאו לתאו שלוש

Col. 39:
(01) [אמות וחצי]

Notes on Readings

2: [רא]שיתמה – Yadin has שיתמה[ ]. **4:** ובימי] – Yadin and Wacholder begin the line with ו֯יו֯אכל֯]. **5:** On the first half Qimron transcribes ר֯י֯ש֯י֯ת֯ and a little later א֯ל֯ ∘∘∘ל | Wacholder does not read לפרי at the end of the line. **6:** Yadin and Wacholder begin the line with את] | א֯ו֯כ֯ל֯י֯ם֯ א֯צ֯ל – Wacholder restores מן הדגן החדש ומהיין] כול פרי ארצמה את הת֯א֯נים] [כ֯ו֯ל֯ עץ אשר י֯ב֯ו֯א֯ והע֯נבים והרמונים] – Yadin reads ה֯עץ אשר י֯א֯כ֯לה .**7:** ...ל. **8:** [לבונה ולשמ֯אול ש֯[ער הצ]פון מנ֯חת ה֯אשמ[ות ה֯קנאות] – Wacholder reads [לבונה ול[וא ימוש ממנה לבונה רק ממנחת הקנאות]. **10:** [את ח]ט֯א֯ות֯ – Wacholder restores [את התבואות]. **12:** סובבת א֯ת הח[צר – Yadin restores ס֯ב֯[י]ב ל֯[חצר.

[23] Qimron, 55.

2.11. Column 39

Col. 39 is preserved on plates 54 and 27* and contains the continuation of the commands to build the middle court.[1]

(1)] [...יׄם.......
(2) ......] [מׄקרת הגׄג] [
(3) .....] [ודלתותיה מצופו[ת ז]הׄבׄ
(4) ◦◦שפׄ] [..◦חצר הזואת] [

Nothing can be discerned at the beginning of line 1. At the end of the line Yadin seems to refer to plate 54, which is dark and unclear. Qimron transcribes מ[דת הׄשׄ]ערים. This can be read quite clearly at the top left corner of plate 27*.[2]

At the beginning of line 2, Yadin uses lines 36:9–10 – וגובה (10) המקרה מן המשקוף ארבע עשרה באמה – for a tentative restoration with the following result, [וגובהמה x באמה מן הסף עד המשקוף וגובה] מקרת הגג מן המשקוף y באמה.[3] This restoration should, however, be considered as highly hypothetical. At the beginning of the line Qimron succeeds to transcribe הׄכׄוׄלׄ,[4] of which some traces can be observed at the top right corner of plate 27*. In addition to this he transcribes עד in front of מׄקרת הגׄג.[5] This reading is very difficult to verify from the mentioned plates above.

Yadin does not transcribe anything at the beginning of line 3. Here Qimron reads אמות עׄ[.[6] At the very end of the line he transcribes מׄ◦ הׄ או[*pro* Yadin's מצופו[ת ז]הׄבׄ.[7]

On line 4 Yadin tentatively suggests [טוב] at the beginning of the line.[8] Using lines 36:13–14 – וככה תהיה מ{ד}ת כל השערים האלה אשר (14) לחצר הפנימית – he suggests the following for the whole line, וככה]

[1] Yadin, 165.
[2] Qimron, 56.
[3] Yadin, 165.
[4] Qimron, 56.
[5] Qimron, 56.
[6] Qimron, 56. There are some traces on plate 27* – *alef* is the clearest letter – which supports this reading. Qimron claims that this *alef* on line 3, ם שפׄ[on line 4, and עש◦ ל◦ on line 5 – which can be discerned on plate 27* – belong to the middle of the lines or to lines 40:3–5. This is a possible solution but difficult to verify.
[7] Yadin, 165; Qimron, 56.
[8] Yadin's suggestion is based on line 36:11, ודלתותיו מצופות זהב טוב. Yadin, 166.

תהיה מדת כול השערים האלה אשר ל]חצר הזואת.[9] On the contrary, Qimron begins the line with]מצופהׄ ז֯הׄב֯.[10] At the end of this line Qimron restores יבואו אל] החצר הזואת כול.[11] Since there is palaeographical evidence for Qimron's reading, we subscribe to his transcription.

(5) ◦ש ולו[ ]. .סה דור רבי[עי] בן
(6) י֯ש֯רׄא֯ל֯ [ ]להשתחוות לפני כול ע֯[ד]ת בנׄיׄ
(7) ישרׄאל . . . [ ]ל֯ו֯א֯ תבוא בׄהׄ אשה וילד עד יום
(8) אשר י֯ש֯ל֯י֯ם֯ חוק [ ]נ֯פ֯ש֯ו֯ ליהיה מחצית השקל חוק עולם
(9) לזכרון ב֯מ֯ו֯ש֯ב֯ו֯ת֯י֯ה֯מ֯ה֯ ע֯ש֯ר֯י֯ם֯ גרׄהׄ הׄשקׄל֯

Qimron continues from line 4, החצר הזואת כׄול (5) קׄהל עדׄת and Yadin, very cautiously reads ולו]א יבוא.[12] Concerning the rest of the line Qimron restores [ישראל והגר אשר יולד בתו]כ֯סה דור רביע֯י֯ מׄבׄן, which is a possible solution.[13] Yadin compares line 5 with Gen 15:16, ודור רביעי ישובו and suggests a tentative restoration on the second part of the line, בשוב[סה.[14] The context, however, is different to the Scroll. At the end of line 5, Yadin seems to be able to read בן (6) י֯ש֯רׄא֯ל֯ without problems and Qimron transcribes מׄבׄן (6) כשריׄם. Qimron reads according to the model from lines 10–11, מבן (11) עשריׄם and continues שנׄהׄ [למעלה וכאשר יבואו.[15] It is difficult to judge between בן or מבן on palaeographical grounds, since the space in front of בן is unclear in the manuscript.[16]

At the beginning of line 6 Yadin's reading י֯ש֯רׄא֯ל֯ seems to be closer to the evidence on plate 27*. Moreover, it is certainly correct

---

[9] As another possibility Yadin suggests [וככה תעשה את כול השערים האלה אשר ל]חצר הזואת. Yadin, 166.

[10] Qimron notes that the new text – his new readings – are visible on "the old transparencies." Qimron, 56. García Martínez agrees with this reading. García Martínez, 1256.

[11] Qimron, 56.

[12] Yadin, 166; Qimron, 56.

[13] Qimron, 56.

[14] Yadin, 166.

[15] This is a creative solution. On the other hand we cannot subscribe to it, since we do not find evidence that supports Qimron's reading at the beginning of line 6.

[16] The small traces at the very end of line 5 could just as easily belong to a *mem* as to a *beit*.

that לְפֵנִי is read with first person singular suffix, לְפֵנִי.[17] Thereafter the transcription is clear to the end of line 7.

Qimron reads line 8 differently as he has noted that Yadin's transcription at the end of the line, חוק עוֹלָם, actually should be חוק עלומיו. According to Qimron, these words were stuck at the back of the Scroll.[18] As a result, he restores the middle of the line to חוק עֹל]ומיו ונתן פדיו]ן נפשו.[19] Yadin suggests [ונתן כופר] *pro* Qimron's ונתן פדיו]ן based on Ex 30:12, ונתנו איש כפר נפשו.[20] Even if the main part of line 9 is very unclear there is no disagreement concerning its restoration. At the end of the line there is a *vacat*.

(10) וכאשר ישאו ממנוֹ את מחצית הש[ק]ל [ ] לי אחר יבואו מבן
(11) עשרים [ ] וה]יוֹ שמ[ות הש]עָרים אשר ל[ח]צֶר הזואת על שמֹ[ות]
(12) בני יש[ר]אֵל שמעוֹן לוי וֹיהודה בקדם מזרח [ר]אֹובן יוסף ובנימין לנגב
(13) דרום יש שכר זבולון וגד לים דן נפתלֹי וֹאֹשֹר לצפון וֹבֹין שער לשער
(14) מדה מן פנה למזרח צפון עד שער שמעוֹן תשׁע ותשעים באמה והשער {שמעון}[21]
(15) שמונה ועשרים באמה ומשער הזה עד שער {ooooo} לוי תשׁע ותשעים
(16) באמה והשער שמונה ועשרים באמה ומשער לוי עד שערֹ יהודה

On the second part of line 10, Yadin tentatively suggests the restoration [כופר נפשם].[22] This reading does not seem to be possible palaeographically, because there is not enough space after the *lamed*. Yadin may have been influenced by Ex 30:16, והיה לבני ישראל לזכרון לפני יהוה לכפר על־נפשתיכם. The לזכרון on line 9 also indicates this. Qimron reads differently with [ישב]ע and notes that יבוא is another alternative instead

---

[17] Yadin, 166. García Martínez interprets לפני without the suffix, that is "to prostrate before all [the assembly." García Martínez, 1257.

[18] Qimron, 56. This is difficult to verify with the photographs.

[19] Qimron, 56. He notes that the *nun sophit* can be discerned on the original. Qimron 1978a, 144.

[20] Yadin, 166. It is, again, difficult to verify Qimron's *nun sophit*, since the plates are so unclear.

[21] Yadin argues that the scribe planned to write ומשער שמעון, but instead wrote ומשער הזה. Afterwards he wrote שמעון above the line only to erase it later. Yadin, 167. Qimron suggests that the traces of שמעון appear to have been stuck from another column. Qimron, 56. Later on the same line something seems to have been erased.

[22] Yadin, 167.

ferently with עׄ[ישב] and notes that יבוא is another alternative instead of יבואו.[23] On palaeographical grounds we prefer Qimron's reconstruction.

There is nearly no disagreement about the first *lacuna* at the beginning of line 11, which should be read as עשרים [שנה ומעלה or עשרים [שנה ולמעלה.[24] Qimron reconstructs the second *lacuna* differently, ושם השעׄרׄים אשר לׄחצר and is supported by García Martínez.[25] This seems to be a possible reading according to plate 27*. Yadin quotes Ezek 48:31, ושערי העיר על־שמות שבטי ישראל, comparing the closeness of style with על שׄמׄ[ות] (12) בני ישׄ[ר]אל.[26]

From here on, there is no disagreement concerning the transcription up to the end of the column. Concerning the order of the tribes, there does not seem to be a close relationship with the biblical texts.[27]

Summary of Col. 39

(1)] מ]דת הׄשׄ[ערים

(2) הׄכׄוׄלׄ]]מׄקרת הגׄגׄ [

(3) א[מות]ודלתותיה . . . .

(4) מצופהׄ זׄהׄבׄ]] החצר הזואת כול

(5) קׄהל עדתׄ [ישראל והגר אשר יולד בתו]כמׄה דור רביעׄי [

(6) יׄשׄרׄאׄלׄ [ ]להשתׄחׄוות לפנׄי כול עׄ[ד]ת בנׄי

(7) ישרׄאל [ ] לׄוׄאׄ תבוא בׄאׄ אשה וילד עד יום

(8) אשר יׄשׄלׄיׄםׄ חוק [ ] נׄפׄשׄוׄ ליהוה מחצית השקל

(9) לזכרון בׄמׄוׄשׄבׄוׄתׄיׄהׄמׄהׄ עׄשׄרׄיׄםׄ גרׄהׄ הׄשׄקׄל *vacat*

(10) וכאשר ישאׄוׄ ממנׄוׄ את מחצית הׄש[ק]לׄ [ישבע] לי אחר יבואו מבן

(11) עשריׄםׄ [שנה] ולמעלה ושם [הש]עׄרׄים אשרׄ לׄ[ח]צר הזואת על שׄמׄ[ות]

(12) בני ישׄ[ר]אל שמעׄון לׄוי וׄיׄהודה בקדם מזרחׄ [ר]אׄובן יוסף ובנימין לנגב

(13) דרום יש שכר זבולון וגד לים דן נפׄתלׄיׄ וׄאׄשׄרׄ לצפון וׄבׄין שער לשער

(14) מדה מן פנה למזרח צפון עד שער שמעׄון תשׄעׄ ותשעים באמה והשער

---

[23] Qimron, 56. According to plate 54, the few traces that are visible could possibly be the remains of an *ayin*.

[24] Qimron inserts an additional *lamed* as Yadin argues that his reading "corresponds exactly" with the *lacuna* and furthermore inserts וה[יׄו. Qimron, 56; Yadin, 167.

[25] Qimron, 56; García Martínez, 1258. The text on plate 27* is, however, very unclear.

[26] Yadin, 167.

[27] See e.g. Ezek 48:31b, שער ראובן אחד שער יהודה אחד שער לוי אחד. The order of the tribes concerning the gates will be discussed in chapter six where courtyards are compared with each other.

(15) שמונה ועשרים באמה ומשער הזה עד שער {°°°°°} לוי תשעׄ ותשעים

(16) באמה והשער שמונה ועשרים באמה ומׄשער לוי עד שערׄ יׄהודה

Notes on Readings

1: מ]דת הׄשׄ[ערים – Yadin has . . . [יׄם. **2:**]מׄקרת הגׄג[– Qimron transcribes עד מׄקרת הגׄג. **3:** א]מות – Qimron transcribes אמות עׄ [– ודלתותיה | – Yadin has]ודלתותיה מצופו[ת ז]הׄבׄ as Qimron reads]ודלתותיה מׄ°הׄ אוׄ[.[28] **4:**]מצופהׄ זׄהׄבׄ[– Yadin transcribes]שׄפׄ°° | החצר [– קׄהל עדתׄ. **5:** יבואו אל] החצר הזואת כול – Qimron restores הזואת כול – Yadin reconstructs ולו]א יבוא | [רביעׄיׄ דור כׄסה]בתו – Yadin restores ישׄרׄאׄל [. **6:** בתו]כׄסה דור רביעׄיׄ מׄבׄן as Qimron has בשוב]סה דור רבי[עי] בן – Qimron reads למעלה וכאשר יבואו [עשריׄם שנׄהׄ. **8:** חוק [– Qimron restores נׄפׄשׄוׄ | חוק עׄולׄ[מיו ונתן פדיו]ן נפשו [– Yadin suggests | ונתן כופר] השקל – Yadin transcribes השקל חוקׄ עולם. **10:** לי [ישבע] – Yadin restores [כופר נפשם]. **11:** עשריׄם [שנה] ולמעלה ושׄם – Yadin reads [שנה ומעלה וה]יו שׄמ[ות הש]עׄרׄים.

---

[28] Concerning Yadin's tentative reconstructions of lines 3-4 that are not based on palaeography, see the text-critical analysis above.

2.12. Column 40

From this column onwards the quality of our text-material becomes better. All of the other columns in this study – with the exception of Col. 30[1] – have the lower part better preserved. Concerning textual evidence of Col. 40 we refer to plates 55 and 28*.[2]

(1)]]ללבוש את הב[גדים [
(2)]]ה להיות מֿשרת[ים [
(3)]]בני ישראל ולוא ימ[[
(4)] החצ]ר הזואת ל . . [[

The context of these first lines is the middle court and the holy garments of the priests. Yadin has pointed out, there is biblical influence here from Lev 6:4, ופשט את־בגדיו ולבש בגדים אחרים.[3] Qimron agrees with Yadin concerning the restoration of line 1 but has another suggestion for the end of line 2. Yadin in his restoration seems to refer to Ezek 44:19, יפשטו את־בגדיהם אשר־המה משרתם בם והניחו אותם בלשכת הקדש ולבשו בגדים אחרים. Qimron restores line 2 to]ה להיות נש[י]א תח[ת אהרון, as he refers to Num 17:17, וקח מאתם מטא מטא לבית אב מאת כל־נשיאהם לבית אבתם שנים עשר מטות and to Ex 29:30, שבעת ימים ילבשם הכהן תחתיו מבניו.[4]

On evaluating these two alternatives, we subscribe to Qimron's restoration due to the following palaeographical reasons: 1. According to plate 28*:1, the next letter after להיות seems to be a *nun pro* Yadin's *mem*. 2. Plate 28*:3, which is the fragment to the left, shows a fairly clear תח[. We would understand these first two lines as Rewritten Bible.

---

[1] In Col. 30 the upper portion has survived better than the lower one.

[2] Yadin tentatively suggests the content of seven lines 01–07 at the very beginning of Col. 40. Since Col. 39 ended with ומשער לוי עד שער יהודה, it could possibly continue with תשע ותשעים באמה והשער שמונה ועשרים באמה. Since there is not enough space to present the rest of the gates – Gad, Dan, Naphtali, and Asher – it seems likely that the author shortened the presentation and may have written something like וככה מדות כול השערים וכמדה הזואת בין שער לשער. Yadin, 169. We will, however, not present a restoration of these lines as we have no palaeographical evidence for this.

[3] Yadin, 169.

[4] Qimron, 57.

There is practically no disagreement concerning the restoration of line 3, except that Yadin suggests [...ולוא ימ]ותו...חוקת עולם at the end of the line. García Martínez supports ימ]ותו. We are in agreement with this. The rest of the line is possible but quite hypothetical.[5]

In the middle of line 4 there is agreement about the word; on the other hand there is disagreement concerning its spelling. Yadin reads הזואת whereas Qimron and García Martínez have הזאת.[6] In the light of plate 55, the first clear discernable trace seems to be a *zayin* and not a left vertical stroke of a *he*. In case of a *he*, the horizontal stroke should pass the left vertical stroke, which is not the case here.[7] On the basis of these observations, we would support Yadin's הזואת.[8]

On the second part of line 4, Qimron discerns two more letters at the end, which are *lamed* and *taw*.

(5)] ועשיתה חצר שליש[י]ת [ ]
(6)] ו]לבנותיהמה ולגרים אשר נולדׄ[ו]
(7)] רו]חב סביב לחצר התיכונה שׄ[ ]
(8) באורך כאלׄףׄ ושש [מאות ב]אׄמׄהׄ מפנה לפנה

At the beginning of line 5 Qimron discerns a *he* and for the rest of the line follows Yadin. At the end of line 5 and at the beginning of line 6 Qimron restores התיכונה] (6) [סובבת את החצר].[9] This seems to be a good solution to fit the space available. On the other hand סובב is a grammatical form that is extant neither in the Bible nor in the DSS literature.[10] We will, therefore, leave the reconstruction at the end of the line open.

---

[5] Yadin refers to Ex 30:21, ולא ימתו והיתה להם חק־עולם לו ולזרעו לדרתם. Yadin, 169; García Martínez, 1258.

[6] Qimron, 57; García Martínez, 1258.

[7] No horizontal stroke of a *he* is seen on the photograph. On the other hand, the top of the letter is broader in a way, which makes it similar with a *zayin*.

[8] The spelling of זואת is not a problem since the order of *waw* and *alef* appear both as הזאות and זואת in Cols. 40:8 and 45:6, respectively.

[9] Qimron, 57.

[10] Indeed, this does not make Qimron's suggestions impossible. Another possibility is מסביב, derived from the word סביב. This word is widely spread in DSS in general and in particular with at least 12 appearances in 11QT. An example is on line 7.

At the end of line 6, Qimron reconstructs differently with נולד̇[ו] בישראל (7) [עד הדור השלישי.[11] Yadin suggests נולד[ו להמה דור שלישי] for the end of line 6 which is based on e.g. Deut 23:9, בנים אשר־יולדו להם דור שלישי and Deut 29:10, טפכם נשיכם וגרך אשר בקרב מחניך.[12]

According to the context both alternatives fit in well. If Yadin's intention is to read the whole phrase at the end of line 6, it seems too long for the space available. On the other hand, it would be possible to move his last word, שלישי, to the beginning of the next line. In any event we will not subscribe to these two suggestions as the palaeographical evidence available does not support them.[13]

In the first half of line 7 Qimron restores ו]ר̊ו̊חב instead of Yadin's רו]חב.[14] At the end of the line Qimron again has another restoration, that is שש̊ מא̊ו̊ת̊ אמה.[15] On the other hand Yadin reads tentatively ש]שים וחמש מאות באמה].[16] This reading is problematic in the light of plate 28*:1, which unfortunately has a hole and some dark stains at this location. We need to conclude, however, that Qimron's reading fits better the traces and into the space available.[17]

On line 8 there is a disagreement concerning the word after the restoration of מאות]. Qimron reads אמ̇ה̇ *pro* Yadin's ב]אמ̇ה̇.[18] On plate 28*:1 there are some traces – similar to the upper tip to the left of a *beit* – before the severely damaged אמ̇ה̇, which make Yadin's reading more likely.

---

[11] Qimron, 57. The reading ב̊י̊ש̊ר̊א̊ל is very difficult to verify palaeographically. It seems that Qimron refers to a fragment, which neither appears on plate 55 nor on 28*.

[12] Yadin, 170.

[13] The two reconstructions will, however, be presented below in Notes on Readings.

[14] Qimron, 57. Both alternatives are possible.

[15] Qimron, 57.

[16] Yadin explains the measurement of 560 cubits in *The Temple Scroll*. Yadin 1983 vol. 1, 415. We will continue this discussion in chapter five.

[17] García Martínez supports Qimron's reading. García Martínez, 1258.

[18] Yadin, 170; Qimron, 57.

(8) לכול רׄוח ורוח כמדה הזאׄתׄ
(9) לׄמזרח ולדׄרׄוׄם ולׄים ולצׄ[פו]ן ורוחב הקׄיר שבע אמות וגובה תשע
(10) ורבעים בׄאמה וׄתׄאים [ע]שוים ביׄן֯ לשעריו מחוץ לעומת המוסד
(11) עׄד עטׄרותׄיׄו שׄלׄושׄהׄ בׄ[ו] שערׄים במזרח ושלושה בדרום ושלושה
(12) לׄים ושלושה לצפון

Concerning the end of line 8, and line 9 there is no disagreement concerning the transcription.

In the middle of line 10, Qimron reads בו ולשעריו *pro* Yadin's ביׄן֯ לשעריו.[19] According to both of the plates, 55 and 28*:1, Qimron's solution seems to be more likely. For example, the space between the second and the third letter suggests that a new word has begun.[20] Furthermore, Yadin notes that בכול שעריו would be another possibility. Although he himself rejects this reading due to palaeographical reasons. There seems to be common terminology concerning the second half of line 10 with Ezek 42:7a, וגדר אשר־לחוץ לעמת הלשכות דרך החצר החיצונה אל־פני הלשכות.

On the next one and a half lines there is no disagreement concerning the transcription. Yadin notes that עטרותיו at the beginning of line 11 also is found in the Bible but it is referring to gold and silver crowns.[21]

(12) ורׄוחב השעׄרים חמשים באמה וגובהמה שבעים
(13) באמה ובין שער לשערׄ [מדה] שלוש מאות וששים באמה מן הפנה עד
(14) שער שמעון ששים ושׄלוש מאות באמה ומשער שמעון עד שער לוי
ו
(15) כמדה הזאת ומשע[ר] לוי עד שער יהודה כמדה הזואת ששים ושלוש

There is no disagreement about the transcription of these last four lines. We note that the scribe has added a supralinear *waw* above the second word on line 15, between *zayin* and *alef*, in order to spell the demonstrative pronoun, הזואת.

Qimron notes correctly concerning the next word on the same line, that there is no space for a *resh* in the MS at the end of the word

---

[19] Qimron, 57.

[20] Moreover, the third letter is similar to a *waw*. A *nun sophit* is usually not as thick at the top as a *waw*. In this case the thickness would suggest a *waw*.

[21] See Zech 6:11, 14. In the context of the Temple Scroll the word refers, however, to a higher part of the temple. Yadin, 171.

that Yadin reads as ומשע[ר].[22] If we take a closer look at plate 28*:1, it is possible to discern a dark stain above the word itself.[23] It seems likely that this trace above *ayin* is a supra linear *resh*.

Summary of Col. 40

(1)]]ללבוש את הב[גדים
(2)]]ה להיות נש[י]א תח[ת אהרון
(3)]]בני ישראל ולוא ימ[ותו
(4)] החצ]ר הׄזואׄת ל . .]
(5)]] ועשיתה חצר שליש[י]ת]
(6)] ו]לבנותיהמה ולגרים אשר נולד̇[ו
(7)] רו]חב סביב לחצר התיכונה ש̇[ש] מׄאׄ[ות] אמה
(8) באורך כאלׄף ושש [מאות ב]אׄמׄה̇ מפנה לפנה לכול רׄוח ורוח כמדה הזואׄת
(9) לׄמזׄרח ולדׄרוׄם ולים ולצׄ[פו]ןׄ ורוחב הקיר שבע אמות וגובה תשע
(10) ורבעים בׄאמה וׄתאים [ע]שוים בוׄ ולשעריו מחוץ לעומת המוסד
(11) עדׄ עטׄרותׄיוׄ שלׄושׄהׄ בׄ[ו] שערׄים במזרח ושלושה בדרום ושלושה
(12) לׄים ושלושה לצפון ורׄוחב השעׄרים חמשים באמה וגובהמה שבעים
(13) באמה ובין שער לשערׄ [מדה] שלוש מאות וששים באמה מן הפנה עד
(14) שער שמעון ששים ושׄלוש מאות באמה ומשער שמעון עד שער לוי
(15) כמדה הזואת ומשעׄר לוי עד שער יהודה כמדה הזואת ששים ושלוש

Notes on Readings

2: להיות נש[י]א תח[ת אהרון – Yadin reads להיות מׄשרת[ים. **3:** ימ]ותו – Yadin restores ימ]ותו...חוקת עולם...]. **4:** הׄזואׄת ל . .]. – Qimron and García Martínez transcribe הזאת | at the end Qimron transcribes ל◦◦◦◦◦◦ לׄ◦◦◦תׄ. **5:** Qimron reads ◦◦◦◦הׄ in the first half of the line | שליש[י]ת] – Qimron reads שלישׄית [סובבת את החצר (6) [התיכונה. **6:** נולד̇[ו – Qimron restores נולד̇[ו בׄישׄרׄאׄלׄ (7) [עד הדור השלישי. **7:** רו]חב – Qimron has ו]רׄוׄחב | ש̇[ש] מׄאׄ[ות] אמה – Yadin restores ש[שים וחמש מאות באמה]. **8:** מאות ב]אׄמׄה̇ – Qimron reads [מאות] אׄמׄה̇. **10:** בוׄ לשעריו – Yadin restores בׄיׄן לשעריו.

[22] Qimron, 57.
[23] The darker colour is less clear on plate 55.

2.13. Column 41

At the top of Col. 41 there is a large v-shaped hole, which prevents us from being certain of the readings at this location. Beginning with line 9 to the end, everything of the text is preserved. The text of the column is found on plates 56, 29*:1 and 38*:5. The last of these fragments has later been published by White in DJD XIII.[1] In our analysis we will use White's definition of the fragment, Frg. 2 Col. ii, which is presented below before we begin the analysis of Col. 41.[2] The theme for this column is the measurements of the outer court. These do not have any parallel in the Bible. Therefore the whole passage can be defined as Individual Composition.

Yadin suggests a possible restoration of the lines 01–05 at the very top of Col. 41. Since we do not have any evidence for this portion, it will only be presented here but not in the summary of the column. Yadin has restored the lines according to the descriptions in Cols. 40 and 41.[3]

(01) [מאות באמה ומשער יהודה עד פנת הדרום כמדה]
(02) [הזואת שלוש מאות וששים באמה ומן הפנה הזואת]
(03) [עד שער ראובן שלוש מאות וששים באמה ומשער]
(04) [ראובן עד שער יוסף כמדה הזואת ששים ושלוש]
(05) [מאות באמה ומשער יוסף עד שער בנימין שלוש]

---

[1] This fragment belongs to the *editio maior* of 4Q365a made by Sidnie White. In that edition the fragment is defined as Frg. 2 Col. ii, which parallels the 11Q19 in lines 41:4-42:3. White 1994, 320, 327.

[2] The passage of Frg. 2 Col. ii – lines 8–11 – which is relevant for Col. 42 will be presented in the next section. – Yadin presents his own transcription of Frg. 2 Col. ii referring to it as Rockefeller 43.366. When his readings differ from White's and it has an influence on the reconstruction of 11Q19, this will be pointed out.

[3] "In general, the restoration seems correct, although there may be deviations here and there." Yadin, 173. The lines in his restoration of lines 01–05 are not as long as in other columns of 11Q19. This is, however, not a problem as all the lines in this column are unusually short.

We will now take a closer look at Frg. 2 Col. ii:[4]

(1) מאות באמה ומשער זבולון עד שער גד ששי֯ם] ושלוש מאות באמה]ו֯מש[ער ג]ד֯ ע֯[ד
(2) וששים באמה ומן הפנה הזואת עד שער דן של֯[וש מאות]וששים באמ֯ה וכ֯כה֯
(3) שער נפתלי ששים ושלוש מאות באמה ומשער נפתלי עד שער אשר שלוש מאו[ת וששים]
(4) ומשער אשר עד פנת מזרח{הִ} שלוש מאות וששים באמה ויוצאים ה◦ [ ]ר֯[
באים
(5) שבע אמות {יו}לפנימה מקיר החצר שש ושלושים באמה ורוחב פתחי השער֯י֯[ם
(6) באמה וגובהמה שמונה ועשרים באמה עד { הִמשקופִ ומן} המשקופ ומקירי֯ם[
(7) ומצופים זהב ודלתותי֯ה֯מה מצופות זהב טהור ובין שער לשער תע֯שה֯[

At the end of line 1, Yadin restores שלוש מאות [עד פנת הצפון] *pro* ע֯[ד. On line 4 we note that the *he* has been erased, which is marked with cancellation dots.[5] At the end of the same line Yadin reads השערים מקיר החצר לחוץ *pro*]ר֯[ ]ה◦. On the first part of line 5 the letters *yod* and *waw* have been erased in the MS. On the second part of line 6 the letters inside the brackets have clearly been erased; המשקופ is then repeated. At the end of line 7 Yadin continues ת]עשה פנימה נשכות[6] וחדרים ופרורים[, *pro* White's תע֯שה֯.[7]

[4] In addition to some short comments about the analysis made by White, we will compare it to the readings with major differences suggested by Yadin. The alternative suggestions made by Wacholder are minor in nature. Wacholder 1991, 34. See the complete "Notes on Readings" in White 1994, 327. The text is printed in a smaller font due to the long lines.

[5] White 1994, 327.

[6] Yadin does not read נשדות as White's misprint suggests. White 1994, 328.

[7] Yadin, 172.

We are now prepared to carry out the analysis of Col. 41.[8]

(1) [מאות וששים באמה ומשער בנימין עד פנת המ]ע̊ר̊[ב]
(2) [שלוש מאות וששים באמה וככה מן הפנה] ה̊ז̊ו̊אׄתׄ
(3) עד שׄ[ער יש שכר שלוש מאות וששים ב]אׄמה ומשער
(4) יש שכר[עד שער זבולון ששים ושלוש] מאות באמה
(5) ומשער זב<u>ולון עד שער גד ששי</u>[ם ו]שׄלׄושׄ מאות
(6) באמהׄ ומׄשׄ[ער] <u>גׄדׄ</u>[9] [עד פנת הצפון] שלוש מאות
(7) וששים באמה *vacat*

Qimron begins his restoration of line 1 a little further than Yadin, that is from the middle of the line, starting with ומשער.[10] Apart from this difference, there is no disagreement concerning the restoration. At the location of the *vacat* in line 7, Yadin notes that two letters, ככ, are visible on the infra-red photograph of mirror-writing on the back of Col. 42. With the reservation that these letters do not belong to this line at all, Yadin tentatively suggests a reading like ו]ככ[ה תעשה] מן הפנה הזואת.[11] The traces of these possible two letters are, however, very unclear and we suggest therefore that the traces do not belong to this line and that a *vacat* on this location is the likely alternative.

[8] Yadin and Qimron do not indicate in the same way the textual material which is common to Col. 41 and 4Q365a. Yadin basically only notes the letters with small brackets (these parts are underlined above, in lines 5 and 6) in Col. 41, which have been restored with the help of 4Q365a, Qimron underlines all the textual material in Col. 41 that overlaps with 4Q365a. We note that Wacholder also indicates all the common material, with the difference that he uses both small brackets around the overlapping textual material in addition to the underlining. Wacholder 1991, 34.

[9] In Yadin's restoration גׄדׄ is underlined, since he seems to be able to discern these letters as certain, but damaged ones. These letters are, however, very unclear on the MS and will not be underlined in the summary. The reading is, in any event, quite certain.

[10] Qimron, 58. Yadin's suggestion from the beginning of the line seems, however, to be a reasonable reconstruction.

[11] Yadin, 174.

(7) ו]מ̇ן̇ ה̇פ̇נ̇ה הזואת עד
(8) שער דן שלוש מאות̇ ו̇ששים באמ̇ה̇ ו̇ככה משער דן עד
(9) שער נפתלי ששים ושלוש מאות באמה ו̇משער נפתלי
(10) עד שער אשר שלוש מאות וששים באמ̇ה̇ ומשער
(11) אשר עד פנת {של(?)} המזרח שלוש מאות וששים באמה

In this passage the transcription is clear until the last line 11. As we note from the restoration by Yadin, he claims that של was written and afterwards erased. He tentatively suggests that that this would have been part of עד פנת שלוש.[12] Qimron has a more likely solution, which is that the scribe at first wrote שער and then corrected the *resh* into a *he,* which belongs to the next word, המזרח.[13] In the middle of the same line, Qimron discerns traces of an erased *he*.[14] However, according to plate 56 this cannot be the case.

(12) ויוצאים השערים מקיר החצר לחוץ שבע אמות
(13) ולפניסה באים מקיר החצר שש ושלושים באמה
(14) ורוחב פתחי השערים ארבע עשרה באמה וגובהמה
(15) שמונה ועשרים באמה עד המשקוף ומקורים
(16) באדשכים עץ ארז ומצופים זהב ודלתותיהמה מצופות
(17) זהב טהור ובין {ע} שער לשער תעשה פנימה נשכות

There are no disagreements concerning the transcription of this last passage that belongs to Col. 41. On line 13 באים was written between the lines in Frg. 2 Col. ii. Concerning המשקוף on line 15, the scribe of the parallel text Frg. 2 Col. ii at המשקוף ומן, but later it was erased and repeated המשקוף.[15] The word at the beginning of line 16, אדשכים, is not a biblical word. Yadin suggests that it may be of Persian origin, but notes also that no parallel has been found. The context suggests a translation of some kind of beams.[16]

At the beginning of line 17, זהב טהור, is clearly discerned. On the other hand the parallel location of Frg. 2 Col. ii, Yadin suggests that the

---

[12] Yadin, 174-175.
[13] Qimron, 58.
[14] Qimron, 58.
[15] Yadin argues that the scribe at first would have written עד הא̇ד̇ש̇כים וכן המשקוף. This is not an impossible solution, but since the scribe erased it, it is not a crucial matter. See also the analysis of 4Q365a Frg. 2 Col. ii at the beginning of this section.
[16] Yadin, 175.

scribe at first wrote טהור but changed it to טוב. We agree with White, that טהור is the correct reading.[17] Concerning line 17, the scribe by mistake wrote an *ayin*, which was later erased. Yadin notes that the last word, נשכות, is only found in Nehemiah in the Bible, where it appears twice. The more common synonym is לשכה.[18]

Summary of Col. 41[19]

(1) [מאות וששים באמה ומשער בנימין עד פנת המ]ע֯ר֯[ב]
(2) [שלוש מאות וששים באמה וככה מן הפנה] ה֯ז֯ו֯א֯ת֯
(3) עד ש֯[ער יש שכר שלוש מאות וששים ב]אמה ומשער
(4) יש שכר[עד שער זבולון ששים ושלוש] מאות באמה
(5) ומשער זב[ולון עד שער גד ששים ו]שלוש מאות
(6) באמה ומש[ער גד עד פנת הצפון] שלוש מאות
(7) וששים באמה *vacat* [ו]מ֯ן֯ הפנה הזואת עד
(8) שער דן שלוש מאות וששים באמה וככה משער דן עד
(9) שער נפתלי ששים ושלוש מאות באמה ומשער נפתלי
(10) עד שער אשר שלוש מאות וששים באמה ומשער
(11) אשר עד פנת {ש֯ע֯}המזרח שלוש מאות וששים באמה
(12) ויוצאים השערים מקיר החצר לחוץ שבע אמות
(13) ולפניסה באים מקיר החצר שש ושלושים באמה
(14) ורוחב פתחי השערים ארבע עשרה באמה וגובהמה
(15) שמונה ועשרים באמה עד המשקוף ומקורים
(16) באדשכים עץ ארז ומצופים זהב ודלתותיהמה מצופות
(17) זהב טהור ובין {ע} שער לשער תעשה פנימה נשכות

Notes on Readings

1: Qimron begins his restoration of the line from ומשער. **7:** וששים באמה – Yadin continues tentatively ו]ככ[ה תעשה] מן הפנה. **11:** אשר עד פנת {ש֯ע֯} – Yadin suggests עד פנת שלוש | המזרח – Qimron transcribes המזרח(ה֯).

[17] Concerning Yadin's suggestion, White notes the reading in e.g. 2 Chr 3:5, ויחפהו זהב טוב. White 1994, 328.

[18] Neh 12:44, הנשכות and 13:7, נשכה. Yadin, 176.

[19] In the summaries the discernable overlapping textual material between 11Q19 and 4Q365a is underlined.

2.14. Column 42

It seems very likely that the rest of 4Q365a Frg. 2 Col. ii contains the top lines of Col. 42.[1] Qimron presents these lines with the line numbers of Frg. 2 Col. ii.[2] We prefer, however, to locate them at the beginning of Col. 42. Concerning the palaeographical evidence, we will refer to the plates 57, 29*:1, and 38*:5.[3]

At first we shall return to White's analysis of the rest of Frg. 2 Col ii, that is the relevant passage for this column, which are lines 8–11. They are presented below:[4]

ח
(8) רוחב הדר עשר באמה ואורכו עשרים באמה וגובהו ארבע֯] עשרה
(9) עץ ארז ורחב הקיר שתים אמות ולחוצה מזה הנשכהׄ ר֯]וחב
(10) עשרים באמה והקיר שתים אמות רוחבו֯ ◦]
(11) עצי ארז ופתחה שלוש אמות רוחב ה֯]

Qimron has suggested several additional reconstructions to these lines.[5] At the end of line 8 he suggests עשרה באמה ומקורה באדשכים].[6]

At the beginning of line 9, Yadin, Wacholder, and Qimron read *tsade* instead of *tsade sophit*.[7] We admit that both readings are possible according to plate 38*:5. On the other hand is *tsade sophit* by no means a less possible – a fact which makes this alternative preferable. At the end of the line Qimron reads הנשכה ר֯]וחב הנשכה עשר באמה ואורכו].[8]

For the second part of line 10 Qimron suggests רוחׄבׄ ו֯]גובהה ארבע עשרה באמה ומקורה באדשכים].[9] In the light of plate 38*:5, there is such a long distance between רוחׄבׄ and ו֯ that Qimron's alternative to read the *waw* with the next word is to be preferred *pro* White's sugges-

---

[1] 4Q365a Frg. 2 Col. ii is defined as 38*:5 in Yadin 1977b.
[2] In any event, he notes that the text is a direct continuation of the previous column. Qimron, 59.
[3] The text that Yadin has used for his construction of Col. 42 from Frg. 2, Col. ii is underlined in this presentation.
[4] White 1994, 327.
[5] These restorations follow mostly the restorations, which Yadin has done in the corresponding locations of Col. 42.
[6] Qimron, 59.
[7] Qimron, 59.
[8] Qimron, 59. Concerning the reading of the first הנשכה, see below the analysis of line 05 of Col. 42.
[9] Qimron, 59.

tion, who reads them together. In his reconstruction of the end of the line, ומקורה באדשכים, Qimron follows the same pattern we find at the end of line 8. This is a possible solution, but it will not have any influence on the restoration of Col. 42 since the MS clearly shows the letters המשק.

We will now move on to the analysis of Col. 42.[10]

(01) [וחדרים ופרורים *vacat*]
(02) רוחב החדר עשר באמה ואורכו עשרים באמה
(03) וגובהו ארב[ע עשרה באמה ומקורה באדשכים]
(04) עץ ארז ורוחב הקיר שתים אמות ולחוצה מזה
(05) הנשכות *vacat*

The beginning of line 01 has been restored according to the model from line 9 below, that is וחדריהמה ופרוריהמה.[11] At the end of the line 03, the restoration [ומקורה באדשכים is derived with the help of the former column, lines 41:15–16, which read ומקורים באדשכים.[12]

At the beginning of line 05, Yadin restores the word with the help of plate 38*:5 to הנשכות.[13] There is indeed a tear in the MS, which makes it difficult to restore the word. It seems more likely to read נשכה, as White and Qimron have suggested.[14]

---

[10] Yadin does not have the lines 01–1 in brackets, even if this would be the logical thing to do: this is instead done in the summary at the end of the column and in chapter three.

[11] Yadin, 177.

[12] Yadin notes that the end of line 03 requires at least two words. Yadin, 177.

[13] Yadin, 178. Wacholder and García Martínez support this reading. Wacholder 1991, 35; García Martínez, 1260.

[14] White 1994, 327; Qimron, 59.

(05) [רוחב הנשכה עשר באמה]
(1) [ואורכו]עשרים באמה והקיר שתים אמות רוחב
(2) [וגובהה ארבע עשרה באמה] עׄדׄ המשקוף ופ֯תחה
(3) שלוש אמות רוחב [וכן תעשה] לכול הנשכות ולחדריה[מה]
(4) ו֯פרו֯[ר רו]חב עשר אמות ובין שער
(5) לשעׄר [תעשה שמונה] עשׂרׄה נשכה וחדריהמה
(6) שמונה] עשרה [*vacat*

Yadin restores the passage from line 05 until the middle of line 2 with the help of 4Q365a. Qimron begins his restoration from line 1 in a different way: he reads only two words, שלו[ש֯ א֯מ֯]ות, suggesting that it is more likely that Frg. 2 Col. ii line 11 would overlap with line 1 instead of lines 2 and 3 as Yadin has suggested.[15]

Qimron continues with his restoration in the middle of line 2 with ג֯וב֯ה֯ המשקוף ופ֯[רוריהמה[16] *pro* Yadin's עד המשקוף ופ֯תחה (3) שלוש אמות רוחב. It seems that Yadin was influenced by the expression עד המשקופ that is found earlier in Frg. 2 Col. ii.[17] Qimron's reconstruction of ג֯וב֯ה֯ is difficult to verify with plate 57. As a matter of fact the trace before המשק, which is found at the lower end of the letters, resembles more Yadin's reading עד with the low endings of *ayin* and *dalet* touching each other. Due to these reasons we consider Yadin's theory of the overlapping material more convincing.

Before לכול on line 3, Qimron restores [מדה אחת instead of Yadin's [כן תעשה].[18] Yadin's suggestion fits in with the pattern, that we see e.g. on line 7, ובית מעלות ת֯עשה or at the beginning of line 11,תעשה עמודים.

At the beginning of line 4, Yadin tentatively suggests ופרו[ריהמה כולמה יהיו רו]חב, which is supported by Qimron.[19]

In the first part of line 5 Qimron suggests לשער ת[היינה שמונה] עשרה *pro* Yadin's לשׄעׄר [תעשה שמונה] עשׂרׄה.[20] Both readings are

[15] Qimron, 60. By mistake Qimron refers to lines 1 and 2 concerning the suggestion made by Yadin. See the passage, which is underlined in Yadin's restoration; Wacholder does not read line 05 at all, but continues from line 04 directly to line 1: ולחוצה מזה] (1) [ואורכה. Wacholder 1991, 35.

[16] Qimron, 60.

[17] García Martínez agrees with Yadin concerning עד המשקוף. García Martínez, 1260. See also the presentation of the beginning of Frg. 2 Col. ii in the analysis of Col. 41.

[18] Qimron, 60; Yadin, 178.

[19] Yadin, 178; Qimron, 60.

[20] Qimron, 60; Yadin, 178.

possible: it seems that Qimron reads תהיינה due to space reasons. This is, however, not necessary since the words can sometimes be written with more space between them.

At the beginning of line 6 Qimron's masculine form of שמונה עשר] referring to וחדריהמה at the end of line 5 seems more logical than Yadin's feminine form of שמונה [עשרה, which seems to refer to the following text.[21]

(7) ובית מעלות תעשה אצל קירות השערים בתוך
(8) הפרור עולים מסבות לתוך הפרור השני ולשלישי
(9) ולגג ונשכות בנוית וחדריהמה ופרוריהמה כתחתונות
(10) שניות ושלישיות כמדת התחתונות

There is no disagreement concerning the transcription of this passage. In the first part of line 8 Yadin notes that the correct reading from a grammatical point of view should be either עולות מסבות or עולים במסבות.[22] On the other hand it is possible that מסבה also was used in masculine.

Concerning the three levels of chambers, which are mentioned in lines 9–10, we have two interesting parallel passages in the Bible, of which the first is 1 Kgs 6:6, היצוע התחתנה חמש באמה רחבה והתיכנה שש באמה רחבה והשלישית שבע באמה רחבה.[23] The other passage is Ezek 42:5-6, (5) והלשכות העליונת קצרות כי־יוכלו אתיקים מהנה מהתחתנות ומהתכונות בנין (6) כי משולשות הנה ואין להן עמודים כעמודי החצרות על־כן נאצל מהתחתונות ומהתיכנות מהארץ. We note here that the terminology is not very dissimilar: both passages speak both about lower chambers and a construction of three levels of chambers. This passage of lines 9–10 is an example of Rewritten Bible.[24]

---

[21] Qimron, 60; Yadin, 178. Yadin, however, claims that his restoration is certain.
[22] Yadin, 179. See also the comments about מְסִבָּה in the analysis of line 30:5. It is interesting to note that the grammar is irregular in all the cases when this word appears in 11Q19: line 30:5 – את is not followed by the determined form with a *he* as usual; line 31:8 – בית מסבה הזואת *pro* the expected בית המסבה הזה; and finally this case in line 42:7.
[23] We note, that the *masorah* in the margin gives the *Qere*-reading היציע, when the textual apparatus suggests the reading הצלע. In any event this does not affect our comparison.
[24] בנוית is indeed a difficult form grammatically in this context. It is possible that the scribe intended the plural-form of בנויות. See also the translation of Col. 42.

(10) ועל גג השלישית
(11) תעשה עמודים ומקורים בקורות מעמוד אל עמוד
(12) מקום לסוכות גבהים שמונה אמות והיו הסוכות
(13) נעשות עליהמה בכול שנה ושנה בחג הסוכות לזקני
(14) העדה לנשיאים לראשי בתי האבות לבני ישראל
(15) ולשרי האלפים ולשרי המאיות אשר יהיו עולים
(16) ויושבים שמה עד {ע}[ע]הלות את עולת המועד אשר
(17) לחג הסוכות שנה בשנה בין שער לשער יהיו

The only disagreement concerning the transcription of this passage is found on line 16. Yadin suggests that the scribe at first wrote *ayin*, which he erased afterwards. Qimron, on the other hand, claims that *he* is the letter that was erased.[25] We would consider it more logical if *ayin* would have been erased. Why would the scribe erase *he* and write *he* once more? However, according to the very light traces both *ayin* and *he* are possible.

Concerning בכל שנה ושנה on line 13, we note what is written in Zech 14:16b, ועלו מדי שנה בשנה להשתחות למלך יהוה צבאות ולחג את־חג הסכות.[26] The expression in line 13 is a *terminus tecnicus*. It is used in the context of the feast of booths, which is also the background in Zechariah. The same influence is seen on line 17, אשר (17) לחג הסוכות, but this is even more relevant, because the celebrating *per se* is the issue. We may interpret line 13 as Rewritten Bible, and line 17 can be understood as Biblical Paraphrase.

At the end of line 13 and at the beginning of line 14 we have the expression לזקני (14) העדה. In comparison Yadin notes Lev 4:15, וסמכו זקני העדה את־ידיהם על־ראש הפר לפני יהוה ושחט את הפר לפני יהוה.[27]

The expression about the elders belongs to a completely different context in Lev 4. On the other hand, זקני העדה, has an essential continuance and we need, therefore, to read it together with the rest on lines 14–15. The elders are followed by other leaders of Israel on different levels on lines 14–15. This may be compared with Num 7:2, ויקריבו נשיאי ישראל ראשי בית אבתם הם נשיאי המטת הם העומדים על־הפקדים.

[25] Qimron, 60.
[26] Yadin, 179.
[27] Yadin, 179.

Beginning with line 16 to the end of Col. 42 we have ויושבים שמה עד {ע}ה(ע)לות את עולת המועד אשר (17) לחג הסוכות שנה בשנה בין שער לשער יהיו. This can be compared with Lev 23:42, בסכות תשבו שבעת ימים כל־האזרח בישראל ישבו בסכות, and with Neh 8:17, ויעשו כל־הקהל השבים מן־השבי סכות וישבו בסכות כי לא־עשו מימי ישוע בן־נון כן בני ישראל עד היום ההוא ותהי שמחה גדולה מאד.[28]

Summary of Col. 42

(01) [וחדרים ופרורים *vacat*]
(02) [רוחב החדר עשר באמה ואורכו עשרים באמה]
(03) [וגובהו ארבע עשרה באמה ומקורה באדשכים]
(04) [עץ ארז ורוחב הקיר שתים אמות ולחוצה מזה]
(05) [הנשכה *vacat* רוחב הנשכה עשר באמה]
(1) [ואורכה עשרים באמה והקיר שתים אמות רוחב]
(2) [וגובהה ארבע עשרה באמה] ע֯ד֯ המשקוף ופ֯תחה
(3) [שלוש אמות רוחב וכן תעשה] לכול הנשכות ולחדריה[מה]
(4) ו֯פרו֯[ריהמה כולמה יהיו רו]חב עשר אמות ובין שער
(5) לשעׄר [תעשה שמונה] עשׄרׄה נשכה וחדריהמה
(6) שמונה[עשר] *vacat*
(7) ובית מעלות תׄעשה אצל קירות השערים בתוך
(8) הפרור עולים מסבות לתוך הפרור השני ולשלישי
(9) ולגג ונשכות בנוית וחדריהמה ופרוריהמה כתחתונות
(10) שניות ושלישיות כמדת התחתונות ועל גג השלישית
(11) תעשה עמודים ומקורים בקורות מעמוד אל עמוד
(12) מקום לסוכות גבהים שמונה אמות והיו הסוכות
(13) נעשות עליהמה בכול שנה ושנה בחג הסוכות לזקני
(14) העדה לנשיאים לראשי בתי האבות לבני ישראל
(15) ולשרי האלפים ולשרי המאיות אשר יהיו עולים
(16) ויושבים שמה עד {ע}ה(ע)לות את עולת המועד אשר
(17) לחג הסוכות שנה בשנה בין שער לשער יהיו

Notes on Readings

05: הנשכה – Yadin, Wacholder and García Martínez read הנשכות. **1:** Qimron reads at the middle of the line שלו]ש֯ א֯מ֯[ות. **2:** עד המשקוף ופ֯תחה – Qimron transcribes ג֯ובׄהׄ המשקוף ופ֯[רוריהמה]. **3:** [וכן תעשה] –

[28] Yadin, 180.

Qimron restores [מדה אחת. **5:** [תעשה שמונה] – Qimron has ת̊[היינה [שמונה. **6:** עשר]שמונה – Yadin restores עשרה]שמונה. **16:** {ע}העלות – Qimron transcribes (ה̇)העלות.

2.15. Column 43

This column is also well preserved. The v-shaped hole has moved a little to the right in comparison with Col. 42. This is due to how the Scroll was rolled. Therefore, it is the upper right part, which needs a certain amount of restoration. Line 6 is the first line that is possible to read with complete certainty. Concerning this column we have plate 58 and 29*:2 as palaeographical evidence. It appears that a discussion about the feast of booths was on the missing lines at the top.[1]

(1)]   ]ה̇ לשש[[
(2)]   ]בימי השבתות ובימ[י   [
(3)]   ]ובימי הבכורים לדגן לת[ירוש וליצהר]
(4) [ובמועד קורבן ה]עצים

Yadin suggests לשש[ת ימי המעשה] as one possibility for line 1, following the pattern on lines 16 and 17, בימי המעשה.[2] This reading is supported by Qimron.[3] There is no disagreement about the readings on the next line, and so the end of the line is restored to ובימ[י החודש].

At the beginning of line 3 Qimron restores [ובימי חג המצות] ובימי הבכורים and continues with לדגן ולתי[רוש].[4] Yadin does not read anything at the beginning of this line but agrees with the rest. Due to space-reasons Qimron's reading would be the most probable.

On the other hand the different festivals are mentioned later in the texts. We do not find חג המצות in those later references.[5] Due to this reason we tentatively follow Yadin and do not read anything at the beginning of line 3. At the end of the line we need, however, to depart from Yadin's reading since he reads וליצהר] on the same line.[6] It is not likely that there would be enough space for this according to the paleographical evidence on plate 58.

Qimron suggests a reading of ול̊[יצהר ובימי ה]עצים at the beginning of line 4, which is a good alternative considering the space avail-

[1] Yadin, 181.
[2] Yadin, 181.
[3] Yadin, 181; Qimron, 61.
[4] Qimron, 61.
[5] חג הבכורים לדגן is mentioned on line 6, מועד התירוש and מועד התירוש והיצהר on lines 8–9.
[6] Yadin, 182.

able.[7] Since we do not advocate Yadin's reading at the end of line 3, it would be difficult to subscribe to his continuation at the beginning of line 4, ובמועד קורבן ה[עצים].[8] Qimron's suggestion includes the same amount of letters. This content also makes his suggestion plausible.[9]

(4) באלה הימים יאכל ולוא יני[חו]
(5) ממנו שנה לשנה אחרת כי ככה יהיו אוכלים אותו
(6) מחג הבכורים לדגן החטים יהיו אוכלים את הדגן
(7) עד השנה השנית עד יום חג הבכורים והיין מיום
(8) מועד התירוש עד השנה השנית עד יום מועד
(9) התירוש והיצהר מיום מועדו עד השנה השנית
(10) למועד יום הקרב שמן חדש ^על^ מזבח

There is no disagreement concerning the transcription of this passage. At the beginning of the passage we have an interesting textual parallel from Lev 7:15, ביום קרבנו יאכל לא יניח ממנו עד־בקר.[10] In comparison with 𝔊 we have καὶ ἐν ᾗ ἡμέρᾳ δῶρειται, βρωθήσεται· οὐ καταλείψουσιν ἀπ' αυτοῦ εἰς τὸ πρωί. The difference we note between these two versions is the verb יניח – καταλείψουσιν: 𝔊 reads it in third person plural as 𝔐 has third person singular.

On the other hand, there is a MS of 𝔊 – that is 53' – which belongs to the *f*-Group and reads the verb in singular, καταλείψεται. Unfortunately, the last word at the end of line 4 is reconstructed, which makes it impossible to use it in the comparison. Several of the verbs in the passage above (lines 4–10) are, however, written in plural form and therefore יני[חו] is a likely restoration.

At the end of line 5 we read ככה יהיו אוכלים אותו. From a grammatical viewpoint Ex 12:11 has a parallel expression. However, it is imperfect and not a composite form, ככה תאכלו אותו. The context is not the same, since Exodus speaks about Passover and 11QT addresses the Feast of Booths.

At the end of line 8 and at the beginning of line 9 we read עד יום מועד (9) התירוש. Yadin has noted Hos 2:11, לכן אשוב ולקחתי דגני בעתו

---

[7] Qimron, 61. This reading is also supported by García Martínez. García Martínez, 1261.
[8] Yadin, 182.
[9] Yadin noted that "the space at the beginning of the line exactly fits the suggested restoration." Yadin, 182.
[10] Yadin, 182.

ותירושי במועדו. In the Scroll, the context is a proper feast but Hosea uses the expression to describe the season for wine in the context of punishment.

At the end of this passage the scribe at first wrote only למזבח and afterwards corrected it by inserting *ayin* and *he* above the line so that the final result would be על המזבח.

(10) וכול אשר
(11) נותר ממועדיהמה יקדש באש ישרף לוא יאכל עוד
(12) כי קדש והיושבים במרחק מן המקדש דרך שלושת
(13) ימים כול אשר יוכלו להביא יביאו ואם לא יוכלו
(14) לשאתו ימכרוהו בכסף והביאו את הכסף ולקחו בו דגן
(15) ויין ושמן ובקר וצאון ואכלוהו בימי המועדים ולוא
(16) יואכלו ממנו בימי המעשה לאונמה כי קודש הוא
(17) ובימי הקודש יאכל ולוא יאכל בימי המעשה

The sentence that begins at the end of line 10 and ends at the beginning of line 12 with כי קדש, has a parallel in Ex 29:34, ואם־יותר מבשר המלאים ומן־הלחם עד־הבקר ושרפת את־הנותר באש לא יאכל כי־קדש הוא.[11] The Scroll is actually not introducing anything new here and is therefore understood as Biblical Paraphrase.

The long section beginning on line 12 with והיושבים and continuing until the end of line 16 has clearly been influenced by Deut 14:24-26, (24) וכי־ירבה ממך הדרך כי לא תוכל שאתו כי־ירחק ממך המקום אשר יבחר יהוה אלהיך לשום שמו שם כי יברכך יהוה אלהיך (25) ונתתה בכסף וצרת בכסף בידך והלכת אל־המקום אשר יבחר יהוה אלהיך בו (26) ונתתה הכסף בכל אשר־תאוה נפשך בבקר ובצאן וביין ובשכר ובכל אשר תשאלך נפשך ואכלת שם לפני יהוה אלהיך ושמחת אתה וביתך.

Yadin suggests that the limitation of three days may come from e.g. Ex 3:18, which is located in the context of God's discussion with Moses.[12] This is indeed a possibility as verse 3:18b reads ועתה נלכה־נא דרך שלשת ימים במדבר ונזבחה ליהוה אלהינו. We note that the Temple Scroll presents the same message but in a shorter manner. Since the circumstances are so different, we cannot understand שלשת ימים as a quotation. This passage in 11QT represents, however, a clear example

[11] Yadin, 183.
[12] Yadin, 183. Another passage is Ezra 10:8, וכל אשר לא־יבוא לשלשת הימים.

of Rewritten Bible that possibly has been influenced by the biblical verses mentioned above.

At the end of line 14 and at the beginning of line 15 we read ולקחו בו דגן (15) ויין ושמן ובקר וצאון ואלכוהו בימי המועדים. Yadin suggests that the author drifted from the point as he adapts a different terminology. On the other hand, this may be seen as support for the idea that the Temple Scroll is Rewritten Bible. The content in the lines 14 and 15 is indeed close to equivalent; only the writer has preferred to use synonyms in some cases, e.g. יין instead of תירוש.[13]

On line 14 Qimron reads ומכרוהו[14] *pro* Yadin's ימכרוהו. As we have noted before, *waw* and *yod* are often difficult to distinguish from each other in these manuscripts. On the other hand, plate 58 shows us how the third letter from the end – obviously a *waw*, of which there is no disagreement – is quite short also. Due to these reasons there are no palaeographical reasons that force us either way. Qimron points out that only rarely an imperfect-form with suffix would lack a *waw* after the first radical.[15] In conclusion we support the reading of ומכרוהו.

On lines 16 and 17 we have the expression בימי המעשה. A phrase close to this is found only once in the Bible, in Ezek 46:1, שער החצר הפנימית הפנה קדים יהיה סגור ששת ימי המעשה.[16] We note that a saying close to a biblical expression is used; on the other hand the context is so different that we would not understand this part as Biblical Paraphrase. According to our definition, this is understood as Rewritten Bible.

At the end of line 17 Yadin suggests that another בימי have been erased. Qimron suggests (לימי) instead.[17]

---

[13] Yadin suggests moreover that the author had another biblical text in mind whilst he wrote. Yadin, 183. We consider this as speculative.

[14] Qimron, 61.

[15] "In the scrolls, a future *o*-form with enclitic pronominal objective suffixes has a *waw* after the first radical or after the second, and only occasionally is the *waw* lacking. Our scroll has no examples whatever of such forms without a *waw* after the initial radical." Qimron 1978b, 172. The present author uses the term imperfect instead of future above; we refer, however, to the same form grammatically.

[16] Yadin, 184.

[17] Yadin, 184; Qimron, 61. This is very difficult to verify from plate 58. Since the word is erased, it is in any event not a crucial matter.

Summary of Col. 43

(1) [   ]ה לשש[ת ימי המעשה]
(2) [   ]בימי השבתות ובימ[י החודש]
(3) [   ]ובימי הבכורים לדגן לת[ירוש]
(4) [וליצהר ובימי ה]עצים באלה הימים יאכל ולוא ינ̊[חו]
(5) ממנו שנה לשנה אחרת כי ככה יהיו אוכלים אותו
(6) מחג הבכורים לדגן החטים יהיו אוכלים את הדגן
(7) עד השנה השנית עד יום חג הבכורים והיין מיום
(8) מועד התירוש עד השנה השנית עד יום מועד
(9) התירוש והיצהר מיום מועדו עד השנה השנית
(10) למועד יום הקרב שמן חדש ^על^ל'מזבח וכול אשר
(11) נותר ממועדיהמה יקדש באש ישרף לוא יאכל עוד
(12) כי קדש והיושבים במרחק מן המקדש דרך שלושת
(13) ימים כול אשר יוכלו לבהיא יביאו ואם לא יוכלו
(14) לשאתו ומכרוהו בכסף והביאו את הכסף ולקחו בו דגן
(15) ויין ושמן ובקר וצאון ואכלוהו בימי המועדים ולוא
(16) יואכלו ממנו בימי המעשה לאונמה כי קודש הוא
(17) ובימי הקודש יאכל ולוא יאכל בימי המעשה {. . . .}

Notes on Readings

3:]ובימי – Qimron restores [ובימי חג המצות] ובימי | לת[ירוש] – Yadin reads [ובמועד קורבן] לת[ירוש וליצהר]. **4:** [וליצהר ובימי ה]עצים – Yadin has ה[עצים. **14:** ומכרוהו – Yadin reads ימכרוהו. **17:** {. . . .} המעשה – Yadin suggests {בימי} המעשה as Qimron has (לי̇מ̇י) המעשה.

2.16. Column 44

This column is missing some of the material at the top. From line 5 downwards, the column is well preserved. For the palaeographical evidence we have used plate 59. Yadin suggests tentatively that the missing lines would have discussed eating the tithes and the dwellers in the holy city.[1]

(1)] [יושבים] [
(2)] [אשר בתוך העיר למ◦] [
(3)] [*vacat* וחלקתה את [הנשכות וחדריהמה(?) משער]
(4) [שמעו]ן̊ עד שער יהודה יהיו לכוהנים] [

It is possible to discern only one word on line 1. At the end of the next line Yadin tentatively restores למ[זרח.[2] This reading is indeed likely and is also supported by Qimron.[3] On the second part of line 3, Yadin follows the pattern of what is written on line 12, הנשכות וחדריהמה.[4] Qimron has a shorter suggestion with [כול הנשכות משער].[5] It seems that this reading was created according to space-restrictions. There is, however, no compulsory reason to disqualify the longer restoration. If this reading is supported, it would make line 3 the longest line in the column. On the other hand it would be only one or two spaces longer than line 10 which is the second longest one on plate 59. We consider, however, a shorter reading more likely in this case.

At the end of line 4 Yadin suggests [בני אהרון] or [בני צדוק], although he prefers the first alternative.[6] בני אהרון is indeed a very common expression in the Bible and appears later in this text, on line 5; on the other hand, it would be difficult to prove explicit biblical influence in this context.

[1] Yadin, 184.
[2] It is possible that assignments belonging to the east side of the city are discussed. Yadin, 185.
[3] Qimron, 62.
[4] Yadin, 185. See also line 4 with נשכה וחדריהמה.
[5] Qimron, 62; García Martínez agrees with this reading. García Martínez, 1298.
[6] Yadin, 186; Also Qimron subscribes to [בני אהרון]. Qimron, 62.

(5) וכׄ[ו]ל° ימין שער לוי ושמאולו לבני אהרון אחיכה תח[לק]
(6) שמונה ומאה נשכה וחדריהמה ושתי סוכותיהמה
(7) אשר מעל הגג ולבני יהודה משער יהודה עד
(8) הפנה ארבע וחמשים נשכה וחדריהמה והסוכה
(9) אשר מעלהמה

There is no disagreement concerning the transcription of this passage. There are actually only two words, which need restoration: at the beginning of line 5 we have one word that needs transcription, that is וכׄ[ו]ל°. This is, nevertheless, a very likely solution. At the end of the same line, the reconstruction of תח[לק] also appears to be certain.[7] Yadin also notes that 𝔐 seems to be defective in Ezek 40:44,[8] ומחוצה לשער הפנימי *pro* 𝔊 with καὶ εἰσήγαγέ με εἰς τὴν αὐλὴν τὴν ἐσωτέραν.

It is evident that the verse in Ezekiel, which is mentioned above, describes the inner court whereas the Scroll describes the outer court.[9] In any event, we agree with Yadin about the idea of priestly chambers to the north and to the south of the gate of Levi is similar to Ezek 40:44-46[10] and therefore interpret this as Rewritten Bible.

(9) ולבני שמעון משער שמעון עד הפנה
(10) השנית נשכותמה וחדריהמה וסוכוׄתהׄמה[11] ולבני ראובן
(11) מן המקצוע אשר אצל בני יהודה עד שער ראובן
(12) שתים וחמשים נשכוׄת וחדריהמה וסוכוׄתמה

We have now arrived to the part of the column that does not need restoration. However, there are some supra linear corrections, which seem to have been done by a scribe: these are located on lines 10 and 12. Yadin suggests that the corrections concerning the booth were not done by the first scribe, but are a result of a misunderstanding.[12] This is indeed pos-

[7] Yadin, 186; Qimron, 62; García Martínez, 1262.
[8] Yadin, 186.
[9] This is actually the third court since the temple in the Temple Scroll is surrounded by three courts.
[10] Yadin, 186.
[11] Yadin notes that the dot above *he* and a possible dot above *waw* indicate erasure. Yadin, 186. A similar dot usually indicates a damaged but certain letter in a transcription.
[12] Furthermore, Yadin claims that at least the supralinear *he* on line 10 is written in another handwriting. Yadin, 186. This is, however, difficult to see from plate 59.

sible, since סוכה appears in singular at the end of line 8. Concerning the correction of נשכה to נשכות on line 12, Qimron notes that נשכה was the original reading.[13]

(12) ומשער
(13) ראובן עד שער יוסף לבני יוסף לאפרים ולמנשה
(14) ומשער̣ יוסף עד שער בנימין לבני קהת מ{ב}נ{י} הלויים
(15) ומשע˺ר˹ בנימין עד פנת המערב לבני בנימין מן הפנה
(16) הזאת עד שער יש שכר לבני יש שכר ומשער

There is no disagreement concerning the last remainder of this column. On line 14 the בני קהת are mentioned. Yadin suggests that the sons of Gershon and Merari could have been mentioned in the missing section at the top of Col. 45.[14] Whether this is the case or not is not crucial, since this in any event quite clearly is a case of Rewritten Bible.

Near the end of line 14 the scribe seems to have written מבני by mistakc, which he afterwards corrected to מנ by erasing *beit* and *yod*. We may compare this change with e.g. Jos 21:20, ולמשפחות בני־קהת הלוים הנותרים מבני קהת ויהי ערי גורלם ממטה אפרים.[15] At the beginning of linc 15 a *resh* was inserted later.[16]

Summary of Col. 44

(1) [ ]יׄושבים[
(2) [ ]אשר בתוך העיר למ[זרח
(3) [ ] *vacat* וחלקתה את [כול נשכות משער
(4) [שמעו]ןׄ עד שער יהודה יהיו לכוהנים [
(5) וכׄ[ו]לׄ ימין שער לוי ושמאולו לבני אהרון אחיכה תח[לק]
(6) שמונה ומאה נשכה וחדריהמה ושתי סוכותיהמה
(7) אשר מעל הגג ולבני יהודה משער יהודה עד
(8) הפנה ארבע וחמשים נשכה וחדריהמה והסוכה
(9) אשר מעלהמה ולבני שמעון משער̣ שמעון עד הפנה
(10) השנית נשכותמה וחדריהמה וסוכׄת˺ה˹מה ולבני ראובן

---

[13] Qimron, 62. The changes on line 10 and 12 do not, however, influence our analysis, since the passages do not have close parallel readings in the Bible.

[14] Yadin vol. 1 1983, 266.

[15] Yadin, 187.

[16] Yadin claims that it seems to have been added by another hand. Yadin, 188. This is not certain, however.

(11) מן המקצוע אשר אצל בני יהודה עד שער ראובן
(12) שתים וחמשים נשלת וחדריהמה וסולתמה ומשער
(13) ראובן עד שער יוסף לבני יוסף לאפרים ולמנשה
(14) ומשער יוסף עד שער בנימין לבני קהת מ{ב}נ{י} הלויים
(15) ומשער בנימין עד פנת המערב לבני בנימין מן הפנה
(16) הזאת עד שער יש שכר לבני יש שכר ומשער

Notes on Readings

3: את [הנשכות וחדריהמה(?) – Yadin restores את [כול נשכות משער משער]. **4:** לכוהנים [ ] – Yadin and Qimron לכוהנים [בני אהרון].

2.17. Column 45

In Col. 45 the lines are clearly longer than the columns in Col. 44. For the palaeographical evidence we will consult plates 60, 30*:1, 39*:1, and 40*:5. The last two fragments have been published as a part of 11Q20 by García Martínez.[1]

At the very top of this column Yadin suggests a possible restoration of lines 01–04. Since we do not have any palaeographical evidence for this portion, it will only be presented below at this point but not in the summary.[2]

(01) [יש שכר עד שער זבולון לבני זבולון ומשער זבולון עד שער]
(02) [גד לבני גרשון מן הלויים ומשער גד עד פנת הצפון לבני גד]
(03) [מן הפנה הזאות עד שער דן לבני דן ומשער דן עד שער נפתלי]
(04) [לבני נפתלי ומשער נפתלי עד שער אשר לבני מררי מן הלויים]

In this context we also need to present Frg. 40:5 so that we would be able to evaluate the interpolations of it into Col. 45.[3]

(1) [ ]°בׄאים
(2) [ ]נ֯שכה
(3) [י]ה֯יה בא
(4) [ב]אלה

The restoration of the beginning of Col. 45 is quite complicated: this is reflected in the amount of different suggested alternatives. Yadin gives a tentative reconstruction of lines 1–2 adding that the content is certain even if a few of the words may need to be changed.[4] We will in this context add lines 3 and 4 so that the comparison with other suggestions becomes easier.[5]

---

[1] In DJD XXIII these fragments are included as follows: 40:*5 as Frg. 20 in 11Q20 Col. 11 and 39*:1 as Frg. 21 i belonging to Col. 12. DJD XXIII, plates XLIV-XLV.
[2] Yadin, 189-190.
[3] The restoration of the two fragments belonging to 11Q20 will not be presented since they rely heavily on 11Q19 and therefore would add little to our analysis.
[4] Yadin, 190.
[5] Since Yadin and Wacholder suggest readings that cover the full length of lines 1–2, these readings are presented separately. Qimron's alternative readings will afterwards be weighed against these. By that we do not consider the Qimron's reading as a

(1) ומש[ער אשר עד פנת המזרח לבני אשר והיו כול הנשכות אשר לשבט הלוי]
(2) שבעים֯ [ומאתים[6] נשכה ולבני ישראל שש ושמונים וחמש מאות נשכה]
(3) וכאשר י[ה]שני יהיה בא לשמאול[ ]
בֹ
(4) יצא הרישון מֹימֹ[י]ן ולוא [יהי]ו֯ מתערבים אלה באלה וכל֯יה[מה]א

Wacholder uses Yadin's suggestion for lines 1 and 2 to some extent and interpolates the fragment, which is presented above in the following way:[7]

(1) ומש[ערים יהיו <u>באים</u> ויוצאים והיו כול הנשכות אשר לשבט לוי]
(2) שבעים [ומאתים <u>נשכה</u> ולבני ישראל שש ושמונים וחמש מאות נשכה]
(3) וכאשר י[בואו המשמרות ויצאו ה]שני <u>יהיה בא</u> לשמאול[ובבואו]
(4) יצא הרישון מֹימֹ[י]ן ולוא [יהי]ו מתערבים אלה ב<u>אלה</u> ובֹכל֯יה[מה ויבו]א

First of all we need to be aware that the suggestion by Yadin above actually includes about ¾ of the fragment, except באים in line 1. He does not, however, mention this in his analysis of the passage.

Secondly, Wacholder's restoration of the first half of line 1 is not impossible but very hypothetical. Furthermore, we note that he supports Yadin's suggestion for the second part of the line. Qimron is cautious and reads only יה]יו <u>באים</u> ... [◦מֹשׁ◦].[8] This seems to be a good solution considering the poor condition of the manuscript. García Martínez suggests וה]יו באים.[9] From an old transparency – actually the same photograph as plate 60 – we can see that the first two letters are *yod* and *he*.

When we arrive to line 2, we note that Wacholder follows Yadin completely. Qimron is more restrictive with שבעים֯ [ומאתים <u>נשכה</u> ...]א֯ ◦ ל ◦ וכליהמה.[10] On line 3 he continues after וכאשר with י[היה] בה

weaker *a priori*: they are shorter which does not, indeed, bear witness of lesser quality. A careful comparison will be carried out in order to find out a reasonable reading.

[6] This number is derived from the total number of the chambers for the priests and the Levites: 108 (priests) + 54 (Kohathites) + 54 (Gershonites) + 54 (Sons of Merari) = 279.

[7] Wacholder 1991, 37. The interpolated words are underlined.

[8] Qimron, 63.

[9] García Martínez 1998, 1262.

[10] Qimron, 63. He seems to be able to read the last complete word without difficulties. We were not able to verify this from the palaeographical evidence.

המשׁ̊]מר.[11] We note above that Wacholder is not very far from this suggestion with וכאשר י]בואו המשמרות ויצאו. There is no disagreement concerning the second part of line 3.

Line 4 is the first clear line in the column; there are, nevertheless, some difficulties at the beginning and at the end of the line. In contrast with Yadin's מׄיׄמׄ[י]ןׄ, Qimron reads מׄעירו.[12] The first, damaged stroke after *mem* should be more vertical in order to be a part of a *yod*. The dark stain at the location of the next letter fits well as a part of the down stroke of an *ayin*. This could, however, also be part of a *mem*. In any event, מעירו seems to be more likely. At the end of the line Wacholder reads ויבו]א whereas Qimron restores ב]א.[13]

Wise suggests a different solution for lines 1–4. This is in fact a restoration of 11Q20 and not of Col. 45 in 11Q19.[14]

(5) משמר אל מקומו וחנו זׄה[ב]אׄ וזה יׄוצא ליום השמיני ומטהרים את
(6) הנשכות זואת אחרי זאות[ל]עׄת תצא הראישונה ולוא תהיה שמה
(7) תערובת

There is no disagreement concerning the transcription of line 5. At the end of that line and at the beginning of line 6 we have ומטהרים את (6) הנשכות זואת אחרי זאות. We could compare this with Neh 13:9, ואמרה ויטהרו הלשכות.[15] This biblical passage is not far from the reading in the Scroll, and so this part of the Scroll is understood as Rewritten Bible. It

---

[11] Qimron refers to this as an unidentified piece of the Scroll. Qimron, 63.
[12] Qimron, 63.
[13] Wacholder 1991, 37; Qimron, 63.
[14] Wise reads מש]פטכה *pro* נׄשכה on line 2 of Frg. 40*:1. Concerning this reading, we need to point out the beginning of *tet*, "inside the letter," does not usually touch the bow at the bottom of the letter. Moreover, משפט is a bit unfamiliar in the present passage. Therefore, we consider נשכה as the likeliest reading. This word has also appeared rather frequently in the present context. Wise argues that the lines need to be divided differently. His suggestion is presented here: (1) [...] ומש]מרות יהיו יוצאים ו]באים (2) [כול שבועה ליום השמיני ומספרמה יהיה] שבעים [שבעים לכול יום ויום כמש]פטכה (3) [...] כאשר י[בואו המשמרות כן יצאו ה]שני יהיה בא (4) לשמאול] ובבואו] יצא הרישון מימין ולוא יהיו מתערבים אלה באלה . Wisc 1990, 77. We will not comment on this restoration further, apart from the fact that Wise has a strange repetition (misprint?) of שבעים on line 2.
[15] Yadin, 191.

is furthermore interesting to note, that זואת is spelled in two different ways on the same line.[16]

In the middle of line 6 Qimron restores [מ]עת *pro* Yadin's reading [ל̇]ע̇ת.[17] Both combinations are extant in the Bible. In the DSS literature עת appears – in singular without a suffix – with a preposition 33 times as a certain reading.[18] The prepositions are the following: -ב 26 times (79 %), -מ 5 times (15 %), and -ל twice (6 %). In 11Q19 there is only one certain reading, that is בעת in line 33:2. As an aside, we note that the meaning of בעת and לעת are actually very similar. Based on the statistics above and the appearance of בעת earlier in our Scroll, we tentatively read [ב]עת תצא הראישונה in the middle of line 6.

Before we analyze the next passage, Frg. 39:1 will be presented below:

(1)] א]ח̊ר̇
(2)]] כי ישכב
(3)] שלוש]ת̊ ימי{ן}ם
(4)]]שוכן בתוכה
(5)] [*vacat*
(6)] ביו]ם השביעי
(7)] ט]מ̇א לנפש לוא
(8)] אש]ר̇ יטהרו וכאשר
(9)]]ק לוא יבוא אל מקדש
(10)]]ר̊וכל/יו̇כ̇ל̇ ואל המקדש

On the last line there are some alternative readings: Yadin suggests א̊כ̇ל̇[and García Martínez reads ר̊וכל[.[19] According to the palaeographical evidence the latter seems to be more likely. Another possibility that fits with Frg. 39*:1 is יו̇כ̇ל̇.[20]

[16] Yadin notes the lack of uniformity in spelling is common in the DSS. Yadin, 191. We add that spelling differences that are so close to each other is, nevertheless, not common in the Temple Scroll.
[17] Qimron, 63.
[18] According to the DSS Concordance.
[19] Yadin, 196; DJD XXIII, 390.
[20] Wacholder 1990, 38; Qimron, 64.

We will now continue with the analysis of the lines 7–10 in Col. 45:

(7) וא[יש] כי יהיה לו מקרה לילה לוא יבוא אל
(8) כול המקדש עד אשר [יש]לים שלושת ימים וכבס בגדיו ורחץ
ורחץ
(9) ביום הראישון וביום השלישי יכבס בגדיו ובאה השמש אחר
(10) יבוא אל המקדש ולוא יבואו בנדת טמאתמה אל מקדשי וטמאו

There is no disagreement concerning the transcription of this passage. Yadin points out the biblical sources of it:[21] those are Deut 23:11-12, (11) כי־יהיה בך איש אשר לא־יהיה טהור מקרה־לילה ויצא אל־מחוץ למחנה לא יבא אל־תוך המחנה (12) והיה לפנות־ערב ירחץ במים וכבא השמש יבא אל־תוך המחנה and Ex 19:10-11, (10) ויאמר יהוה אל־משה לך אל־העם וקדשתסהיום ומחר וכבסו שמלתם (11) והיו נכנים ליום השלישי כי ביום השלישי ירד יהוה לעיני כל־העם על־הר סיני.

When we get to line 8, we note that the temple has taken the place of the camp. Furthermore, the waiting period of three days reminds us of the passage from Exodus. This command makes the reading in the Scroll more severe in comparison to Deuteronomy.

It is interesting to note the supra linear ורחץ on line 9: this line seems more to rely on Ex 19, which includes יכבס. Then we get an additional ורחץ, which is to be read before ובאה השמש. The possible conclusion is that the author wishes to increase the severity of the biblical commands: it is not enough to wash your clothes – you need to bathe also! In any event, lines 8 and 9 may be interpreted as Rewritten Bible. Moreover, we note that א[ח̊רׄ from Frg. 39*:1, line 1 can be interpolated at the end of line 9 of the present column.

Line 10 seems to be Individual Composition. This emphasizes the importance of what has been said before: the unclean shall stay out of the temple's premises.

[21] Yadin, 192.

(11) ואיש כיא ישכב עם אשתו שכבת זרע לוא יבוא אל כול עיר
(12) המקדש אשר אשכין שמי בה שלושת ימים כול איש עור
(13) לוא יבואו לה כול ימיהמה ולוא יטמאו את העיר אשר אני שוכן
(14) בתוכה כי אני יהוה שוכן בתוך בני ישראל לעולם ועד *vacat*

The transcription of the passage above is clear. We may note that Yadin has chosen not to point out the *vacat* at the beginning of line 11.[22] This is, however, not crucial.

Near the beginning of line 11, כיא ישכב, is also found on line 2 of Frg. 39*:1. In the section that contains the lines 11–14 we need to take a look at several biblical verses.[23] For line 11 there is a biblical echo from Lev 15:18, ואשה אשר ישכב איש אתה שכבת־זרע ורחצו במים וטמאו עד־הערב. The first half of the line is here interpreted as Biblical Paraphrase.[24] After this we have a section of Individual Composition, which ends with a short *vacat* close to the end of line 12. We note also that line 3 of Frg. 39*:1 can be interpolated before this *vacat*.

After the *vacat* a new command is presented that continues until the end of the passage: blind people are not allowed into the Temple city. Yadin suggests that the author did not intend the ban for the blind only, but for blemished persons in general.[25] The biblical background for this is found in Lev 21:18, כי כל־איש אשר־בו מום לא יקרב איש עור או פסח או חרום או שרוע.[26] The context of this verse is connected with the priests. It is, nevertheless, possible that the Scroll relies on 2 Sam 5:8b, על־כן יאמרו עור ופסח לא יבוא אל־הבית, and so shows that the ban was extended to all of Israel – not only to the priests.[27] This is interpreted as Rewritten Bible. It is, moreover, worthwhile to note the expression at the beginning of line 13: לוא יבואו לה. In comparison with Deut 23:3b, לא־יבא לו בקהל יהוה.

Beginning in the middle of line 13, ולוא יטמאו את העיר אשר אני שוכן (14) בתוכה, we have a quotation from Num 5:3, ולא יטמאו

[22] Yadin, 193.
[23] Lev 15:18, 21:18, 2 Sam 5:8, Deut 23:3, and Num 5:3. Yadin, 193.
[24] In this context the focus in the Temple city. In lines 29:3-4 we have a similar passage that relates to the temple, בْבית אשׁ֯ר א[שכין] (4) שמי עליו.
[25] Yadin, 193.
[26] In this context there is no need to continue the quotation, even if the list continues in Leviticus.
[27] Yadin, 193.

את־מחניהם אשר אני שוכן בתוכם. A comparison with the biblical text-traditions shows that ɯ and 𝔊 agree with 𝔐.

At the end of line 13 and at the beginning of line 14, (14) שוכן בתוכה can be interpolated from line 4 of Frg. 39*:1.

At the end of this section we read אני יהוה שוכן בתוך בני ישראל לעולם ועד which reminds us about Ex 15:18, יהוה ימלך לעלם ועד.

(15) וכול איש אשר יטהר מזובו וספר לו שבעת ימים לטהרתו ויכבס ביום
(16) השביעי בגדיו ורחץ את כול בשרו במים חיים אחר יבוא אל עיר
(17) המקדש וכול טמא לנפש לוא יבואו לה עד אשר יטהרו   וכול צרוע
(18) ומנוגע לוא יבואו לה עד אשר יטהרו וכאשר יטהר והקריב את

There is no disagreement concerning the transcription of this last passage. Lines 15 and 16 are clearly influenced by the first half of Lev 15.[28] If we take a closer look at this passage, we may especially note 𝔐 of Lev 15:13, וכי־יטהר הזב מזובו וספר לו שבעת ימים לטהרתו וכבס בגדיו ורחץ בשרו במים חיים וטהר. ɯ is nearly identical with this: the only difference is that it reads ורחץ את בשרו.[29]

There are, moreover, some MSS belonging to 𝔊, which add ζωντὶ after τὸ σῶμα ὕδατι Thus they agree with 𝔐 concerning this passage.[30] In conclusion we note that the Scroll partly quotes the Bible, that is יטהר ... מזובו וספר לו שבעת ימים ... בגדיו ורחץ בשרו במים חיים לטהרתו. In addition, 11Q19 follows 𝔐 and some minor manuscripts of 𝔊. We note also that the Scroll reads את as does ɯ, even if the Scroll adds כול.[31] As a conclusion line 15 is partly interpreted as a Biblical Quotation. The end of line 15 and the first half of line 16 is then interpreted as Rewritten Bible, since the explaining ביום השביעי is added.

In line 17 we read about becoming unclean through contact with dead corpses and lepers. This may be compared with Num 5:2, צו את־בני ישראל וישלחו מן־המחנה כל־צרוע וכל־זב וכל טמא לנפש.[32] We note here that the context is not very dissimilar: the city in the Scroll and the camp in Numbers – these are similar entities according to our definition, as we try to detect biblical influence. On the other hand, the con-

---

[28] Yadin refers to the whole passage of Lev 15:2-13. Yadin, 194.

[29] On the other hand, ɯ reads וכבס בגדיו without את.

[30] In the footnote apparatus of 𝔊, these MSS are defined as *reliqui*, which means "the remaining ones". With other words neither e.g. A nor B supports this reading.

[31] We will continue the analysis of this in chapter four.

[32] Yadin, 194.

text in the Bible deals with sending away the unclean, and the Temple Scroll speaks about cleansing. This is therefore interpreted as Rewritten Bible.

Yadin argues about the supra linear letter on top of waw on line 18, that the scribe wrote יטהרו, due to מנוגע and צרוע earlier and the plural in Num 5:3. Then somebody marked the *waw* with a cancellation dot due to the singular in Lev 13-14.[33]

The end of line 18 speaks about sacrificing after the cleansing. This may have been influenced by Lev 14:10-12, (10) וביום השמיני יקח שני־כבסים תמימים וכבסה אחת בת־שנתה תמימה ושלשה עשרנים סלת מנחה בלולה בשמן ולג אחד שמן (11) והעמיד הכהן המטהר את האיש המטהר ואתם לפני יהוה פתח אהל מועד (12) ולקח הכהן את־הכבש האחד והקרוב אתו לאשם ואת־לג השמן etc.[34]

Summary of Col. 45

(1) יה[יו באים

(2) שבעים [ומאתים נשכה

(3) וכאשר י[ה]שני יהיה בא לשמאול[בבואו

ב

(4) יצא הרישון מעירו ולוא [יהי]ו מתערבים אלה באלה וכליה[מה

(5) משמר אל מקומו וחנו זה[ב]א וזה יוצא ליום השמיני ומטהרים את

(6) הנשכות זואת אחרי זאות[ב]עת תצא הראישונה ולוא תהיה שמה

(7) תערובת *vacat* וא[יש] כי יהיה לו מקרה לילה לוא יבוא אל

(8) כול המקדש עד אשר [יש]לים שלושת ימים וכבס בגדיו ורחץ

ורחץ

(9) ביום הראישון וביום השלישי יכבס בגדיו ובאה השמש אחר

(10) יבוא אל המקדש ולוא יבואו בנדת טמאתמה אל מקדשי וטמאו

(11) ואיש כיא ישכב עם אשתו שכבת זרע לוא יבוא אל כול עיר

(12) המקדש אשר אשכין שמי בה שלושת ימים כול איש עור

(13) לוא יבואו לה כול ימיהמה ולוא יטמאו את העיר אשר אני שוכן

(14) בתוכה כי אני יהוה שוכן בתוך בני ישראל לעולם ועד *vacat*

(15) וכול איש אשר יטהר מזובו וספר לו שבעת ימים לטהרתו ויכבס ביום

(16) השביעי בגדיו ורחץ את כול בשרו במים חיים אחר יבוא אל עיר

(17) המקדש וכול טמא לנפש לוא יבואו לה עד אשר יטהרו וכול צרוע

(18) ומנוגע לוא יבואו לה עד אשר יטהרו וכאשר יטהר והקריב את

[33] Yadin, 195. This is a possible solution.

[34] Yadin, 195.

Notes on Readings

1: Qimron continues with]◦מש◦[at the end of the line | Yadin reads ומש]ער אשר עד פנת המזרח לבני אשר והיו כול הנשכות אשר לשבט הלוי[. Wacholder suggests ומש]ערים יהיו <u>באים</u> ויוצאים והיו כול הנשכות אשר לשבט לוי[. **2:** שבעיׄם]ומאתים <u>נׄשכה</u> – Qimron continues the line with]אׄ וכליהמה ◦ל◦ ◦[| Yadin and Wacholder read שבעיׄם]ומאתים נשכה ולבני ישראל שש ושמונים וחמש מאות נשכה[. **3:** וכאשר י[– Qimron restores וכאשר י]היה[בה המשׄ]מר. **4:** מׄעירו – Yadin and Wacholder transcribes מימׄ]י[ן . | At the end of the line Wacholder has ויבו]א as Qimron restores ב]א **6:** ב]עׄת – Yadin restores ל]עׄת as Qimron has מ]עׄת.

2.18. Column 46

In this column we will do the same as we did with Col. 42. It seems quite clear that the end of Frg. 39*:1 is the immediate continuation of Col. 45, so this material will begin our analysis of the present column with the following numbers of 01, 02 and so forth. The two last lines from the fragment above are repeated below:

(9)]]ק לוא יבוא אל מקדש
(10)]]ר̊וכל/יֹוכל ואל המקדש

In addition to the main plate 61, we will also consult the plates 39*:2, 39*:3, and 39*:4 for palaeographical evidence.[1] In the text-critical analysis the textual material will be presented as we get to the lines, which are affected by the interpolations.

(01) [חטאתו ביום השמיני יקרב אל הטהרה בתוך עיר המקדש רק לוא יבוא אל המקדש̊]
(02) [ולוא יוכל מן הקודשים ובבוא השמש ביום השמיני מן הקודשים יֹוכֹל ואל המקדש̊ יבוא][2]

Qimron's restorations for these two lines are very long in comparison with the other lines in the column, although he claims not to be reconstructing the beginning of the Col. 46 but actually restoring the last two lines of plate 39*:1. Even so, we cannot accept a reconstruction, which is as long as this.

Wacholder suggests the following reading for 01–02[3]: [קורבנו לפני יהוה וכול איש אשר בו נגע צרעת נתק לוא יבוא אל] (02) [המק̊ד̊ש̊. We note that the length of the suggested line 01 is more reasonable, even if this suggestion also seems to be too long.[4] We conclude that these suggestions are in any case too hypothetical. We will, therefore, not include them in the summary of Col. 46.[5] Wacholder continues his restoration with [לוא יֹוכֹל ואל המקדש̊ לוא יבוא] (03) [כול קודש.

If we compare the position of the interpolated words from plate 39*:1 with Col. 45, we note that as we continue the analysis, every line

---

[1] Yadin, 195.
[2] This restoration is made by Qimron. Qimron, 64.
[3] Wacholder 1991, 38.
[4] The line is shorter since Wacholder reads the last word המקדש̊ on the next line, that is 02.
[5] Neither will Qimron's restoration in this case be included concerning lines 01–02 since it actually refers to 11Q20 and not to the beginning of Col. 46.

is moved a little bit to the left. Taking this into consideration, we would approximately get the following location for the interpolated text into the lines 01–03:

(01)] רק לוא יבוא אל[
(02)]הַמקדש ר֯וכל/יׄוׄכׄלׄ[
(03)]ואל המקדש

At this point plates 40*:3 and 39*:2 need to be presented, since their content can be interpolated on the following lines, beginning with line 04.[6]

Plate 40*:3

(1)] ...]נ֯ה שלנחושת[
(2)] ...]כ֯ולו אשר לוא[
(3)] ...] לׄחׄצר החׄיׄ[צונה

Wacholder and García Martínez read]ב֯ה *pro*]נ֯ה on line 1.[7] At the beginning of line 2 García Martínez suggests ג]ב֯ולו *pro*]כ֯ולו. At the end of the same line we note that he agrees with Yadin's restoration and continues with אשר לוא] ישכון כול[.[8]

Plate 39*:2

(1)] ...] אני שוכן[
(2) *vacat*
(3)] ... פ]תׄחי השערי[ם
(4)] ... א]לׄיו לבוא אל מקׄ[דש
(5)] ...]לׄ בין מקדש
(6)] ...]וקדשו את מ[קדשי

[6] Qimron has chosen to restore line 1 of plate 40*:3 and plate 40*:6 on a different page in his edition: מכו]נה שלנחושת] ...]למכונה֯. Moreover, he notes that García Martínez reads]בה֯[ ]. Qimron, 65. Qimron is hereby restoring 11QT^{b} 22 and 29. It seems that the latter number of the fragment should be 36?

[7] Wacholder 1991, 39; DJD XXIII, 390. See also the restoration of line 04 and the commentary.

[8] García Martínez has interpolated the underlined letters from Col. 46, line 1. DJD XXIII, 390. See also the restoration of line 1.

With the necessary fragments presented above we are prepared to continue the text-critical analysis of Col. 46:[9]

(04)	]	<u>מכונ̊ה שלנחושת</u> [
(1)	] [. . .]	לו]א יע̊ו̊ף [כול]
(2)	עוף טמא על מקד̇[שי	]. . . . גגי השערים [אשר]
(3)	לחצר החיצונה וכ̇ול̇[	]היות בתוך מקדשי לעו[לם]
(4)	ועד כול הימים אשר א̊[ני שוכ]ן בתוכ̇ם̇	

The underlined part of the line is interpolated from plate 40*:3, line 1. The restoration to מכונה on line 04 is a reasonable reading.[10] *Nun* seems to be more likely here, as the horizontal base stroke is relatively short and the vertical line stands close to 90 degrees in relation to the base. The "vertical" stroke of a *beit* is usually slightly turned to the left. Furthermore, Qimron uses another fragment, 40*:6, which is not utilized by others, and transcribes למכונ̇ה[at the end of the line with the final result of למכונ̇ה[ ] מכו]נה שלנחושת.[11] This seems to be a possible solution.

Line 1 is badly preserved. At the end of the line Wacholder interpolates line 2 from plate 40*:3, combining this with Yadin's reading, which gives <u>כולו אשר לו]א</u> יע̊ו̊ף [כול].[12] Qimron, on the other hand, is able to read]שר ה̊[on the first half of line 1. This reading has palaeographical support on an old transparency. Moreover, Qimron interpolates 40*:3, line 2, but reads differently at the end of the line, <u>כ̇ולו אשר לו]א</u> ישכ̇[ון].[13] García Martínez suggests a close variation, that is גבולו אשר לו]א ישכ[ון כול].[14]

In the middle of line 2 Yadin suggests tentatively מקד̇[שי ועשיתה שפודים על קיר החצר ועל] גגי.[15] According to the space available on plate 61, this reading is much too long. Wacholder and Qimron restores the same passage as מקד̇[שי אשר בחצר הפנימית ו]ע̊ל גגי.[16] This is a possible

---

[9] From line 1 onwards Yadin's analysis is the one that other suggestions are related to.

[10] Qimron, 65.

[11] Qimron, 65.

[12] Wacholder 1991, 40.

[13] Qimron, 66.

[14] García Martínez, 1264.

[15] Another suggestion by Yadin before ג̊ג̊י is עטרות. Yadin, 197.

[16] Wacholder 1991, 40; Qimron notes that ע̊ל is found on an early infra-red photograph. Qimron, 66.

solution. Yadin points out Lev 20:25, והבדלתם בין־הבהמה הטהרה לטמאה ובין־העוף הטמא לטהר as a comparison from the Bible.[17]

At the beginning of line 3 it is possible to interpolate line 3 of plate 40*:3. There is no disagreement concerning the restoration of the line, לחצר החיצונה וכׄוׄל [עוף טמא לוא יוכל ל]היות בתוך מקדשי לעו[לם].

At the end of this passage we are able to interpolate line 1 from plate 39*:2, אנו שוכן. Yadin notes the biblical expression, כל־הימים אשר, which is found in e.g. 1 Sam 20:31 and 2 Chr 6:31.[18] These are, nevertheless, in other contexts than the Scroll's. It is therefore regarded as Rewritten Bible.

Furthermore, we need at this stage to present a new fragment, which in DJD XXIII is identified as 24.[19]

(1) [...]בׄנׄי ישׄ[ראל
(2) [...]אשר יהיה[
(3) [...]ל[

Continuing the analysis of Col. 46:

(5) ועשיתה רובד סביב לחוץ מחצר החיצונה רחב
(6) ארבע עשרה באמה על פי פתחי השערים כולמה ושתים
(7) עשרה מעלה תעשה לו אשר יהיו עולים בני ישראל אליו
(8) לבוא אל מקדשי

There is no disagreement concerning the transcription of this passage. Yadin notes that the phraseology in line 6, על פי פתחי השערים, may have been influenced by Prov 8:3, ליד־שערים לפי־קרת.[20] Line 1 of fragment 24 can be interpolated quite at the end of line 7 of Col. 46.

On lines 6 and 7–8 it is possible to interpolate lines 3, פ[תׄחי השערי[ם, and 4, א]ליו לבוא אל מקׄ[דש, from plate 39*:2. Wacholder, on the other hand, interpolates a fragment, that he identifies as 11QT^b 34, beginning on line 7. This fragment is presented below:[21]

---

[17] Yadin, 196.
[18] Yadin, 197.
[19] García Martínez interpolates it into 11Q20 Col. 12, lines 20–21. DJD XXIII, 391.
[20] Yadin, 197.
[21] Wacholder 1991, 40. Line 2 would according to Wacholder's suggestion fit into line 9 of Col. 46.

(1) [עשר]ה מעׄ[לה]

(2) [ ]ח֯[יל][22]

This fragment is defined as 15c in García Martínez publication of 11Q20. It was utilized in the restoration of Col. 9 of 11Q20 which overlaps with Col. 32 of 11Q19.[23] Wacholder's alternative is possible, even if this would create a long line: in fact the lines in Col. 9 are long also. We need, however, to be aware that the trace at the bottom of the fragment is so tiny, that it is difficult to decide between a *chet* or a *he*.[24] In the light of this evidence, we do not find it necessary to abandon García Martínez' joining of the fragments 15a, 15b, and 15c.[25]

(9) ועשיתה חיל סביב למקדש רחב מאה באמה אשר יהיה

(10) מבדיל בין מקדש הקודש לעיר ולוא יהיו באים בלע אל תוך

(11) מקדשי ולוא יחללוהו וקדשו את מקדשי ויראו ממקדשי

(12) אשר אנוכי שוכן בתוכמה

We may once more note that there is no disagreement concerning the transcription of this passage. On the other hand we have again some interpolations from fragments, which belong to 11Q20.

At the end of line 9 it is possible to interpolate Frg. 24, line 2. Near the beginning of line 10 we can, furthermore, interpolate line 5 from plate 39*:2. In Lev 16:33 we have a comparable saying with וכפר־את מקדש הקדש ואת־אהל מועד.[26] The context is quite different: desecration in the Scroll and atonement in the Leviticus, therefore we can interpret the end of line 9 and the beginning of line 10 as Rewritten Bible.

Later on line 10 it is possible to interpolate the *lamed* from line 3 of Frg. 24.[27] On lines 10–11 there seems to be biblical influence from Num 4:20, ולא־יבאו לראות כבלע את־הקדש ומתו.[28] The 𝔊 can be a help

[22] These two last fragments, 15c and 24, are not included in Yadin 1977b.

[23] DJD XXIII, 386.

[24] In Col. 32 the trace at the bottom is interpreted as a *he*. This is, however, not a crucial issue.

[25] DJD XXIII, plate XLIV.

[26] Yadin notes that this is the only location where מקדש הקודש is mentioned in the Temple Scroll. Yadin, 198.

[27] We note, however, that Qimron has not chosen to do that.

[28] Yadin, 198.

to understand לראות כבלע: ἰδεῖν ἐξάπινα can be translated as "to see suddenly."[29] Since the Scroll speaks about desecration instead of death as in the Bible, we understand the text of the Scroll as Rewritten Bible.

ולוא יחללוהו on line 11 may be compared with Ezek 22:26, כהניה חמסו תורתי ויחללו קדשי.[30] As Ezekiel speaks about the sins of the priests, there seems to be a connection. This is, however, a description of what has already happened. In Lev 21:12 we read ולא יחלל את מקדש אלהיו.[31]

The following expression, וקדשו את מקדשי, may be interpolated from line 6 of plate 39*:2. This is an echo of 2 Chr 29:5, וקדשו את־בית יהוה אלוהי אבתיכם[32] and is interpreted as Rewritten Bible. At the end of line 11 we have ויראו ממקדשי: this can be compared with Lev 19:30, את־שבתתי תשמרו ומקדשי תיראו אני יהוה.[33]

Before we move to the next passage, fragment 39*:3 will be presented.

(1) [... מקו]ם֯ יד חוץ מ[
(2) [... ו]ב֯ורות בתוכ֯[מה
(3) [... ש]ל֯[ושת

Yadin does not transcribe anything on line 3 of this fragment. The *lamed* is, however, a likely reading. We will now continue with the analysis of Col. 46.

(13) ועשיתה להמה מקום יד חוץ מן העיר אשר יהיו יוצאים שמה
(14) לחוץ לצפון המערב לעיר בתים ומקורים ובורות בתוכמה
ולוא
(15) אשר תהיה הצואה יורדת אל תוכמה תהיה נראה לכול רחוק
(16) מן העיר שלושת אלפים אמה

First of all we note that there is no disagreement concerning the transcription of this passage. On line 13 we see a clear biblical influence from Deut 23:13, ויד תהיה לך מחוץ למחנה ויצאת שמה חוץ.[34] Concerning 39*:3, we can interpolate line 1 on line 13.

---

[29] Yadin, 198. The literal translation of כבלע is also a help: "in a swallowing."
[30] Yadin, 198.
[31] Yadin, 198.
[32] Yadin, 198.
[33] Yadin, 198. See also the analysis in chapter 4.4.13.
[34] Yadin, 199.

On line 14 we note a difference in comparison with Deut 23:13, מחוץ למחנה: the command in the Scroll is to make the latrine inside, in a small building with a roof. On the other hand, חוץ in Deuteronomy in this context is to be interpreted as outside the camp, not outside in general. We note that the Scroll makes the command stricter: it is not enough to only take it outside the city / camp – the excrements cannot even be visible for somebody who happens to pass by. At the end of this line, line 2 of 39*:3 can be interpolated.

Line 15 can be compared with Deut 23:15, ולא־יראה בך ערות דבר.[35] This is not far from the biblical context: the reason, that God may pay a visit is not mentioned explicitly. On the other hand line 12 is clear enough as it reminds the reader that God dwells among them. On line 16 the *lamed* belonging to שלושת from line 3 of 39*:3 can be interpolated.

Before we complete the analysis of Col. 46, two different fragments will be presented: 39*:4 and 39*:1.[36]

Plate 39*:4

(1) [... שלו]שׁ̊ה̊[

(2) [...]והאנשים אשר יה̊[יו

(3) [...[37]]ל̇[

In his restoration of 11Q20 line 13:1 García Martínez transcribes the first line from 39*:4 as וע[שי̊]תה, which would overlap with the word at the end of line 16 of Col. 46.

We would consider שלו]שׁ̊ה̊[a more likely reading due to two reasons: firstly, שה is a more solid alternative palaeographically, i.e. the trace to the left of the possible *shin* is indeed very long and reaches lower down than the alleged *shin*. This casts doubt on the *yod* and makes a *he* more likely. Secondly, the line length of the fragment: even if the exact line-length is difficult to verify, it seems possible that the interpolation of *shin* into עשיתה makes the line too long.[38]

---

[35] Yadin, 199.

[36] For this column we need only to present the first line of 39*:1 since the rest of this fragment will be interpolated into Col. 47 and is therefore presented in the context of that column.

[37] At this location Wacholder restores אלפ[י̊ם̊. Wacholder 1991, 43.

[38] We note that García Martínez inserts a *vacat* on line 1 of 11Q20 Col. 13. DJD XXIII, 394. Even without the *vacat* the line consists of 64 spaces.

Plate 39*:1 ii[39]

(1) יה̇ו̇באים

This is Qimron's suggestion, which seems to be a likely solution. He points out the באים first was written and that the rest of the letters were added afterwards in the right margin.[40] Wacholder suggests וה|באי̊ם and argues that the *waw* and *he* were written in the margin.[41] This solution is possible, as well. We prefer Qimron's reading since it is possible to interpolate these words at the end of Col. 46.

We will now do the analysis of the last passage belonging to this column.

(16) עשיתה
(17) שלושה מקומות למזרח העיר מובדלים זה מזה אשר יהיו
(18) באים המצורעים והזבים והאנשים אשר יהיו להמה מקרה

There is no disagreement concerning the transcription of this passage. Yadin compares the separation of three places at the end of line 16 and at the beginning of line 17 with Deut 19:2a, 4a: שלוש ערים תבדיל לך ... וזה דבר הרצח אשר־ינוס שמה וחי.[42] As we can see, the biblical command concerns greater violations of the law than what is the issue in our Scroll in this passage. The text in the Scroll will, however, be interpreted as Rewritten Bible instead of Individual Composition, since the use of language is quite close in style to the parallel in the Hebrew Bible. On line 18 we have biblical influence from Num 5:2, וישלחו מן־המחנה כל־צרוע וכל־צב.[43]

We note here that lines 1 and 2 of plate 39*:4 can be interpolated on lines 17 and 18. Line 1 from 39*:1 ii can, furthermore, be interpolated at the end of line 17 and at the beginning of line 18.[44]

---

[39] ii indicates here the second column of the fragment.
[40] Qimron, 66.
[41] Wacholder 1991, 43.
[42] Yadin, 200.
[43] Yadin, 200.
[44] All the interpolations are indicated by underlining the text in the summary of the column.

Summary of Col. 46

(01) [רק לוא יבוא אל]
(02) [המקדש רֹוכל/יֹוכֹל]
(03) [ואל המקדש
(04) [מכו]נה שלנחושת [ ]למכונה [
(1) [ ]שׂר הׄ[כֹולו אשר לו]א[
(2) עוף טמא על מקדׄ[שי אשר בחצר הפנימית ועל] גגי השערים [אשר]
(3) לחצר החיצונה וכׄולׄ [עוף טמא לוא יוכל ל]היות בתוך מקדשי לעו[לם]
(4) ועד כול הימים אשר אׄ[ני שוכ]ן בתוכם *vacat*
(5) *vacat* ועשיתה רובד סביב לחוץ מחצר החיצונה רחב
(6) ארבע עשרה באמה על פי פתחי השערים כולמה ושתים
(7) עשרה מעלה תעשה לו אשר יהיו עולים בני ישראל אליו
(8) לבוא אל מקדשי *vacat*
(9) ועשיתה חיל סביב למקדש רחב מאה באמה אשר יהיה
(10) מבדיל בין מקדש הקודש לעיר ולֵוא יהיו באים בלע אל תוך
(11) מקדשי ולוא יחללוהו וקדשו את מקדשי ויראו ממקדשי
(12) אשר אנוכי שוכן בתוכמה *vacat*
(13) ועשיתה להמה מקום יד חוץ מן העיר אשר יהיו יוצאים שמה
(14) לחוץ לצפון המערב לעיר בתים ומקורים ובורות בתוכמה
(15) אשר תהיה הצואה יורדת אל תוכמה תהיה ^ולוא^ נראה לכול רחוק
(16) מן העיר שלֵושת אלפים אמה *vacat* עשיתה
(17) שלושה מקומות למזרח העיר מובדלים זה מזה אשר יהיו
(18) באים המצורעים והזבים והאנשים אשר יהיו להמה מקרה

Notes on Readings

01–02: רק לוא יבוא אל] (02) [המקדש – Wacholder restores [קורבנו לפני יהוה וכול איש אשר בו נגע צרעת נתק לוא יבוא אל] (02) [המקדשׁ כול קודש] (03) [לוא יֹוכֹל. **02–03:** רֹוכל/יֹוכֹל] (03) [ואל המקדש – Wacholder has ואל המקדשׁ לוא יבוא. **04:** [מכו]נה שלנחושת [ ]למכונה [– Wacholder has בׄהׄ שלנחושת. **1:** כֹולו אשר לו]א[– Yadin reads [כול] יׄעׄוׄףׄ לו]א as כֹולו אשר לו]א. Wacholder has [כול] יׄעׄוׄףׄ כולו אשר לו]א. Qimron restores גבולו אשר לו]א ישכ[ון כול] while García Martínez reads ישכֹ[ון]. **2:** מקדׄ[שי אשר בחצר הפנימית ועל] – Yadin has מקדׄ[שי ועשיתה שפודים על קיר החצר ועל].

2.17. Column 47

This is the last column that will be analyzed in the present study because the material concerning the temple and its context ends here. In this passage the focus is on the temple city in relation to the surrounding cities.

As in the former column, it seems possible to restore some of the fragmentary material. This can be located between columns 46 and 47. These lines will as usual be numbered as 01, 02 and so forth. In addition to the main plate 62, we also have palaeographical evidence on plate 31*. Furthermore, we will use fragment 39*:1 ii in order to discover possible material between the columns.

Before we begin with the analysis of Col. 47, the rest of fragment 39*:1 ii will be presented.[1]

At the end of this analysis an additional fragment, which may belong to the Temple Scroll, will be presented. It belongs to a group that is usually defined as 11Q21 or 11QTemple^{c}. In his edition Qimron locates this between Cols. 47 and 48. García Martínez defines it as Frg. 3.[2] We will not include this fragment in the summary of the columns, since its interpolation would introduce a lot of speculation.

---

[1] The beginning of line 1 was already presented and interpolated in the former column. García Martínez has restored this as 11Q20 Col. 13. DJD XXIII, 394. Qimron seems to restore the text of the fragment, but not necessarily Col. 13. Qimron, 67. The restorations belong to Qimron.

[2] DJD XXIII, 413, and plate XLVIII.

(1) [לילה][3]
(2) רחוק֯ מ֯[ן העיר שלושת אלפים אמה *vacat*(?)
(3) וכול ע֯[ריהמה יהיו טהורות
(4) דבר ומצ֯[רעת
(5)
(6) וח֯מ֯[לתי
(7) וחורד֯[תי
(8) עריה֯[מה

On line 4 García Martínez transcribes]דבר ומש֯, which is another possible reading.[4] At the beginning of line 6 Wacholder suggests וחמ]שים / [/ וחמ]ש מאות.[5] This is possible palaeographically, even if it represents a rather strange reading from the contextual point of view.[6] On line 7 García Martínez restores והורדת֯]מה ... למעלה ולוא למטה.[7] Qimron suggests that there possibly is an overlap between lines 6–8 above and lines 1–3 of Col. 47.

We note that the restoration of the lines before line 1 of Col. 47 is very complex in the light of the textual evidence. It is likely that line 1 above can be defined as 01 of Col. 47 as it follows right after לילה. We will not, however, continue the restoration of the 0X-lines due to shortage of palaeographical material. Wacholder also has a suggestion for the lines 02–04.[8] The suggestion is not, however, repeated in the summary, since it is quite uncertain. The lines 01–04 are presented below:

[3] García Martínez refers to this line as line 2. DJD XXIII, 394. For restoration of Col. 13 this is a correct alternative. However, his definition of line 3 where he transcribes the first word on 39*:1 ii as וה|באים, creates unnecessary difficulties. In the former column we noted already that Qimron's reading of יהיו באים is the preferred solution. As we still maintain that, we suggest that the line beginning with רחוק should be identified as line 3 in the context of 11Q20 or line 2 (as it is) in the context of the transcription of fragment 39*1 ii. This difference is obviously reflected in the definition relating to the numbering of the rest of the lines. We refer below to the lines according to Qimron's numbering, since that seems to be the most likely.
[4] DJD XXIII, 394.
[5] Wacholder 1991, 44.
[6] Any restoration is actually quite speculative in these last three lines since so few letters have survived.
[7] DJD XXIII, 394. The underlined letters are interpolated from Col. 47, line 2.
[8] Wacholder agrees with the restoration of line 01 as well. Wacholder 1991, 44.

(01) [לילה רחוק֯ מ֯ן העיר שלושת אלפים אמה[9]

It is obvious that this restoration is uncertain as well. On the other hand, the content follows quite closely the end of the former column. In the following we will take a look at Wacholder's reading of the lines 02–04.[10]

(02) [ל֯ וכול עריהמה]
(03) [דבר ומצורע / ומצורעים /]
(04) [וחמישים / וחמש מאות /]

At the beginning of line 02 Wacholder has interpolated the *lamed* from line 3 of fragment 39*:4.[11] We will now continue the analysis of Col. 47, beginning from line 1.[12]

(1) [ ]◦◦[ ]
(2) [ל]מעלה ולוא למט[ה] *vacat*
(3) [והיו]ע֯ר֯יהמה טהורות וש֯[ ]ה לעולם

Qimron notes a trace near the beginning of line 1. Moreover, he is able to discern]ו֯ב֯[at the location where Yadin notes two dots.[13] At the end of the line Wacholder interpolates [והורדתמה, as he reads line 7, from fragment 39*:1 ii.[14]

On line 2 it is possible that we have an influence from Deut 28:13, ונתנך יהוה לראש ולא לזנב והיית רק למעלה ולא תהיה למטה.[15] The significance of this connection is difficult to prove, because the immediate context in the Scroll is not known. Yadin suggests tentatively that the *vacat* was preceded by [לראש ולוא לזנב], reminding us about the passage from Deut.[16] Qimron suggests [ויהיו רק ל]מ֯עלה at the beginning

[9] Wacholder interpolates י֯ם֯ in אלפים. Wacholder 1991, 44.
[10] Wacholder 1991, 44.
[11] This *lamed* should have a dot, that is ל֯, on top of it since the letter is clearly damaged on the MS. This restoration will not be commented upon further.
[12] Once again we begin with the transcriptions by Yadin.
[13] Qimron, 68.
[14] Wacholder 1991, 44.
[15] Yadin, 202.
[16] Yadin, 202.

of the line. This is a possible solution. We would, however, understand this as Rewritten Bible.

Yadin suggests an approximate reconstruction for the *lacuna* at the middle of line 3, וש[כנתי ... אתמ]ה לעולם or וש[כנתי ... בתוכמ]ה לעולם.[17] Qimron restores line 3 in the following way with a fuller alternative: [ויהי]ו̊ עריהמה טהורות וש̇[כנתי שמי בתוכ]מ̇ה לעולם.[18]

Wacholder's suggestion comes very close, as he follows Yadin with the restoration [והיו].[19] From the context it seems that the imperfect – that is Qimron's alternative – is more probable to be correct. It is, nevertheless, also possible to have a consecutive perfect-form in this passage, since it would carry the same content as an imperfect. This is, however, not a crucial issue. We note also that it is possible to interpolate line 8 of 39*:1 ii near the beginning of this line.

(3) והעיר
(4) א̇שר אקדיש לשכין שמי ומקד̇[שי בתוכה] ת̇ה̇יה קודש וטהורה
(5) מכול דבר לכול טמאה אשר יטמאו בה כול אשר בתוכה יהיה
(6) טהור וכול אשר יבוא לה יהיה טהור יין ושמן וכול אוכל
(7) וכול מושקה יהיו טהורים

There is no disagreement concerning the transcription or restoration of these lines. On line 4 we have לשכין, which is equivalent to להשכין.[20] The passage לכול טמאה אשר יטמאו בה on line 5 may be compared to Lev 5:3, או כי יגע בטמאת אדם לכל טמאתו אשר יטמא בא.[21] Line 5 is therefore quite close to a quotation, but is here defined as Biblical Paraphrase. In the middle of line 6 we have the expression אשר יבוא לה, which in Yadin's opinion is influenced by some biblical passages, that is e.g. Deut 23:3b, גם דור עשירי לא־יבא לו בקהל יהוה.[22] The contexts are, nevertheless, so different that we need to understand the passage as Individual Composition.

---

[17] Yadin, 202.
[18] Qimron, 68.
[19] Wacholder 1991, 44.
[20] Yadin, 202.
[21] Yadin, 202.
[22] Other passages could be Jer 51:48, כי מצפון יבוא־לה or Zech 9:9, הנה מלכך יבוא לך. Yadin, 202.

The word מושקה is less familiar: Yadin suggests "foodstuff" with the help from lines 49:7–8, וכול אוכל אשר יוצק עליו מֹ[י]םׄ יטמא כול המושקה יטמא (8).[23] This seems to be a good solution.

(7) כול עור בהמה טהורה אשר יזבחו
(8) בתוך עריהמה לוא יביאו לה כי בעריהמה יהיו עושים
(9) בהמה מלאכתמה לכול צורכיהמה ואל עיר מקדשי לוא יביאו
(10) כי כבשרמה תהיה טהרתמה

In the middle of line 8 and at the end of line 9 Yadin transcribes יביאו, supported by García Martínez.[24] Qimron prefers יבוֹאו, even if he admits that Yadin's alternative is better from a palaeographical point of view.[25] We prefer to follow the palaeographical evidence, which enables the transcription יביאו. There may be a distant influence concerning the verb להביא from Lev 17:9, ואל־פתח אהל מועד לא יביאנו לעשות אתו ליהוה.[26] It is, however, understood as Individual Composition. Apart from this discussion, there is no disagreement concerning the transcription of the passage.

In the middle of line 9 we have צורכיהמה: it is worthwhile to note that צורך is *hapax legomenon* in the Bible, that is in 2 Chr 2:15, ככל־צורכך.[27]

(10) ולוא תטמאו את העיר אשר
(11) אנוכי משכן את שמי ומקדשי בתוכה כי בעורות אשר יזבחו
(12) במקדש בהמה יהיו מביאים את יינמה ואת שמנמה וכול
(13) אוכלמה לעיר מקדשי

There is no disagreement concerning the transcription of this passage. Yadin notes two interesting biblical parallels concerning lines 10–11.[28] Firstly the connection to Ezek 43:7, אשר אשכן־שם בתוך בני־ישראל לעולם. We note the 𝔊 has a slightly different reading with ἐν οἷς

[23] Yadin, 203.
[24] Yadin, 203; García Martínez, 1264.
[25] Qimron supports the other view, mainly due to grammatical reasons. Qimron 1978b, 170. With the short stroke above the *waw*, Qimron notes that both readings are possible.
[26] Yadin, 203.
[27] Yadin, 203.
[28] Yadin, 204.

κατασκηνώσει τὸ ὄνομά μου ἐν μέσῳ οἴκου Ισραηλ τὸν αἰῶνα. We note that both the Scroll and Ezekiel has a context of defilement of the temple. Furthermore, line 11 seems to be closer to 𝕲 than to 𝔐 in this case. In conclusion we understand lines 10–11 as Biblical Paraphrase.

Secondly, Neh 1:9, אל־המקום אשר בחרתי לשכן את־שמי שם. The context of Nehemiah is different from Col. 47, and it seems that the only common denominator is the expression, "to settle my name."

(13) ולוא יגאלו את מקדשי בעורות זבחי
(14) פגוליהמה אשר יזבחו בתוך ארצמה ולוא תטהרו עיר
(15) מתוך עריכמה לעירי כי כטהרת בשרו כן יטהרו העורות

We note that first of all there is a problem with the transcription, that is to tell the difference between *yod* and *waw*. This difficulty will follow us still into the next textual passage. The palaeographical evidence is not offering much help to discern between these two letters. In a case like this, the context becomes more important. Yadin's translation is odd at the end of line 14 and at the beginning of line 15: "And you shall not purify a city of your cities to (the degree of) my city."

A better alternative, suggested by Baumgarten, Qimron, and García Martínez,[29] is to read עור at the end of line 14. Then we would agree with the readings לעירי[30] and בשרו on line 15. This gives us the following reasonable translation: "You shall not purify a skin (15) from your cities for my city." Instead of בשרו, Qimron seems to prefer בשרי since he transcribes it as בשרִ.[31] "My flesh" would, nevertheless, not fit the context.

---

[29] Qimron, 68; García Martínez, 1266.
[30] עירי is *hapax legomenon* in the Bible and appears in Isa 45:13b, הוא־יבנה עירי. Yadin, 204
[31] Qimron, 68.

(15) אם

(16) במקדשי תזבחוהו יטהר למקדשי ואם בעריכמה תזבחוהו וטהר

(17) לעריכמה וכול טהרת המקדש בעורות המקדש תביאו ולוא תטמאו

(18) את מקדשי ועירי בעורות פגוליכמה אשר אנוכי שוכן בתוכה

On line 16 we still have slight problems to determine which transcription is the correct one. Firstly there is the word that Yadin reads as יטהר.[32] Palaeographically this is a likely reading. Again, we need to remember the difficulty to discern between *yod* and *waw*.

Qimron argues from a grammatical point of view: in a similar syntactical construction beginning with אם in DSS literature, the likelihood for וטהר would be greater.[33] García Martínez accepts this reading.[34] Qimron's contextual argumentation is strong but we choose, nevertheless, to follow the palaeographical evidence and therefore we read יטהר. This reading could be correct, even if it is not *so* correct from a grammatical point of view.

Secondly, we have וטהר at the end of line 16: the *waw* is actually very long and there is no disagreement concerning its transcription.

Finally, 11Q21, Frg. 3 will be presented:[35]

(1) ∘ה

(2) לבוא אל עירי

(3) תרנגול לוֹ̊א̊ תגדֹל̊[ו

(4) בכול המקדֹש̊∘∘∘

(5) המקֹ]דש

García Martinez supports Qimron's transcription completely apart from that the former restores] מ̊ה̊ [ ] on line 1.[36] We agree with Qimron that the location of Frg. 3 between Cols. 47 and 48 seems to be the only possibility.

---

[32] Yadin, 205.

[33] As a comparison, the ratio between וקטל and יקטל in the Qumran Scrolls is 32 to 2 (or 3), respectively. Qimron 1978b, 171.

[34] García Martínez, 1266.

[35] Qimron, 69.

[36] DJD XXIII, 413.

Summary of Col. 47

(1)]]ׄׄ[
(2)] ל]מעלה ולוא למט[ה [*vacat*
(3) [והיו]עׄרׄיהמה טהורות וש֯[כנתי שמי בתוכ]מׄה לעולם והעיר
(4) אׄשר אקדיש לשכין שמי ומקדׄ[שי בתוכה] תׄהׄיה קודש וטהורה
(5) מכול דבר לכול טמאה אשר יטמאו בה כול אשר בתוכה יהיה
(6) טהור וכול אשר יבוא לה יהיה טהור יין ושמן וכול אוכל
(7) וכול מושקה יהיו טהורים כול עור בהמה טהורה אשר יזבחו
(8) בתוך עריהמה לוא יביאו לה כי בעריהמה יהיו עושים
(9) בהמה מלׄאכתמה לכול צורכיהמה ואל עיר מקדשי לוא יביאו
(10) כי כבשרמה תהיה טהרתמה ולוא תטמאו את העיר אשר
(11) אנוכי משכן את שמי ומקדשי בתוכה כי בעורות אשר יזבחו
(12) במקדש בהמה יהיו מביאים את יינמה ואת שמנמה וכול
(13) אוכלמה לעיר מקדשי ולוא יגאלו את מקדשי בעורות זבחי
(14) פגוליהמה אשר יזבחו בתוך ארצמה ולוא תטהרו עור
(15) מתוך עריכמה לעירי כי כטהרת בשרו כן יטהרו העורות אם
(16) במקדשי תזבחוהו יטהר למקדשי ואם בעריכמה תזבחוהו וטהר
(17) לעריכמה וכול טהרת המקדש בעורות המקדש תביאו ולוא תטמאו
(18) את מקדשי ועירי בעורות פגוליכמה אשר אנוכי שוכן בתוכה

Notes on Readings

1: Wacholder restores [והורדתמה at the end of the line. **2:**] ל]מעלה – Qimron has [ויהיו רק ל]מׄעלה. **3:** [והיו]עׄרׄיהמה – Qimron restores [ויהי]ו֯ עריהמה | וש֯[כנתי שמי בתוכ]מׄה – Yadin suggests וש[כנתי ... בתוכמ]ה לעולם or ... אתמ]ה לעולם וש[כנתי. **8, 9:** יביאו – Qimron transcribes יבו֯או. **14:** עור – Yadin reads עיר. **15:** בשרו – Qimron transcribes בשרי֯. **16:** יטהר – Qimron and García Martínez read וטהר.

CHAPTER THREE

Text and Translation of Columns 29:3b–47:18

3.1. Text

3.1.1. Column 29

(3)] בׄבית אשׁׄרׄ א[שכין]
(4) שמי עליו [ויקריבו בו] עולת֯ [יום] ב֯יומו כתורת המשפט הזה
(5) תמיד מאת בני ישראל לבד מנדבות֯מה לכול אשׁר יקרי֯בוׄ
(6) לכול נדריהמה ו֯ׄלכול מת֯נותמה אשׁר יב֯יאו לי לרצון לה[מה]
(7) ורציתׄ֯יׄ֯םׄ֯ ו֯ה֯י֯ו֯ לי לעם ואנוכי אהיה להם לעולם [ו]שכנתי
(8) אתמה לעולם ועד ואקדשה [את מ]ק֯דשי בכבודי אשר אשכ֯ין
(9) עליו את כבודי עד יום הבריה אשר אברא אני את מק֯דשי
(10) להכינו לי כול ה֯ימים כברית אשר כרתי ע֯ם יעק֯וב בבית אל

3.1.2. Column 30

(1) [ושכנ]תי ואקדש[ ]
(2) [ ]
(3) [ ]עשות ועשׂי[תה בית]
(4) למעלות משׁׄ[ני צדי השע]רׄ֯יׄ֯ם אשׁ֯ר בבית אשר תבנה [להיות שמ]י
(5) עליו֯ *vacat?* [וע]שׂׄי֯תה [בי]ת֯ מסבה צפון להיכל֯ בית מרובע
(6) מ֯פנה אל֯ פ֯נה֯ עשרים באמה לעומת ארבע פנותיו ורח֯וק מקיר֯
(7) [ה]היכל֯ שב֯ע֯ אמ֯ות֯ ב֯מערב צפונו ועשית֯ה רוחב ק֯יר֯ו֯ ארבע
(8) אמות [וגבוהו ארבעים אמה] כ֯ה֯יכל ותוכו מ֯מקצוע א֯ׄל֯ מקצוע
(9) שתים עשר[ה באמה] ועמוד בתוך באמצעו מרובע רוחבו֯ ארבע
(10) א֯מוׄת֯ ל֯כׄוׄל֯ ר֯וחותיו ורוחב המסבה עולה מעלות א[

3.1.3. Column 31

(1) [ ] ◦ת

(2) [ ] ◦ השער

(3) [הכוה]ן המשיׄחׄ[1]

(4) [ ]הכוהן המשנה

(5) [הכוהן הג]דול *vacat*

(6) ובעלית הב[ית הזה תעשה שע]רׄ פתוח לׄגג ההיכל ודׄרׄךׄ עשוי

(7) בׄשער הזה {א}לפרׄוׄר [ה]הׄיׄכל אשר יהיו באיׄם בו לעלית ההיכל

(8) [כו]לׄ בית המסבה הזואת צפו זהב קירותיו ושעׄרׄיׄו וגגו מבית

(9) [ומ]חוץ ועמודו ומעלותיו ועשה ככול אשר אנוכי מדבר אליכה

(10) וׄעשיתה בית לכיור נגב מזרׄחׄ מרובע לכול רוׄחׄותיו אחת ועשרים

(11) אמה רׄחׄוׄקׄ מהמׄזבׄחׄ חמשים אמה ורחב ה[ק]יׄר שׄלוש אׄמות וגבה

(12) [ע]שׄרׄיׄםׄ אמׄהׄ[שלוש]הׄ שׄעׄרים עשו לה מהמזרח ומהצפון

(13) ומהמערב רׄחב השערים ארבע אמות וגובהמה שׄבׄעׄ

3.1.4. Column 32

(1) [ ] שלוש אׄמותׄ [ ]

(2) [ ] . . . . [ ]

(3) [ ]שלוׄש[ ]

(4) [ ]יהמה[ ]

(5) [ ]מׄה לׄמזבח עש[ ]

(6) [ ]אשמׄםׄ לכפר על העםׄ ובעלות

(7) [ ] לׄמׄנ[חת]ם להקטיר על המזבח

(8) העו[לה]רות . . . . וׄעׄשׄיׄ[ת]הׄ (?) בקיר הבית

(9) הזה בׄתׄ[ ] אׄמה לאמה ומׄצׄ[ ] מן [ ] אׄמה וגובהמה

(10) מן הארץ ארבע אמ[ות] מצופות זהב אׄשר יהיו מניחים עליהמה

(11) את בגדיהמׄה אשר יהי[ו באי]םׄ [בה]ם למעלה מׄעל לׄבׄיׄתׄ הׄ[

(12) בׄבואם לשׄרׄת בקודש [ו]עשיתה תעׄלׄהׄ סׄביבׄ לכיור אצל מׄזבׄחׄ הׄעׄוׄלׄהׄ

(13) הׄולכתׄ [ ] הכיור וׄמחלה יורדת לׄמׄטה אל תוך הארץׄ אׄשׄר

(14) יהיו המים נשפכים והולכים אׄליה ואובדים בתוך הׄארץ ולוא

(15) יהיה נוגעים בהמׄה כול אדם כי מדם הׄעולה מתערב במה

[1] Another possible reading is שמ]ן המשיׄחׄה.

3.1.5. Column 33

(1)]]יים באים [

(2)]] ובעת אש[ר

(3)] י]ומם ואת[

(4)]]אשר עליהמה ומני[חים

(5)]]בי[ת] הכיור ומ[ ]ם לכיו[ר

(6) [יהיו באי]ם אל הכיור והיוצאים בהמה אל [החצר התיכונה ולוא]

(7) יהיו מקדשים את עמי בבגדי הקודש אשר [ישרתו בהמה]

(8) *vacat* ועשיתמה בית למזרח בית ה[כ]יו[ר] כמדת [בית הכי]ור

(9) ר[ח]וק קירו מק[י]רו שבע אמות ו[כ]ול בנינו ומקרותיו כבית הכיור

(10) ושנים שערים לו מצפונו ומדרומו זה נוכח זה כמדת שער בית

(11) הכיור וכול הבית הזה כולו קירו עשוי חלונים פנימה אטומים

(12) שתי אמות רוחבמה בשתי אמות וגובהמה ארבע אמות

(13) מדולתים בתים לכלי המזבח למזרקים ולקשוא[ת] ולמחתות

(14) ולכוננות הכסף אשר יהיו מעלים במה את הקרבים ואת

(15) הרגלים על המזבח *vacat* ובכלותמה לקטיר

3.1.6. Column 34

(1)] מצו]פים בלוח נחו[שת

(2)]]ובין העמוד לע[מוד

(3)]]אשר בין העמודים[

(4) [ומביאים את] הפרים אל תוך הגלג[לים

(5) [הגלג]לים וסוגרים את הגלגלים וא[

(6) ואוסרים את קרני הפרים אל הטבעות ו[ ]בטבעות

(7) אחר יהיו טובחים אותמה ויהיו כונסים א[ת כול הדם] במזרקות

(8) וזורקים אותו על יסוד המזבח סביב *vacat* ופותחים

(9) את הגלגלים ומפשיטים את עורות הפרים מעל בשרמה ומנתחים

(10) אותמה לנתחיהמה ומולחים את הנתחים במלח ומרחצים את

(11) הקרבים ואת הכרעים ומולחים במלח ומקטירים אותמה על

(12) האש אשר על המזבח פר ופר ונתחיו אצלו ומנחת סולתו עליו

(13) ויין נסכו אצלו וממנו עליו והקטירו הכוהנים בני אהרון את הכול

(14) על המזבח אשה ריח ניחוח לפני יהוה *vacat*

(15) ועשיתה שלשלות יורדות מן מקרת שני עשר העמודים

3.1.7. Column 35

(1) [אל קוד]שׄ הקודשי֯[ם
(2) [   ]ה כול איש אשר לואׄ[
(3) [   ]◦ כול איש אׄשר לואׄ[ק]ו֯דש
(4) [   ]ה ממׄנה וכוׄל [איש מבני ישראל אשר יבוא איתם ו]הוא אין
(5) הׄואׄ כ֯ו֯ה֯ן֯ יׄ[ו]מת וכול אׄישׄ מׄהׄ[כוהנים בני אהרו]ן אשר יבוא
(6) איתם והוא אין הׄואׄ לׄבוש בג֯[די הקודש   ] מלא את
(7) ידיו גם המה יומתו ולוא יחׄל[לו את מק]ד֯ש אלוהׄיהמה לשאת
(8) עׄוון אשמה למות וקדשת{מ}ה את סׄ[בי]ב למזבח ולהיכל ולכיׄור
(9) ולׄפׄרוׄר והיה קודש קודשים לעולם ועד *vacat*
(10) ועשיתה מקום למערב ההיכל סביב פׄרור עמודים עומדים
(11) לחטאת ולאשם מובדלים זה מזה לחטאת כוהנים ולשעירים
(12) ולחטאות העם ולאשמותמה ולוא יהיו מערבים כולו אלה
(13) באלה כי מובדלים יהיו מקומותמה זה מזה למען לוא
(14) ישוגו הכוהנים בכול חטאת העם ובכול אלי אשמות לשאת
(15) חטא אשמה *vacat* והעוף על המזבח יעשה התורים

3.1.8. Column 36

(1) [   ]א[
(2) [   ]שׄע֯רים [
(3) [   ]◦ מן המׄקצוׄעׄ[
(4) [עד פנ]תׄ הׄשעׄ[ר עשרים ומאה באמה ו]השער רחב אר֯ב֯ע֯י֯ם֯
(5) אמׄהׄ לׄכול רוחו֯תׄי֯ו֯ [כמדה הזאת] וׄ[רו]חׄב קיׄ[רו] שׄׄבע אמׄוׄתׄ
(6) [וגוב]ה֯וׄ חמש [וארבעים אמה עד מק]רת גגׄ[ו ורוח]בׄ בׄא֯[יו] ששׄ
(7) וׄעׄשרׄיׄםׄ בׄאמה מׄמקצוע אל מקצוע והש[ע]רׄיׄםׄ הבאיׄםׄ בׄמׄה
(8) וׄהׄ[יו]צאים במה רוחב השער ארבע [עש]רׄה באמה וגובהמׄהׄ
(9) שמונה וׄ[ע]שׄרים באמה מן הס{◦}ף עד הׄמשקוף וגובה
(10) המקרׄהׄ מׄן המשקוף ארבע עשרה באמה ומקורה כיור
(11) ארז מׄצופׄהׄ זהב טהור ודלתותיו מצופות זהב טוב *vacat*
(12) *vacat* וׄמׄפנת השער עד המקצוע השני לחצר עשרים
(13) ומאה באמׄה וככה תהיה מדת כול השערים האלה אשר
(14) לחצר הפנׄיׄמית והשערים באים פנימה אל תוך החצר

3.1.9. Column 37

(01) [ ]◦◦◦מׄ◦◦◦◦
(1) [ ]◦◦◦ ◦יׄיׄןׄ הׄ ◦◦◦◦◦
(2) [יין] חׄדש מׄהׄגׄנותׄ לׄכׄולׄ השנה]
(3) [ת]בׄנׄהׄ בׄיׄן [אר]בׄעׄתׄ]
(4) [קיר החצר] הׄפנימׄית לׄעזרת ה[מז]בׄחׄ אׄשׄרׄ [יהיו אוכלים / זובחים
(5) [שמה א]תׄ זׄבׄחׄיׄ שלמי בׄני ישראל ול[ ]לה]
(6) ◦◦◦ עש [ ] פׄנׄות(?) הפרור הׄתׄחׄתון עׄשׄוׄיׄםׄ]
(7) הׄמׄעׄלות אׄצׄלׄ [קירות ה]שׄ[ע]רים מׄשׄני [עברי] הׄשׄער *vacat*
(8) וׄע[ש]יתמה בחׄ[צר פ]נימה בׄ[י]תׄ מ[ו]שבות לכוהׄנׄים ושולחנות
(9) לׄפׄנׄיׄ המושבות בפרור הפנׄימי אצל קיר הׄחׄצׄר החיצון
(10) מקומות עשוים לכוהנים לז[ב]חׄיהמה ולבכורׄים ולמעשרות
(11) ולזבחי שלמיהמׄהׄ אשר יהיו זובחים ולׄואׄ [י]תערבו זבחׄיׄ
(12) שלמי בני ישראל בזבחי הׄכׄוהׄנים *vacat*
(13) ובארבעת מקצועות הׄחצר עׄשׄית[ה][2] להמׄהׄ מקׄוׄםׄ לכׄיׄרים
(14) אשר יהיו מבשלים שמה אׄתׄ זבחיהמה את הׄחׄאטות[3]

3.1.10. Column 38

(01) [ ]במקצׄוׄע המזרחי צפונהׄ ואתׄ]
(1) [ ] יׄהׄיׄו אוכלׄיׄםׄ]
(2) [ ] . . [רא]שיתמה . .]
(3) [ ]יהׄיו אוכלים ושותׄיׄםׄ]
(4) [ובימי הבכורים] לדגן לתירוש ולׄ[יצהר
(5) . . . . [בני ישראל וביום הבכורים לפרי]
(6) . . . . . .לׄ. . .ל שער המערב [את כול פרי ארצמה את התׄאׄנׄים]
(7) . . . . . . .הׄעץ אשר יׄאׄכׄל וׄ[לימין השער הזהׄ מנחת הקורבנות]
(8) [הבׄאה] עׄלׄיה לבונה ולשׄמׄאול שׄ[ער הצ]פון מנׄחת הׄאשמ[ות הׄקנאות]
(9) ולׄימׄ[ין ה]שׄער הזה כול ה‎מנחהׄ ושׄעׄיׄרׄ[י ה]חטאת אשר יקׄריבו בׄנׄיׄ
(10) [י]שראׄלׄ שׄמה יהיו אוכלים [את ח]טׄאׄותׄ העוׄףׄ ולתורים ולבני היונהׄ
(11) *vacat*
(12) ועשיתׄהׄ [ח]צר שנׄית סובבת אׄת הח[צר הפנ]ימׄית רחוב מאה באמהׄ
(13) ואורך לרׄוח הקדם שמונים וארבע מׄאות באמהׄ וׄכׄכׄהׄ רוחב ואורך לכול
(14) רוחותיׄהׄ לׄנׄגׄב ולים ולצׄ צפון וׄרוחב קירהׄ [אר]בׄע אמׄות וגובה שמונׄ[ה]
(15) ועשרׄים באמה ותאים עשוים לקיר מחוץ ובין התאו לתאו שלוש

---

[2] Another alternative is [ל]עׄשׄות.
[3] Another alternative is הׄחׄאטת.

3.1.11. Column 39

(01) [<u>אמות וחצי</u>]

(1) [מ]דת הׄשׄ[ערים

(2) הׄכׄוׄלׄ[ ]מׄקרת הגׄגׄ [

(3) א[מות]ודלתותיה . . . .

(4) מצופהׄ זׄהׄבׄ[ ] החצר הזואת כול

(5) קׄהל עדׄתׄ [ישראל והגר אשר יולד בתו]כׄסׄה דור רביעׄיׄ [

(6) יׄשׄרׄאׄלׄ [ ]להשׄתׄחׄוות לפנׄי כול עׄ[ד]ת בנׄיׄ

(7) ישׄראׄלׄ [ ] לׄוׄאׄ תבוא בׄאׄ אשה וילד עד יום

(8) אשר יׄשׄלׄיׄםׄ חוק [ ] נׄפׄשׄוׄ ליהוה מחצית השקל

(9) לזכרון בׄמׄוׄשׄבׄוׄתׄיׄהׄמׄהׄ עׄשׄרׄיׄםׄ גׄרׄהׄ הׄשׄקׄלׄ *vacat*

(10) וכאשר ישׄאוׄ ממנוׄ את מחצית הׄש[ק]לׄ [ישבע] לי אחר יבואו מבן

(11) עשרׄיׄםׄ [שנה] ולמעלה ושׄם [הש]עׄרׄים אשׄרׄ לׄ[ח]צר הזואת על שׄמׄ[ות]

(12) בני ישׄ[ר]אל שמעׄון לוי וׄיׄהודה בקדם מזרחׄ [ר]אׄובן יוסף ובנימין לנגב

(13) דרום יש שכר זבולון וגד לים דן נפתלׄיׄ וׄאׄשׄרׄ לצפון וׄבׄין שער לשער

(14) מדה מן פנה למזרח צפון עד שער שמעׄון תשׄעׄ ותשעים באמה והשער

(15) שמונה ועשרים באמה ומשער הזה עד שער {∘∘∘∘∘} לוי תשׄעׄ ותשעים

(16) באמה והשער שמונה ועשרים באמה וׄמשער לוי עד שׄעׄרׄ יׄהׄודה

3.1.12. Column 40

(1) [ ]ללבוש את הב[גדים

(2) [ ]ה להיות נש[י]א תח[ת אהרון

(3) [ ]בני ישראל ולוא ימ[ותו

(4) [החצ]ר הׄזואׄת ל . . [

(5) [ ] ועשיתה חצר שליש[י]ת [

(6) [ו]לבנותיהמה ולגרים אשר נולדׄ[ו

(7) [רו]חב סביב לחצר התיכונה שׄ[ש] מׄאׄ[ות] אמה

(8) באורך כאלׄףׄ ושש [מאות ב]אׄמׄהׄ מפנה לפנה לכול רׄוׄח ורוח כמדה הזאוׄתׄ

(9) לׄמזרׄח ולדׄרׄוׄםׄ ולים ולצׄ[פו]ן ורוחב הקׄיר שבע אמות וגובה תשע

(10) ורבעים בׄאמה וׄתׄאים [ע]שוים בוׄ ולשעריו מחוץ לעומת המוסד

(11) עדׄ עטׄרותׄיׄוׄ שׄלׄושׄהׄ בׄ[ו] שעׄרׄים במזרח ושלושה בדרום ושלושה

(12) לים ושלושה לצפון וׄרוחב השעׄרים חמשים באמה וגובהמה שבעים

(13) באמה ובין שער לשערׄ [מדה] שלוש מאות וששים באמה מן הפנה עד

(14) שער שמעון ששים ושׄלוש מאות באמה ומשער שמעון עד שער לוי

(15) כמדה הזואת ומשעׄרׄ לוי עד שער יהודה כמדה הזואת ששים ושלוש

3.1.13. Column 41

(1) [מאות וששים באמה ומשער בנימין עד פנת המ]ע֯ר֯[ב]
(2) [שלוש מאות וששים באמה וככה מן הפנה] ה֯ז֯ו֯א֯ת֯
(3) עד ש֯[ער יש שכר שלוש מאות וששים ב]א֯מה ומשער
(4) יש שכר[עד שער זבולון ששים ושלוש] מאות באמה
(5) ומשער זב[ולון עד שער גד ששים ו]ש֯ל֯ו֯ש֯ מאות
(6) באמה ומ֯ש֯[ער גד עד פנת הצפון] שלוש מאות
(7) וששים באמה *vacat* [ו]מ֯ן֯ ה֯פנה הזואת עד
(8) שער דן שלוש מאות וששים באמה וככה משער דן עד
(9) שער נפתלי ששים ושלוש מאות באמה ומשער נפתלי
(10) עד שער אשר שלוש מאות וששים באמה ומשער
(11) אשר עד פנת {שע}המזרח שלוש מאות וששים באמה
(12) ויוצאים השערים מקיר החצר לחוץ שבע אמות
(13) ולפניםה באים מקיר החצר שש ושלושים באמה
(14) ורוחב פתחי השערים ארבע עשרה באמה וגובהמה
(15) שמונה ועשרים באמה עד המשקוף ומקורים
(16) באדשכים עץ ארז ומצופים זהב ודלתותיהמה מצופות
(17) זהב טהור ובין {ע} שער לשער תעשה פנימה נשכות

3.1.14. Column 42

(01) [וחדרים ופרורים *vacat*]
(02) [רוחב החדר עשר באמה ואורכו עשרים באמה]
(03) [וגובהו ארבע עשרה באמה ומקורה באדשכים]
(04) [עץ ארז ורוחב הקיר שתים אמות ולחוצה מזה]
(05) [הנשכה *vacat* רוחב הנשכה עשר באמה]
(1) [ואורכה עשרים באמה והקיר שתים אמות רוחב]
(2) [וגובהה ארבע עשרה באמה] ע֯ד֯ המשקוף ופ֯תחה
(3) [שלוש אמות רוחב וכן תעשה] לכול הנשכות ולחדריה[מה]
(4) ו֯פרו֯[ריהמה כולמה יהיו רו]חב עשר אמות ובין שער
(5) לשע֯ר [תעשה שמונה] עשר֯ה נשכה וחדריהמה
(6) שמונה[עשר *vacat*]
(7) ובית מעלות תעשה אצל קירות השערים בתוך
(8) הפרור עולים מסבות לתוך הפרור השני ולשלישי
(9) ולגג ונשכות בנוית וחדריהמה ופרוריהמה כתחתונות
(10) שניות ושלישיות כמדת התחתונות ועל גג השלישית
(11) תעשה עמודים ומקורים בקורות מעמוד אל עמוד
(12) מקום לסוכות גבהים שמונה אמות והיו הסוכות
(13) נעשות עליהמה בכול שנה ושנה בחג הסוכות לזקני

(14) העדה לנשיאים לראשי בתי האבות לבני ישראל
(15) ולשרי האלפים ולשרי המאיות אשר יהיו עולים
(16) ויושבים שמה עד {ע}ה˹ע˺לות את עולת המועד אשר
(17) לחג הסוכות שנה בשנה בין שער לשער יהיו

3.1.15. Column 43

(1) [ ]ה לשש[ת ימי המעשה]
(2) [ ]בימי השבתות ובימ[י החודש]
(3) [ ]ובימי הבכורים לדגן לת[ירוש]
(4) [וליצהר ובימי ה]עצים באלה הימים יאכל ולוא ינ֯י[חו]
(5) ממנו שנה לשנה אחרת כי ככה יהיו אוכלים אותו
(6) מחג הבכורים לדגן החטים יהיו אוכלים את הדגן
(7) עד השנה השנית עד יום חג הבכורים והיין מיום
(8) מועד התירוש עד השנה השנית עד יום מועד
(9) התירוש והיצהר מיום מועדו עד השנה השנית
(10) למועד יום הקרב שמן חדש ˹על˺מזבח וכול אשר
(11) נותר ממועדיהמה יקדש באש ישרף לוא יאכל עוד
(12) כי קדש והיושבים במרחק מן המקדש דרך שלושת
(13) ימים כול אשר יוכלו לבהיא יביאו ואם לא יוכלו
(14) לשאתו ומכרוהו בכסף והביאו את הכסף ולקחו בו דגן
(15) ויין ושמן ובקר וצאון ואכלוהו בימי המועדים ולוא
(16) יואכלו ממנו בימי המעשה לאונמה כי קודש הוא
(17) ובימי הקודש יאכל ולוא יאכל בימי המעשה {. . . .}

3.1.16. Column 44

(1) [ ]יושבים[
(2) [ ]אשר בתוך העיר למ[זרח
(3) [ ] *vacat* וחלקתה את [כול נשכות משער
(4) [שמעו]ן֯ עד שער יהודה יהיו לכוהנים [
(5) וכ֯[ו]ל֯ ימין שער לוי ושמאולו לבני אהרון אחיכה תח[לק]
(6) שמונה ומאה נשכה וחדריהמה ושתי סוכותיהמה
(7) אשר מעל הגג ולבני יהודה משער יהודה עד
(8) הפנה ארבע וחמשים נשכה וחדריהמה והסוכה
(9) אשר מעלהמה ולבני שמעון משער שמעון עד הפנה
(10) השנית נשכותמה וחדריהמה וסוכ֯ת˹ה˺מה ולבני ראובן
(11) מן המקצוע אשר אצל בני יהודה עד שער ראובן
(12) שתים וחמשים נשכ֯ת וחדריהמה וסוכ֯תמה ומשער
(13) ראובן עד שער יוסף לבני יוסף לאפרים ולמנשה

(14) ומשער יוסף עד שער בנימין לבני קהת מ{ב}נ{י} הלויים
(15) ומשע^ר^ בנימין עד פנת המערב לבני בנימין מן הפנה
(16) הזאת עד שער יש שכר לבני יש שכר ומשער

3.1.17. Column 45

(1) יה[יו באים
(2) שבעים [ומאתים נשכה
(3) וכאשר י[ה]שני יהיה בא לשמאול[בבואו
ב
(4) יצא הרישון מעירו ולוא [יהי]ו מתערבים אלה באלה וכליה[מה
(5) משמר אל מקומו וחנו זה[ב]א וזה יוצא ליום השמיני ומטהרים את
(6) הנשכות זואת אחרי זאות[ב]עת תצא הראישונה ולוא תהיה שמה
(7) תערובת *vacat* וא[יש] כי יהיה לו מקרה לילה לוא יבוא אל
(8) כול המקדש עד אשר [יש]לים שלושת ימים וכבס בגדיו ורחץ
ורחץ
(9) ביום הראישון וביום השלישי יכבס בגדיו ובאה השמש אחר
(10) יבוא אל המקדש ולוא יבואו בנדת טמאתמה אל מקדשי וטמאו
(11) ואיש כיא ישכב עם אשתו שכבת זרע לוא יבוא אל כול עיר
(12) המקדש אשר אשכין שמי בה שלושת ימים כול איש עור
(13) לוא יבואו לה כול ימיהמה ולוא יטמאו את העיר אשר אני שוכן
(14) בתוכה כי אני יהוה שוכן בתוך בני ישראל לעולם ועד *vacat*
(15) וכול איש אשר יטהר מזובו וספר לו שבעת ימים לטהרתו ויכבס ביום
(16) השביעי בגדיו ורחץ את כול בשרו במים חיים אחר יבוא אל עיר
(17) המקדש וכול טמא לנפש לוא יבואו לה עד אשר יטהרו וכול צרוע
(18) ומנוגע לוא יבואו לה עד אשר יטהרו וכאשר יטהר והקריב את

3.1.18. Column 46

(01) [רק לוא יבוא אל]
(02) [המקדש רוכל/יוכל]
(03) [ואל המקדש
(04) [מכו]נה שלנחושת [ ]למכונה [
(1) [ ]שר ה[כולו אשר לו]א[
(2) עוף טמא על מקד[שי אשר בחצר הפנימית ועל] גגי השערים [אשר]
(3) לחצר החיצונה וכול [עוף טמא לוא יוכל ל]היות בתוך מקדשי לעו[לם]
(4) ועד כול הימים אשר א[ני שוכ]ן בתוכם *vacat*
(5) *vacat* ועשיתה רובד סביב לחוץ מחצר החיצונה רחב
(6) ארבע עשרה באמה על פי פתחי השערים כולמה ושתים
(7) עשרה מעלה תעשה לו אשר יהיו עולים בני ישראל אליו
(8) לבוא אל מקדשי *vacat*

(9) ועשיתה חיל סביב למקדש רחב מאה באמה אשר יהיה
(10) מבדיל בין מקדש הקודש לעיר ולוא יהיו באים בלע אל תוך
(11) מקדשי ולוא יחללוהו וקדשו את מקדשי ויראו ממקדשי
(12) אשר אנוכי שוכן בתוכמה *vacat*
(13) ועשיתה להמה מקום יד חוץ מן העיר אשר יהיו יוצאים שמה
(14) לחוץ לצפון המערב לעיר בתים ומקורים ובורות בתוכמה
(15) אשר תהיה הצואה יורדת אל תוכמה ~~ולוא~~ תהיה נראה לכול רחוק
(16) מן העיר שלושת אלפים אמה *vacat* עשיתה
(17) שלושה מקומות למזרח העיר מובדלים זה מזה אשר יהיו
(18) באים המצורעים והזבים והאנשים אשר יהיו להמה מקרה

3.1.19. Column 47

(1)] °°[ ]
(2)] ל]מעלה ולוא למט[ה [*vacat*
(3) [והיו]עׄרׄיהמה טהורות ושׄ[כנתי שמי בתוכ]מׄה לעולם והעיר
(4) אׄשר אקדיש לשכין שמי ומקדׄ[שי בתוכה] תׄהׄיה קודש וטהורה
(5) מכול דבר לכול טמאה אשר יטמאו בה כול אשר בתוכה יהיה
(6) טהור וכול אשר יבוא לה יהיה טהור יין ושמן וכול אוכל
(7) וכול מושקה יהיו טהורים כול עור בהמה טהורה אשר יזבחו
(8) בתוך עריהמה לוא יביאו לה כי בעריהמה יהיו עושים
(9) בהמה מלאכתמה לכול צורכיהמה ואל עיר מקדשי לוא יביאו
(10) כי כבשרמה תהיה טהרתמה ולוא תטמאו את העיר אשר
(11) אנוכי משכן את שמי ומקדשי בתוכה כי בעורות אשר יזבחו
(12) במקדש בהמה יהיו מביאים את יינמה ואת שמנמה וכול
(13) אוכלמה לעיר מקדשי ולוא יגאלו את מקדשי בעורות זבחי
(14) פגוליהמה אשר יזבחו בתוך ארצמה ולוא תטהרו עור
(15) מתוך עריכמה לעירי כי כטהרת בשרו כן יטהרו העורות אם
(16) במקדשי תזבחוהו יטהר למקדשי ואם בעריכמה תזבחוהו וטהר
(17) לעריכמה וכול טהרת המקדש בעורות המקדש תביאו ולוא תטמאו
(18) את מקדשי ועירי בעורות פגוליכמה אשר אנוכי שוכן בתוכה

3.2 Translation

3.2.1. The Temple and the Glory of the LORD

29:3 […] in the house in which I w[ill establish] **4** my name. In it they shall present burnt-offerings, [day] after day according to the instruction of this regulation, **5** continually, from the children of Israel, besides their freewill offerings, namely, everything that they shall offer, **6** all their vows, and all their presents, which they shall bring to me (so) that [they] will be accepted. **7** I will (then) be pleased with them and they will be my people. I will be theirs for ever and I will dwell **8** among them for ever and ever.

I will sanctify my [te]mple with my glory. On the temple I will make **9** my glory dwell until the day of creation, when I will create my temple **10** in order to establish it for myself for all times, according the covenant, which I made with Jacob at Bethel … **30:1** […] I will [dwell] and sanctify […] **2** […] **3** […]do.

3.2.2. The Construction

[You] shall make [a house] **4** for the stairs from b[oth sides of the gat]es, which are in the building that you shall erect [that] my [name will be] **5** in it. (*vacat*?) You sh[all] make a house (for) a spiral[4] staircase to the north of the sanctuary, a square building **6** from one corner to another, twenty cubits measuring, for each of its four corners.[5] Its distance from the wall **7** [of the] sanctuary (shall be) seven cubits, to the northwest of the temple. You shall make the wall four **8** cubits thick [and forty cubits high] like the sanctuary, and the inner side, from one (inner) corner[6] to another, **9** twelv[e cubits]. Inside (there will be) a square column at the centre, its thickness (being) four **10** cubits on each side. The width of the spiral staircase (with) ascending steps ®[…]

31:1 […]…® **2** […]… the gate **3** […] the [oi]l the anointed [pries]t **4** […]the deputy priest **5** […the]high [priest.] (*vacat*) 6 In the

---

[4] Yadin translates מסבה as "staircase" only. Yadin, 131. We agree with García Martínez' suggestion "spiral staircase." García Martínez, 1251.

[5] With other words: each side was twenty cubits, all around the building.

[6] Here we have the word מקצוע, which describes the corner on the inside of a building.

upper chamber of [this] buil[ding you shall make a gat]e that opens to the roof of the sanctuary and a passageway[7] leading **7** through this gate to the *stoa* [of the] sanctuary. Through the passageway one may enter the upper chamber of the sanctuary. **8** Cover [al]l of this staircase building with gold, its walls, its gates and its roof from inside **9** [and from] outside, its column and its stairs. Do it all as I have told you. **10** You shall make a square house for the laver in the southeast, with all its sides twenty-one **11** cubits, at a distance of fifty cubits from the altar. The [thick]ness of the wall (shall be) three cubits and the height **12** twenty cubits[…] Make [thre]e gates for it, to the east, to the north, **13** and to the west. The width of the gates (shall be) four cubits and their height seven … **32:1** […] three cubits […] **2** […]…[…] **3** […]three[…]

4 […]their[…] **5** […]®® to the altar ®®[…] **6** […]their guilt-offering to make atonement for the people as they go up **7** […] for their cereal-o[ffering] to burn on the altar **8** of the burnt-[offering…]®®®… On the wall of this building you shall [ma]ke (?) **9** ®®[…] cubit by cubit and ®®[…] from […] cubits and their height **10** from the ground (shall be) four cub[its], covered with gold, in which they shall put **11** their clothes, w[ith] which [they] will [g]o up on the top of the house ®[…] **12** as they come to minister in the sanctuary. You shall make a channel around the laver, beside the altar of the burnt-offering, **13** the channel shall lead […] the laver. A pit leads down into the ground so that **14** the water can be poured out and run into it and disappear into the ground. No one **15** should touch it[8] since it has been mixed with the blood of the burnt-offering…

33:1 […]®®® they come […] **2** […] and at the time tha[t…] **3** […da]ily and ®®[…] **4** […]which are upon them and (so) they [lay…] **5** […]the hou[se] of laver and ®[…]® to the lave[r…] **6** [they shall] co[me] to the laver and continue in them[9] into [the middle courtyard and they shall not] **7** sanctify my people in the sacred clothes [in] which [they will minister.] **8** (*vacat*)

To the east of the house of [l]av[er] you shall make a building, the same size as [the house of la]ver. **9** The di[st]ance of its wall from the w[a]ll of the laver building (shall be) seven cubits and its [wh]ole structure including its ceilings (shall be) as the laver building. **10** It

[7] Yadin translates "way." Yadin, 1251. We follow García Martínez' rendering "passageway." García Martínez, 1251.

[8] The water.

[9] The sacred clothes.

should have two gates, to the north and to the south, one facing the other, the same size as the gate to the house **11** of the laver. This whole building shall have blocked windows (on) its every wall towards the inside. **12** They shall be two cubits wide, two cubits deep and four cubits high. **13** (It shall have) doors and serve as (storing) rooms for the utensils of the altar: for the (sprinkling) bowls, the jars,[10] the fire-pans, **14** and the silver scoops, with which the entrails and the limbs are brought **15** upon the altar. (*vacat*) When they have burned down … **34:1** [...cove]red with a panel of bro[nze...]

3.2.3. Offerings

2 [...]and between one column and another co[lumn...] **3** [...]which is between the columns[...] **4** [they shall bring] the bulls between the whee[ls...] **5** [the whee]ls and they shall close the wheels and®[...] **6** the horns of the bulls shall be tied to the rings and [...]in the rings. **7** Then they shall slaughter them, and [all of t]he [blood] shall be gathered in the bowls **8** and (then) it shall be thrown around the base of the altar. (*vacat*) (Then) they shall open **9** the wheels and skin the hides of the bulls from their flesh and cut **10** them up into pieces, salt the pieces and wash **11** the entrails and the legs, salt (them) and burn them on **12** the fire, which is on the altar, one bull after the other, with its pieces and the cereal-offering with finest flour upon it **13** and wine as its drink-offering, of which (will be poured) upon it. The priests, the sons of Aaron, shall burn everything **14** on the altar. (This will be) an offering by fire, (which has) a pleasing scent before the LORD. (*vacat*)

15 You shall make chains hanging from the ceiling (above) the twelve columns … **35:1** [to] the [hol]y of holi[es...] **2** [...]® any man who is not [...] **3** [...]® any man who is not[...h]oly **4** [...]® from it. Any [man, belonging to the children of Israel, who enters with them] not being **5** a priest shall [be p]ut to death and any man of the [priests, the sons of Aaro]n, who enters **6** with them without being dressed in [the holy] cl[othes...] consecrated, **7** also they shall be put to death. [They] shall not profa[ne] the tem[ple] of their God causing **8** a sin, (which is) punished by death. You shall sanctify the are[a aro]und of the altar, the sanctuary, the laver, **9** and the *stoa* and (so) it will be most holy for ever and ever. (*vacat*) **10** You shall make a place west of the

[10] Possibly for the drink-offering.

sanctuary, a circular *stoa* of standing columns, **11** for the sin-offering and for the guilt-offering, separated from each other: for the sin-offering of the priests and for the male-goats **12** and for the sin-offerings of the people and for their guilt-offerings. There shall not be any exchanges from one of the places **13** to the other: the places have to be separated from each other so that **14** the priests would not err with any of the sin-offerings of the people with any of the rams of the guilt-offerings and (so) causing **15** a sin, (which should be) punished. (*vacat*) The birds shall be prepared for the altar: the turtledoves

3.2.4. The Inner Courtyard

36:1 […]®[…] **2** […]gates […] **3** […]… from the (inner) corner[…] **4** [to the (outer) cor]ner[11] of the gat[e one hundred and twenty cubits.] The gate (shall be) forty **5** cubits wide to all its sides [according to this size]. The [thick]ness of [its] wa[ll] (shall be) seven cubits, **6** its [heig]ht [forty]five [cubits to the raf]ters of [its] ceiling, [and the wid]th of [its] chamber[s twenty six **7** cubits, from an (inner) corner to another. The ga[t]es through which they enter **8** and through which they leave, (shall be) four[te]en cubits wide, and **9** [tw]enty eight cubits high from the threshold to the lintel. The height **10** of the ceiling from the lintel (shall be) fourteen cubits and (the gate shall be) roofed (by) a platform[12], **11** (made of) cedar (and) overlaid with pure gold and its doors (shall as well) be overlaid with pure gold. (*vacat*) **12** (*vacat*)

From the (outer) corner of the gate to the second (inner) corner of the courtyard (the distance shall be) hundred and twenty **13** cubits; the measurement shall be in the same way for all these gates, which **14** (are located) in the inner courtyard. The gates shall open towards the inside of the courtyard … **37:01** […]…®…[…] 1 […]… …wine ®… […] **2** […] new [wine] from the gardens for the whole year […] **3** […you shall]build between the [fo]ur […] **4** [the wall] of the inner [courtyard] to the extension of the [al]tar [that they shall be eating / sacrificing] **5** [there th]e peace-offerings of the children of Israel and ®[…]®® […] **6** … ®® […] the corners? of the lower *stoa* shall be

---

[11] On this location we have פנה, which is the word for the outer corner.

[12] Yadin translates כיור as "platform" as García Martínez suggests "framework." Yadin, 155. García Martínez, 1255.

made […] **7** the steps by [the walls of the] g[a]tes, on both [sides] of the gate. (*vacat*)

3.2.5. Eating Offerings

8 You shall [ma]ke s[i]tting pl[ac]es for the priests [i]nside the co[urt] and tables **9** in front of the seats in the inner *stoa* by the outer wall of the courtyard. **10** Make also places for the priests, for their s[a]crifices, for the first-fruits, and for the tithes, **11** and for their peace-offering, which they shall sacrifice. There shall be no mixing between the peace-offerings **12** of the children of Israel and the sacrifices of the priests. (*vacat*) **13** In the four (inner) corners of the courtyard you shall make for them a place for the stoves, **14** on which they shall cook their sacrifices, the sin-offerings … **38:01** [… in the (inner) corn]er, to the north-east, and the […] **1** […] they shall eat[…] **2** […]...their [firs]t-fruits… […] **3** […]they shall eat and drink[…] **4** [and on the days of the first-fruits,] of the grain, of the wine, and of the [oil …] **5** …[the children of Israel. On the day of the first-fruits of the fruit] **6** …®…® the western gate [all the fruit of their land, the figs] **7** …of the tree shall be eaten and [to the right of this gate (there shall be) a cereal-offering] **8** upon which frankincense (shall be) [added.] To the left [of the no]rthern g[ate] (you shall set) the guilt-offering[s of jealousy] **9** and to the ri[ght of] this gate, all of the cereal-offering and the male-goat[s for the] sin-offering, which the children [of I]srael shall sacrifice. **10** There they shall eat the bird, the turtledoves, and the young pigeons (as) the [sin]-offerings. **11** (*vacat*)

3.2.6. The Middle Courtyard

12 You shall make a second [co]urt that surrounds [the in]ner co[urt] (at) a distance of one hundred cubits. **13** The length on the east side (shall be) four hundred end eighty cubits; the distance and the length of all **14** its sides (shall be made) in the same fashion to the south, to the west, and to the north. Its wall (shall be) [fo]ur cubits thick and the height twenty eigh[t] **15** cubits high and the chambers (shall) be made in the wall on the outside. Between one chamber and another (there shall be) three **39:01** [and a half cubits…] **1** […the mea]surement of the ga[tes…] **2** everything[…]the ceiling of the roof […] **3** cu[bits …]and its doors… **4** covered with gold[…] this courtyard, all **5** the assembly of the congregation [of Israel and the foreigner that was born in] their [mid]st (until the) fourth generation [...] **6** Israel [...]to worship before me, (the) whole ass[em]bly of the children **7** of Israel. [...]

No woman shall enter it, nor a young man before the day **8** he fulfills the law [...] to the LORD, half a shekel **9** as a memorial in their villages, the shekel (being) twenty gerahs.[13] (*vacat*) **10** When they collect the half she[k]el, sworn to me from each one, only then[14] they shall enter, from the age of **11** twenty one [years] and older. There [the g]ates, which (belong) to this co[urt] (shall be) according to the nam[es] **12** of the children of Is[ra]el: Simeon, Levi, and Judah, to the east; [Re]uben, Josef, and Benjamin, to the south; **13** Issachar, Zebulun, and Gad, to the west; Dan, Naphtali, and Asher, to the north. Between one gate and another **14** the measurement from the (outer) corner to the northeast until the gate of Simeon (shall be) ninety nine cubits; and the gate (itself shall be) **15** twenty eight cubits and from this gate until the gate of Levi, ninety nine **16** cubits (with) the gate twenty eight cubits (as well); from the gate of Levi until the gate of Judah... **40:1** [...]to put on the ga[rments...] **2** [...]® to be a lea[de]r inst[ead of Aaron...] **3** [...]the children of Israel, (so that) [they] will not d[ie...] **4** [...]this [cou]rt ®...[...]

3.2.7. The Outer Courtyard

5 [...] You shall make a thi[r]d courtyard [...] **6** [...and] to their daughters and to the foreigners, which [were] born [...] **7** [...the wi]dth around the middle courtyard (shall be) si[x] hun[dred] cubits, **8** in length, about one thousand and six [hundred cu]bits from one (outer) corner to another. Every side (shall be) according to this measurement: **9** to the east and to the south, to the west and to the n[or]th. Its wall (shall be) seven cubits thick and forty nine **10** cubits high. Chambers (shall) [be] made in it and to its gates, on the outside against the foundation **11** up to its ornaments;[15] it (shall) h[ave] three gates to the east and three to the south, three **12** to the west and three to the north. The width of the gates (shall be) fifty cubits and their height seventy **13** cu-

[13] Gerah is an ancient weight that equals 1/20 of a shekel.
[14] The literal translation would here be "afterwards" for אחר.
[15] The literal translation would be "crowns." It seems that some kind of a decoration is the issue.

bits. [The measurement] between one gate and another (shall be) three hundred and sixty cubits.

From the (outer) corner until **14** the gate of Simeon, three hundred and sixty cubits (as well), and from the gate of Simeon to the gate of Levi, **15** according to this (same) measurement. From the gate of Levi until the gate of Judah, (there will also be) this same measurement, three (hundred) and sixty **41:1** [(three) hundred and sixty cubits; from the gate of Benjamin until the (outer) corner to the w]es[t], **2** [three hundred and sixty cubits; in the same fashion from] this [outer corner] **3** until the ga[te of Issachar, three hundred and sixty cu]bits; from the gate **4** of Issachar [until the gate of Zebulun, three] hundred [and sixty] cubits (as well); **5** from the gate of Ze[bulun until the gate of Gad], three hundred [and sixty] **6** cubits; from the ga[te of Gad until the (outer) corner to the north], three hundred **7** and sixty cubits (as well). (*vacat*) From this (outer) corner until **8** the gate if Dan, three hundred and sixty cubits; in the same fashion from the gate of Dan until **9** the gate of Naphtali, three hundred and sixty cubits; from the gate of Naphtali **10** until the gate of Asher three hundred and sixty cubits (as well); from the gate **11** of Asher until the (outer) corner to the east, three hundred and sixty cubits. **12** The gates shall stick out seven cubits from the wall of the courtyard. **13** They shall (moreover) go in thirty six cubits from the wall of the courtyard. **14** The width of the openings of the gates (shall be) fourteen cubits and their height **15** twenty eight cubits up to the lintel; they shall be roofed **16** by beams[16] of cedar wood, (which is) covered with gold. Their doors shall be covered **17** with pure gold.

3.2.8. The Chambers, the Rooms, and the *Stoas*

On the inside, between one gate and another, you shall make chambers, **42:01** [rooms, and *stoas*. (*vacat*)] **02** [The rooms (shall be) ten cubits wide, twenty cubits long **03** [and fourteen cubits high. (The room) shall be roofed by beams] **04** [of cedar wood. The wall (shall be) two cubits thick, and on the outside from that], **05** [the chambers (shall be made). (*vacat*) The chamber (shall be) ten cubits wide], **1** [twenty cubits long, the wall two cubits thick] **2** [and fourteen cubits high] up to the lintel.

[16] The word אדשכים is not extant in the Bible. Yadin suggests that it would have Persian origin and translates it as "beams." Yadin, 175.

Its entrance **3** [(shall be) three cubits wide. In such a way you shall make] all the chambers and [thei]r rooms. **4** [All their] *sto*[*as* shall be] ten cubits [wi]de, and between one gate **5** and (another) [you shall make eight]een chambers with their rooms. **6** Eight[een…] (*vacat*) **7** You shall make a stair house by the walls of the gates, inside **8** the *stoa*, (in which) spiral staircases shall go up to the second and the third *stoa* and **9** (up) to the roof. The chambers shall be built,[17] and their rooms and their *stoas* (shall be) like those below, **10** the second and the third ones, according to the measurement like those below.

On the roof of the third (chamber) **11** you shall make columns, roofed by beams from column to column, **12** (this is) a place for the booths. The (columns shall be) eight cubits high, and the booths shall be **13** built on them every single year on the feast of booths for the elders **14** of the congregation, for the leaders, for the heads of families, for the children of Israel, **15** for the commanders of the thousands and for the commanders of the hundreds, who will come up **16** and sit there until the sacrificing of the festival burnt-offering, that of **17** the feast of booths, year after year. Between one gate and another one they shall …

43:1 […]® for the si[x working days] **2** […]on the days of the sabbaths and on the day[s of the new moon] **3** […]and on the days of the first fruits of the grain, of the w[ine,] **4** [and of the oil, and on the days of the] trees. On these days it shall be eaten and [they] shall not lea[ve] **5** of it from one year to the next year. Therefore they shall eat it in this way: **6** from the feast of the first fruits of the grain of wheat they shall eat the grain **7** to the next year, until the feast of the first fruits; the wine from the day **8** of the feast of the wine until the next year, until the day of the feast **9** of the wine; and the oil, from the day of its feast until the next year **10** until the feast, the day of the offering of new oil /o/n /the/ altar. All that **11** remains from their feasts shall be consecrated, burnt on fire; it shall never be eaten **12** because it is holy.

Those who live further from the temple than a distance of three **13** days shall bring all they can bring. If they are unable to **14** carry it, they shall sell it for money, bring the money and with it buy grain, **15** and wine, and oil, and cattle, and sheep; they shall eat it on the days of the feasts. But **16** they shall not eat of it on the working days (or) in

---

[17] In the MS בנוית is clearly discernable. Since this is a very difficult reading grammatically, both singular and *status constructus*, we read the plural instead, that is בנויות.

their sorrows,[18] for it is holy. **17** But on the holy days it shall be eaten, and it shall not be eaten on the working days … **44:1** […]residents[…] **2** […]that is inside the city to the e[ast…] **3** […] (*vacat*) You shall divide [all the chambers: those from the gate of] **4** [Simeo]n to the gate of Judah shall be for the priests […]

3.2.9. The Booths

5 The en[ti]re right (side) and the left (side) of the gate of Levi you shall as[sign] to the sons of Aaron, your brother, **6** one hundred and eight chambers and their rooms, and their two booths **7** which are on the top of the roof. To the sons of Judah from the gate of Judah to the **8** (outer) corner, forty-five chambers and their rooms and the booth **9** that is above them. To the sons of Simeon from the gate of Simeon to the second corner, **10** their chambers and their rooms and their booths. To the sons of Reuben **11** from the (inner) corner, which is next to the sons of Judah, to the gate of Reuben **12** fifty-two chambers and their rooms and their booths. From the gate **13** of Reuben to the gate of Joseph, to the sons of Joseph, Ephraim and Manasseh. **14** From the gate of Joseph to the gate of Benjamin, to the sons of Kohath, of the Levites. **15** From the gat/e/ of Benjamin to the western corner, to the sons of Benjamin. From this corner **16** to the gate of Issachar, to the sons of Issachar. From the gate.

3.2.10. Purification Rules

45:1 [They] shall [enter…] **2** [two hundred and] seventy, [a chamber…] **3** and as ®[… the] second shall enter to the right.[When he enters, **4** the first shall go out from his city. They shall not intermingle, (neither) share th[eir] vessels (with each other) […] **5** course to its place, and they shall encamp. One[ent]ers, and the other goes out, on the eighth day. They shall purify **6** the chambers, one after another[wh]en the first one goes out; there shall not be any **7** mingling. (*vacat*)

If a m[an] has had a nocturnal emission, he shall not enter into **8** any part of the temple until three days have [passed]. He shall wash his

[18] "Their sorrows." Yadin 1983 vol 1, 116. We prefer this translation against García Martínez interpretation "their strength." García Martínez, 1263. We admit to the difficulty of the translation. It seems, however, that the idea is to encourage the joy during the feasts and therefore not to eat during times of sorrow.

clothes and take a bath **9** on the first day. On the third day he shall wash his clothes /and take a bath/. After the sunset **10** he shall come into the temple. They shall not come into my temple with their unclean impurity and defile (it). **11** (*vacat*) If a man lies with his wife and has an ejaculation of semen, he shall not come into any part of the city of **12** the temple, where I will set my name, for three days. (*vacat*) No blind man **13** shall enter it (during) all of their days, so that they will not defile the city in which I dwell; **14** since I am LORD, who dwells among the children of Israel for ever and ever. (*vacat*)

15 Every man who cleanses himself of his discharge shall count for himself seven days for his cleansing, and wash his clothes on the seventh **16** day and bathe his whole body in running water. After (that) he shall come into the city of **17** the temple. Any one unclean (through contact with) the d/ea/d shall not enter until they have cleansed themselves. Any leper or **18** infected[19] person shall not enter it until he has cleansed himself. When he has been cleansed, he shall sacrifice … **46:01** […surely shall not enter into] **02** [the temple … trader / will be able] **03** [and into the temple…] **04** […ba]se of bronze […] to a base […] 1 […]®® ®[…all of it which (shall) no]t[…] **2** unclean bird over [my] templ[e which is in the inner courtyard and on] the roofs of the gates [of] **3** the outer courtyard. [No unclean bird shall] be [allowed] inside my temple for e[ver] **4** and ever, all the days that [I dwel]l among them. (*vacat*) **5** (*vacat*)

You shall make a terrace around, outside the outer courtyard **6** fourteen cubits wide, according to the entrances of all the gates and twelve **7** steps you shall make to it, for the children of Israel to ascend **8** as they come into my temple (*vacat*). **9** You shall make a trench around the temple, one hundred cubits wide that will **10** separate between the holy temple and the city, so that they shall not suddenly enter into **11** my temple (in order) not to desecrate it. They shall consecrate my temple and fear my temple **12** since I dwell among them. (*vacat*)

13 You shall make them a place of latrine outside the city unto which they shall go **14** out, to the northwest of the city, roofed houses with pits within them, **15** into which the excrement will go down (so that) /it will not/ be visible at any distance **16** from the city, three thou-

---

[19] We translate "infected" with García Martínez against Yadin's version "diseased." García Martínez, 1265; Yadin, 194.

sand cubits. (*vacat*) You shall make **17** three places to the east of the city, separated one from another, into which shall **18** come the lepers, and those who have a discharge, and the men who have had a (nocturnal) emission … **47:1** […]…[…] **2** […u]pwards and not downwar[ds…] (*vacat*)

3.2.11. The Temple City

3 [Let]their cities [be] clean and I shall establish my name in [their] midst for ever. The city **4** that I will consecrate by establishing my name and [my] temp[le within it], shall be holy and clean **5** of any unclean thing with which they may be defiled. Everything that is in it shall be **6** clean, and everything that will be brought to it shall be clean: wine, and oil, and all food, **7** and all the *mushké*[20] shall be clean.

Every skin from clean animals that will be slaughtered **8** within their cities, they shall not bring into it. Instead, in their cities they shall work **9** with these (hides in order) to (fill) all their needs. Into the city of my temple they shall not bring (thcm), **10** for as (unclean as) their flesh (is), (so) will their cleanness be. You shall not defile the city in which **11** I establish my name and my temple. (No), but in the skins (of the animals) that they will slaughter **12** in the temple, in them they shall bring their wine, and their oil, and all **13** their food to the city of my temple, so that they will not defile my temple with skins of their **14** detestable offerings, which they will sacrifice in their land. You shall not purify a skin **15** from your cities for my city, since as clean as the flesh is, as clean will the skins be. If **16** you slaughter it in my temple, it will be clean for my temple; but if you slaughter it in your cities, it will be clean **17** for your cities. All the pure items you shall bring in the temple skins, in order not to defile **18** my temple and my city in which I establish my name, with your detestable skins.

[20] This is probably a term for the food on which liquid was poured upon. Yadin, 203.

CHAPTER FOUR

A Comparison between the Scroll and Biblical Traditions

4.1. Aims

In this chapter we will develop the analysis from chapter two. The analysis will be placed into the following sections: 4.2 Biblical Quotations (BQ). 4.3 Biblical Paraphrase (BP). 4.4 Rewritten Bible (REWB). 4.5 Individual Composition (IC).[1] Since a deeper analysis of this last group easily becomes quite subjective, we will mainly deal with Individual Composition according to its quantity and not to its quality.[2]

Obviously, there are other possibilities to approach a division of the textual material.[3] We have chosen the present categories with similar definitions to compare the results from this study with the outcome of my dissertation. Secondly, more complex categories of textual material bring higher amounts of subjectivity.[4] Thus, we suggest that the chosen method is well suitable for dividing textual material in the context of parabiblical literature.

---

[1] Elledge advocates two main categories in his article: 1) Citation Formulae and 2) Commentary Formulae. Elledge 2003, 167. This classification is not suitable for the present study since the Temple Scroll does not contain any characteristics that could be identified in terms of Citation Formulae or Commentary Formulae.

[2] The method for this is explained in greater detail in section 4.5 Individual Composition.

[3] Saukkonen refers to the division of Jewish exegetical literature in three main categories: 1) Rewritten Scriptural Text, 2) Commentary, and 3) Anthological Style. Saukkonen 2005, 148. These categories are a good way to categorize the text, because the amount of subjective choice is low and the groups are few.

[4] Some examples of more subtle categories are presented: Kaufman divides the Scroll into at least six compositional patterns ranging from lengthy original composition – with no direct biblical source – to extended quotations of a single biblical text, 1) Original Composition, 2) Paraphrastic Conflation, 3) Fine Conflation, 4) Gross Conflation, 5) Modified Torah Quotation, and 6) Extended Torah Quotation. Kaufman 1982, 34. Wise uses 11 categories of analysis, which could be considered as a developed version of Kaufman's pattern. Wise's categories go from Free Composition to Extensive Verbatim Quotation. Wise 1990, 208-213.

In places it will be a matter of interpretation to make a distinction between BP, REWB, and IC. The line below shows the relationship between these categories and the biblical sources. There is greater dependency on the biblical sources in the direction of the arrow.

FIG. 1. DEPENDENCY ON BIBLICAL SOURCES

4.2. Biblical Quotations

In this analysis we will try to distinguish between primary and secondary[5] readings. In other words the text criticism will be developed in columns 29:3b–47:18 in the sections where biblical parallels have been found.

The cases where texts are similar to each other do not help us much, since we know that textual traditions often overlap. As a consequence, we are now interested in possible secondary readings. One of the aims for this section is to find passages with at least two readings – including the one in 11QT[6] – that agree with each other but disagree with the alternative considered as primary. Moreover, we are trying to find out as much as possible of the biblical text, from which the author was quoting from as he worked with this Scroll.[7]

When the textual material is re-analyzed we need to keep in mind that the comparison is sometimes limited to only half a line or even less. Thus, the possible answers we get may be based on a quite unsteady base. Owing to this, the data will reflect more a trend than an objective fact.

---

[5] It will be pointed out when the reading is interpreted as secondary.

[6] A secondary reading is defined as a later reading than the reading it is compared with, or as a less original reading, or sometimes even a less correct reading. On the other hand a secondary reading may also be the "more correct" one from the point of view of the reader. If this is the case, there is a reason to believe that the secondary reading has been created for grammatical or contextual reasons. Consequently, we will also try to give arguments for why a particular reading should be considered as secondary. Riska 2001, 147.

[7] If there is no reference to a biblical Qumran text, it means that the corresponding passage is not as yet found in Qumran or that it is too short to help us towards a meaningful analysis.

4.2.1. Column 34

Lines 11b–12a – Lev 1:8b: 11QT = 𝔐 = ⅏ = 𝔊 (376) ≠ 𝔊 (BA)
על (12) האש אשר על המזבח. In Lev 1:8b we read על־העצים אשר על־האש אשר על־המזבח. As we have noted in the text-critical analysis there is a minuscule MS, 376, which follows 𝔐 and ⅏, ἐπὶ τοῦ πυρὸς τοῦ ἐπὶ τοῦ θυσιαστηρίου. The 𝔊-reading according to B and A is slightly different since it reads τᾶ ὄντα *pro* τοῦ. It seems, however, that the variation does not stem from a different Hebrew text, but that it is a inner Greek variant due to another way of translating אשר.

Another example of this is found a little later, in Lev 1:12, which according to 𝔐 has the same reading as above, that is אשר על־האש אשר על־המזבח. In BA of the 𝔊, it reads ἐπὶ τοῦ πυρὸς τὰ ἐπὶ τοῦ θυσιαστηρίου and here we note even another variation of translating אשר.

4.2.2. Column 45

Line 15 – Lev 15:13a: 11QT = 𝔐 = ⅏ = 𝔊
מזובו וספר לו שבעת ימים לטהרתו. Lev 15:13a has וכי־יטהר הזב מזובו וספר לו שבעת ימים לטהרתו וכבס בגדיו. All the textual witnesses that are quoted in 11QT represent the same text tradition. The readings are identical with each other.

Line 16b – Lev 15:13b: 11QT = 𝔐 = ⅏ = 𝔊 (*reliqui*) ≠ 𝔊 (BA)
במים חיים. In Lev 15:13b we read ורחץ בשרו במים חיים וטהר. Firstly we note that 11QT agrees with 𝔐 and ⅏. In addition, we can note that 11QT tends to define commandments in a stricter manner than the Bible. Therefore, it is no surprise that the Scroll reads במים חיים. It is furthermore interesting to observe that B and A do not agree with some of the manuscripts of 𝔊 that read ὕδατι ζωντὶ. It is thus possible that this reading, of במים חיים, is a secondary reading. The shorter reading – ὕδατι or במים in the Hebrew *Vorlage* to 𝔊 – at times has a tendency of being the more original one.

4.2.3. Conclusion

We note that there are very few direct Biblical Quotations according to our definition in the text of this study. We conclude that the material contains two primary readings and a possible of secondary reading, ὕδατι ζωντὶ. Therefore, the low number of quotations brings our focus to the other categories.[8]

4.3. Biblical Paraphrase

In this section we will present those cases, from the text-critical analysis, that have been interpreted as BP.[9]

4.3.1. Column 29

Lines 7–8a – Ezek 43:27, Ex 29:45, Ezek 37:23
(7) ורציתים והיו לי לעם ואנוכי אהיה להם לעולם [ו]שכנתי (8) אתמה לעולם ועד. There are two biblical passages that are close to lines 7–8. The context of Ezek 43 deals with the temple, the altar, and its consecration. Sacrifices are brought forward by the priests so that God will accept the children of Israel – ורציתי אתכם. 11QT in general also speaks about sacrifices making the people acceptable in the eyes of God. In Ex, 29 the presence of the LORD among his people is the issue: ושכנתי בתוך בני ישראל. His presence, [ו]שכנתי אתמה, is also an important topic in the whole Col. 29. Concerning Ezek 37 the vocabulary is quite similar; but on the other hand the context is a little different. Ezek 37 has the context of deliverance whereas the Scroll has the context of offerings.

Even if the biblical passages above do not mention the expression לעולם ועד, these lines can be interpreted as BP.

Lines 9b–10a – Ex 15:17b
אברא אני את מקדשי (10) להכינו לי. In Ex 15:17b we read מקדש אדני כוננו ידיך. This is a good example of BP as the content – God builds, is the same but rephrased in the Scroll.

---

[8] That is Biblical Paraphrase, Rewritten Bible, and Individual Composition.
[9] Our definition for paraphrase is: 1) The original elements from the biblical text remain but are arranged in a new order. 2) No new ideas. 3) The context is the same as in the biblical text.

4.3.2. Column 34

Lines 7b–8a – Lev 1:5b

אֹ[ת כול הדם] במזרקות (8) וזורקים אותו עַל יסוד המזבח סביב. In Lev 1:5b we read וזרקו את־דם על־המזבח סביב. The end of line 7 is included even though it is a reconstruction because it completes our understanding of what was thrown around the base of the altar, the blood. Furthermore, we note that the Scroll describes the location more specifically, that is על יסוד. In the text-critical analysis we observed, that the passage is close to a quotation. The words, however, are in a different sequence; therefore we have interpreted this text as BP.

Lines 9b–10a – Lev 1:6a

ומנתחים (10) אותמה לנתחיהמה. When we compare this passage with Lev 1:6a ונתח אתה לנתחיה, we note that the Scroll systematically put numbers in plural. The content is close to a quotation but we have interpreted it as BP.

Lines 10b–11a – Lev 2:13a, 1:9a

ומולחים את הנתחים במלח ומרחצים את (11) הקרבים ואת הכרעים. When we match these lines with the Leviticus-passages – Lev 2:13a, וכל־קרבן מנחתך במלח תמלח and Lev 1:9a וקרבו וכרעיו ירחץ במים – we note that actually no new ideas are included in the Scroll. It does not use קרבן but it is implicitly implied. Therefore the passage is BP.

Lines 13b–14a – Lev 1:9b: 11QT ≈ 𝔊 ≠ 𝔐 ≈ ɯ

והקטירו הכוהנים בני אהרון את הכול (14) על המזבח אשה ריח ניחוח לפני יהוה. With regard to the beginning of this passage, we note that 𝔊 reads καὶ ἐπιθήσουσιν οἱ ἱερεῖς, which is adjacent to והקטירו הכוהנים. The verbs included in both textual traditions are, however, not lexically equivalent. Lev 1:9 has והקטיר הכהן את־הכל המזבחה עלה אשה ריח־ניחוח ליהוה. 𝔐 and ɯ are nearly identical with each other, apart from ɯ does not have את. From here to the end of line 14 we are close to a BQ. 𝔊 reads ἐπὶ το θυσιαστήεριον· κάρπωμα ἐστιν, θυσία, ὀσμὴ εὐωδίας τῷ κυρίῷ.[10] This is more similar to 11Q19 than 𝔐 and ɯ. Therefore the passage is understood as BP.

---

[10] The differences in 𝔐 in comparison with line 34:14 are המזבחה *pro* על המזבח and ליהוה *pro* לפני יהוה.

4.3.3. Column 43

Lines 4b–5a – Lev 7:15
באלה הימים יאכל ולוא יני[חו] (5) ממנו שנה לשנה אחרת. In Lev 7:15 we read ביום קרבנו יאכל לא יניח ממנו עד־בקר. The same verb with negation is used here both in the Scroll and Lev 7. We interpret this as BP.

Lines 10b–12a – Ex 29:34
וכול אשר (11) נותר ממועדיהמה יקדש באש ישרף לוא יאכל עוד (12) כי קדש. This passage has a longer parallel in Ex 29:34, that is ואם־יותר מבשר המלאים ומן־הלחם עד־הבקר ושרפת את־הנותר באש לא יאכל כי־קדש הוא. Since nothing new is presented in terms of content on lines 10b-12a, they are interpreted as BP.

4.3.4. Column 45

Lines 7–8a – Deut 23:11
וא[יש] כי יהיה לו מקרה לילה לוא יבוא אל (8) כול המקדש. In Deut 23:11 we read כי־יהיה בך איש אשר לא־יהיה טהור מקרה־לילה ויצא אל־מחוץ למחנה לא יבא אל־תוך המחנה. This passage is a good example of BP because we do not have any new elements in the text. We note that the Scroll deals with the מקדש *pro* the מחנה in Deut 23. However, we have considered it to be the same context according to our definition.

Line 11 – Lev 15:18a
ואיש כיא ישכב עם אשתו שכבת זרע. This passage is clearly a BP of the first half of verse 18, that is ואשה אשר ישכב איש אתה שכבת־זרע.

Lines 13b–14a – Num 5:3b: 11QT ≠ (≈) 𝔐 = ⅏ = 𝔊
ולוא יטמאו את העיר אשר אני שוכן (14) בתוכה. In Num 5:3b we read ולא יטמאו את־מחניהם אשר אני שוכן בתוכם. According to our definition of a quotation this passage does not qualify – even though it is close to one – because the object in the Scroll is העיר and corresponding biblical object is מחנה. Due to the plural of the camps, the Bible reads plural at the end of the verse, that is בתוכם / ἐν αὐτοῖς. ⅏ and 𝔊 agrees with 𝔐. The context is, however, the same as the issue is to keep the camp / city clean since God dwells in it. This is, therefore, understood as BP.

Line 15a – Lev 15:13a
וכול איש אשר יטהר. Lev 15:13a has וכי־יטהר. This is understood as BP.

4.3.5. Column 46

Line 11a – Lev 21:12a
ולוא יחללוהו. In comparison with Lev 21:12a, ולא יחלל את מקדש אלהיו, we note that it is BP.

Line 15b – Deut 23:15b
ולוא
תהיה נראה לכול רחוק. In Deut 23:15b we read ולא־יראה בך ערות דבר. The immediate context in the Scroll deals with the הצואה as Deuteronomy includes ערות. These two words have the same function in their context and thus we understand our passage as a BP.

Lines 17b–18 – Num 5:2a
אשר יהיו (18) באים המצורעים והזבים. A comparison to Num 5:2a, וישלחו מן־המחנה כל־צרוע וכל־צב, reveals that this is a BP.

4.3.6. Column 47

Line 5 – Lev 5:3a
לכול טמאה אשר יטמאו בה. In Lev 5:3a we read או כי יגע בטמאת אדם לכל טמאתו אשר יטמא בא. This is not far from being a quotation. However, according to the criteria of this study it is understood to be a BP.

Lines 10b–11 – Ezek 43:7b: 11QT ≈ 𝔊 ≠ 𝔐
אשר (11) אנוכי משכן את שמי ומקדשי בתוכה. 𝔐 of Ezek 43:7 reads אשר אשכן־שם בתוך בני־ישראל לעולם. 𝔊, on the other hand, has ἐν οἷς κατασκηνώσει τὸ ὄνομά μου ἐν μέσῳ ὄικου Ισραηλ τὸν αἰῶνα. The 𝔊 is a little closer to the Scroll. In any event this is paraphrase of the Bible. In any event, according to the criteria of this study it is BP.

4.3.7. Conclusion

In the examples of BP, which have been presented above, we are able to make the following observations concerning their most typical features in our study:

1) The same Hebrew stem that was used in the biblical text is preserved in the Scroll. The stem can be slightly changed, e.g. with an addition of a suffix, such as מקדש may appear as מקדשי.
2) Another quality for a BP can be that a number is changed. In terms of our examples, often the Scroll reads the number in plural when the Bible has it in singular.
3) Sometimes a section of the Scroll can be very close to a quotation but cannot be identified as such due to our strict definition of a quotation, i.e. it needs to be the same literally word by word. If the Scroll text includes a minor difference to the biblical text, i.e. a different tense or different suffix, it has been defined as BP. Synonymous words or expressions would have been expected to characterize paraphrase. According to the analysis, they were, however, not typical.

4.4. Rewritten Bible

4.4.1. Column 29

Lines 4–6 – Lev 23:37b-38, 1 Chr 23:31b, Lev 17:5a, Ex 28:38b
[ויקריבו בו] עולתׄ [יום] בׄיומו כתורת המשפט הזה (5) תמיד מאת בני ישראל לבד מנדבותׄמה לכול נדריהמה ולׄכול מתׄנותמה אשר יקרׄיבוׄ (6) לכול אשר יקרׄיבוׄ לכול נדריהמה וׄלׄכול מתׄנותמה אשר יבׄיאו לי לרצון לה[מה]. This is a rather long passage that seems to be influenced by several biblical texts. In Lev 23:37-38 we read להקריב אשה ליהוה עלה ומנחה זבח ונסכים דבר־יום ביומו (38) מלבד שבתת יהוה ומלבד מתנותיכם ומלבד כל־נדריכם ומלבד כל־נדבותיכם אשר תתנו ליהוה, and in 1 Chr 23:31b במספר כמשפט עליהם תמיד לפני יהוה. On lines 4–5 we may note inspiration from these passages, e.g. להקריב...דבר־יום ביומו and כמשפט עליהם תמיד.

In line 6 a known feature of the Temple Scroll can be observed. There is the change from third person to first person singular; so Lev

17:5a, והביאם ליהוה has changed to אשׁר יבׅיאו לי. At the end of the same line we see the influence of Ex 28:38b, תמיד לרצון להם לפני יהוה. Therefore we interpret lines 4–6 as REWB.

Line 8b – Ex 29:43b: 11QT ≈ 𝔊 ≠ 𝔐 = 𝔪

ואקדשה [את מ]קׄדשי בכבודי. Concerning Ex 29:43b, ונקדש בכבדי we have noted that 𝔪 agrees with 𝔐. In comparison with these readings, 𝔊 has a slightly different version as it reads καὶ ἁγιασθήσομαι ἐν δόξῃ μου. Since both the Scroll and 𝔊 have included the subject in the sentences, they seem to be a bit closer to each other in comparison with 𝔐 and 𝔪. From the point of view of 𝔊, we can conclude that this BP. From 𝔐 and 𝔪 viewpoints we conclude that this is REWB, because they lack the subject and because a new element has been included in the Scroll: the acting subject "I will."

Line 8b–9a – Ex 24:16a

אשר אשכין (9) עליו את כבודי. In Ex 24:16a we read וישכן כבוד־יהוה על־הר סיני. The context is different with the plans for a temple in the future in the Scroll compared to Moses going up to the mountain top in Exodus. It is, therefore, understood as REWB.

Line 10 – Gen 28:19a, Lev 26:42a

כברית אשר כרתי עֽם יׄעׄקוב בבית אל. In Gen 28: 19 we read ויקרא את־שם־המקום ההוא בית־אל and in Lev 26:42a, וזכרתי את־בריתי יעקוב. This is REWB.

4.4.2. Column 31

Line 8–9a – 1 Kgs 6:21a

(8) [כו]לׄ בית המסבה הזואת צפו זהב קירותיו ושעׄרׄיׄו וגגו מבׅית (9) [ומ]חוץ ועמודו ומעלותיו. We have noted that צפו זהב is part of the terminology for building the temple. In 1 Kgs 6:21a we find a similar sentence, ויצף שלמו את־הבית מפנימה זהב סגור. Nonetheless, the expression צפו זהב is not found in the Bible. This is, therefore, understood as REWB.

Line 9b – Ezek 44:5a: 11QT ≈ 𝔐 = 𝔊

ועשה ככול אשר אנוכי מדבר אליכה. In Ezek we read ובאזניך שמע את כל־אשר אני מדבר אתך and 𝔊 we read καὶ τοῖς ὠσίν σου ἄκουε πάντα, ὅσα ἐγὼ λαλῶ μετὰ σοῦ. This passage is very close to a quotation but cannot be interpreted as such since the context is different. It is, therefore, regarded as REWB.

Line 10a – Ex 30:18, 1 Kgs 7:39b
ועשיתה בית לכיור נגב מזרׄחׄ מרובע. In Ex 30:18 we read ועשית כיור נחשת וכנו נחשת לרחצה ונתת אתו בין־אהל מועד ובין המזבח and in 1 Kgs 7:39b ואת־הים נתן מכתף הבית הימנית קדמה ממול נגב. However, the expression בית לכיור is not found in the Bible. In the text-critical analysis we noticed that Ex speaks about the כיור and 1 Kgs mentions the ים. It is interesting, however, that both the Scroll and 1 Kgs mention the same positioning, that is south-east. Line 10 is interpreted as REWB.

4.4.3. Column 32

Lines 10b–12a – Ezek 42:14a
אשר֯ יהיו מניחים עליהמה (11) את בגדיהמׄה אשר יהי[ו באי]ם֯ [בה]ם למעלה מ֯על ל֯ביׄת ה֯[ ] (12) בׄבׄואם לׄשׄרׄת בקודש. For the comparison we notc that Ezek 42:14a reads ושם יניחו בגדיהם אשר־ישרתו בהן. Due to the additional information on line 11, we cannot interpret lines 10 and 12 as BP. This passage is, therefore, understood as REWB.

4.4.4. Column 33

Lines 6b–7 – Ezek 44:19a
ו֯ה֯יוצאים ב֯המה אלׄ [החצר התיכונה ולוא] (7) י֯ה֯י֯ו֯ מקדשים את עמׄיׄ בׄבגדיׄ הקׄוׄדׄש . In Ezek 44:19a we read ובצאתם אל־החצר החיצונה ... אל־העם יפשטו את־בגדיהם אשר־המה משרתם בם והניחו אותם בלשכת הקדש. The common denominator here is the movement and the mentioning of clothes. This is REWB.

Line 11b – Ezek 40:16a: 11QT ≈ 𝔐 ≈ 𝔊
חלונים פנימה אטומים. In Ezek 40:16 we read וחלנות אטמות אל־התאים ואל אליהמה לפנימה לשער סביב סביב וכן לאלמות and in 𝔊 we read καὶ θυρίδες κρυπταὶ. The contexts in line 11b and Ezek are different: when Ezekiel refers to the chambers, the Scroll is referring to the house of laver. This is REWB. It is, however, interesting to note the closeness of the expressions in both texts, which tends towards, but not significantly, to BP.

Lines 13–15a – Ex 27:3a, 38:3a, Num 4:14a

(13) מדולתים בתים לכלי המזבח למׄזורקים ולקשוא֯ה ולׄמׄחתות (14) ולכוננות הכסף אשר יהיו מעלׄים במׄה את הקרבים ואת (15) הר֯גלים על המזבח. At the beginning of line 13 we observe the only known occurrence of מדולתים. In comparison with the biblical texts we note the following passages: in Ex 27:3a we read ועשיתה סירתיו לדשנו ויעיו ומזרקתיו ומזלגתיו ומחתתיו, in Ex 38:3a ויעש את־כל־כלי המזבח את־הסירת ואת־היעים ואת־המזרקת ואת־המזלגת ואת־המחתת, and in Num 4:14a ונתנו עליו את־כל־כליו אשר ישרתו עליו בהם את־המחתת את־המזלגת ואת־היעים ואת־המזרקת כל כלי המזבח. They are speaking of different buildings, compared to line 11. This is REWB.

4.4.5. Column 35

Line 2a – Lev 21:18a: 11QT = (53*-129) ≠ 𝔐 = ɯ = 𝔊(B)

כול איש אשר לוׄא. In Lev 21:18a we read כי כל־איש אשר־בו מום לא יקרב. This is close to being quotation. However, the context is probably different. We cannot be sure, since the column has suffered tear damage. On the other hand, we know that the holy of holies is mentioned on line 1. We therefore understand this passage as REWB.

Line 3 – Lev 21:18a, 22:3a

כול איש אׄשר לוׄא[ק]ו֯דש. In Lev 22:3a we read אל־הקדשים כל־איש אשר־יקרב מכל־זרעכם, which is part the laws prohibiting for the unclean from approaching the altar. Since there is a need for restoration with the Scroll, we are prevented from saying too much about this passage, other than it is nearly identical with line 2. We understand it as REWB.

Line 7b – Lev 21:12a

ולוא יחׄל[לו את מק]ד֯ש אלוהׄיהמה. This passage does not meet our definition of a quotation.[11] However, we have it as if it was a Biblical Quotation because it is so close to a citation. Nonetheless, we will not include it in our statistics of Biblical Quotations.

In Lev 21:12a we read ולא יחלל את מקדש אלהיו. Our comparison in this case is concentrated on the last word only, אלוהׄיהמה. The rest of

[11] The context is not the same. See the text-critical analysis.

the line above is very similar to Lev 21:12a, apart from the verb that has been restored into plural, due to the context.[12]

אלוהׂיהמה is matched by the equivalent reading in a 𝔊-reading from the *f*-group. This textual parallel is τοῦ θεοῦ αὐτῶν. There is difference in number but this is not caused by plural of the verb in 𝔊, because this is in singular. In any event, the last word in line 7b is equal to the reading of 53*-129 and this reading is understood as a secondary reading because it is a variant resulting from contextual and grammatical reasons.

Lines 7b–8a – Lev 22:16a

לשאת (8) עֿוון אשמה למות. At the end of line 7 and at the beginning of line 8 we have a passage that is close to Lev 22:16a, והשיאו אותם עון אשמה באכלם את־קדשיהם. The biblical context is the person allowed to eat of the offerings whereas the Scroll's context deals with the issue of profaning the sanctuary by improper clothing. Therefore, as there is difference in content and context, we understand this as REWB.

Lines 8–9a – Ex 30:29a, 40:10b

וקדשת{מ}ה את סֿ[בי]ב למזבח ולהיכל ולכיֿוֿר (9) וֿלֿפֿרוֿר והיה קודש קודשים לעולם ועד. In Ex 30:29a we have וקדשת אתם והיו קדש קדשים and 40:10b we have וקדשת את־המזבח והיה המזבח קדש קדשים. These verses from the Bible both refer to the consecration of the altar or the utensils. Since the Scroll also mentions the word פרור,[13] we understand lines 8-9a as REWB.

Lines 10–11a – Ezek 46:19b-20a

(10) ועשיתה מקום למערב ההיכל סביב פֿרור עמודים עומדים (11) לחטאת ולאשם מובדלים זה מזה. In Ezek 46:19b-20a we read as follows: והנה־שם מקום בירכתם ימה (20) ויאמר אלי זה המקום אשר יבשלו־שם הכהנים את־אשם ואת־החטאת. The words in common between the Scroll and Ezekiel are מקום, ימה / מערב, and חטאת and אשם. However, there is also once again פרור, which makes lines 10–11a REWB.

[12] See also the text-critical analysis of line 35:7.

[13] פרור is not extant in the Bible in the meaning of "stoa" as it is used in the Scroll. On the other hand, the Bible has פָּרוּר in the meaning of "pot" (e.g. Num 11:8, Judg 6:19).

Line 15b – Lev 1:14

והעוף על המזבח יעשה התורים. We need to bear in mind that a dot or a semi-colon is very likely after יעשה. Thus התורים belong to the next sentence. In Lev 1:14 we read ואם מן־העוף עלה קרבנו ליהוה והקריב מן־התרים או מן־בני היונה את־קרבנו. There is undeniably a connection between these texts. However, as there is also new information included, we understand line 15b as REWB.

4.4.6. Column 36

Line 8 – Ezek 40:48b: 11QT ≈ 𝔊 ≠ 𝔐

והׄ[יו]צאים במה רוחב השער ארבע [עש]רׄה באמה. In Ezek 40:48 of 𝔊 we read τὸ εὖρος τοῦ θυρώματος πηχῶν δέκα τεσσάρων. In the text-critical analysis we have observed that 𝔐 does not include the measurement, ארבע עשרה. In addition we have observed that the biblical context is the vestibule entrance of the temple and the Scroll's context is one of the gates of the inner court. It is, however, interesting that 𝔊 includes the same measurement as the Scroll. This is REWB.

4.4.7. Column 37

Line 5a – Lev 10:14

[שמה א]ת֯ זׄבחׄיׄ שלמי בני ישראל. In Lev 10:14 we read ואת שוק התרומה תאכלו במקום טהור אתה ובניך ובנתיך אתך כי־חקך וחק־בניך נתנו מזבחי שלמי בני ישראל. We note that line 37:5a looks like a BQ of the end of Lev 10:14. The context in the Scroll, however, concerns the building of different structures and Lev 10 deals with instructions for priests. We, therefore, conclude that זבחי שלמי בני ישראל is a kind of formula, used for different circumstances. This is understood as REWB.

Line 13a – Ezek 46:22a

ובארבעת מקצועות הׄחצר. In Ezek 46:22a we read בארבעת מקצועות החצר חצרות קטרות. This is also close to a BQ. It will, however, be interpreted as REWB, because 37:13a still deals with building stoves this time and Ezek 46:22a is a part of Ezekiel's vision.

4.4.8. Column 39

Line 5b – Gen 15:16a

] דור רביע֯י֯. In Gen 15:16a we read ודור רביעי ישובו הנה. Since the context is different, we understand line 5b to be REWB instead of a BQ.

Lines 8–11a – Ex 30:12-13, 16b

חוק [ ] נ֯פ֯ש֯ו֯ ליהוה מחצית השקל [ ] (9) לזכרון ב֯מ֯ו֯ש֯ב֯ו֯ת֯י֯ה֯מ֯ה֯ ע֯ש֯ר֯י֯ם֯ ג֯ר֯ה֯ ה֯ש֯ק֯ל֯ (*vacat*) (10) וכאשר ישא֯ו֯ ממנ֯ו֯ את מחצית ה֯ש[ק]ל֯ [ישבע] לי אחר יבואו מבן (11) עשרי֯ם֯ [שנה] ולמעלה. In Ex 30:12-13 we read ונתנו איש כפר נפשו ליהוה בפקד אתם ולא־יהיה בהם נגף בפקד אתם (13) זה יתנו כל־העבר על־הפקדים מחצית השקל בשקל הקדש עשרים גרה השקל and in Ex 30:16b we read והיה לבני ישראל לזכרון לפני יהוה לכפר על נפשתיכם. From these we note that there seems to be the same biblical influence on lines 8–11, for example, we find the expressions מחצית השקל and לזכרון. The expression בפקד אתם, however, is a new element in comparison with the biblical passage. Therefore we understand lines 8–11a as REWB.

Lines 11b–12a – Ezek 48:31a

על ש֯מ֯[ות] (12) בני יש֯[ר]אל. The restoration of this passage is certain. In Ezek 48:31 we read ושערי העיר על־שמות שבטי ישראל. This is REWB.

Lines 12–16 – Ezek 48:31b-34

שמ֯עון ל֯וי ו֯יהודה בקדם מזרח֯ [ר]אובן יוסף ובנימין לנגב (13) דרום יש שכר זבולון וגד לים דן נפתל֯י֯ ו֯א֯ש֯ר֯ לצפון ו֯ב֯ין שער לשער (14) מדה מן פנה למזרח צפון עד שער שמ֯עון תש֯ע ותשעים באמה והשער (15) שמונה ועשרים באמה ומשער הזה עד שער {ₒₒₒₒₒ} לוי תשע ותשעים (16) באמה והשער שמונה ועשרים באמה ומשער לוי עד שע֯ר י֯הודה.

In Ezek 48: 31b-34 we read שער ראובן אחד שער יהודה אחד שער לוי אחד (32) ואל־פאת קדימה חמש מאות וארבעת אלפים ושערים שלשה ושער יוסף אחד שער בנימן אחד שער דן אחד (33) ופאת־נגבה חמש מאות וארבעת אלפים מדה ושערים שלשה שער שמעון אחד שער יששכר אחד שער זבולן אחד (34) פאת־ימה חמש מאות וארבעת אלפים שעריהם שלשה שער גד אחד שער אשר אחד שער נפתלי אחד. The tribes are listed in different orders. However, there are similarities and so we understand it as REWB.

4.4.9. Column 40

Lines 1–2 – Lev 6:4a, Ezek 44:19, Num 17:17a, Ex 29:30a

(1) [ ]ללבוש את הב[גדים] (2) [ ]ה להיות נש[י]א תח]ת אהרון. There are several passages from the Bible that are relevant to compare with: Lev 6:4a, ופשט את־בגדיו ולבש בגדים אחרים; Ezek 44:19, יפשטו את־בגדיהם אשר־המה משרתם בם והניחו אותם בלשכת הקדש ולבשו בגדים אחרים; Num 17:17a וקח מאתם מטא מטא לבית אב מאת כל־נשיאהם לבית אבתם שנים עשר מטות and Ex 29:30a, שבעת ימים ילבשם הכהן תחתיו מבניו. The common vocabulary shared with these biblical verses, e.g., בגדים, נשיא, תחת, make it possible to understand this as REWB.

Lines 10–11a – Ezek 42:7a

[ע]שוים בוׄ לשעריו מחוץ לעומת המוסד (11) עד עטׄרותׄיׄו. In Ezek 42:7a we read וגדר אשר־לחוץ לעמת הלשכות דרך החצר החיצונה אל־פני הלשכות. Due to common terminology we understand this passage as REWB.

4.4.10. Column 42

Lines 9–10 – 1 Kgs 6:6a, Ezek 42:5-6

ונשכות בנוית וחדריהמה ופרוריהמה כתחתונות (10) שניות ושלישיות כמדת התחתונות. Three levels of chambers are presented here. For this we find comparison with two biblical parallels, in 1 Kgs 6:6a, היצוע התחתנה חמש באמה רחבה והתיכנה שש באמה רחבה והשלישית שבע באמה רחבה, and in Ezek 42:5-6, (5) והלשכות העליונת קצרות כי־יוכלו אתיקים מהנה מהתחתנות ומהתכנות בנין (6) כי משלשות הנה ואין להן עמודים כעמודי החצרות על־כן נאצל מהתחתונות ומהתיכנות מהארץ. The terminology used in both the Scroll and the biblical passage is similar. This is REWB.

Line 13 – Zech 14:16b

בכול שנה ושנה בחג הסוכות. This is in fact a *terminus tecnicus*. In Zech 14:16b we read ועלו מדי שנה בשנה להשתחות למלך יהוה צבאות ולחג את־חג הסכות. The context in both 11QT and Zechariah is the feast of booths and the expressions are close to each other. However, the activity described in the passages is different, that is building booths in the Scroll and pilgrimage to Jerusalem in the Bible. Line 13 is understood as REWB.

Lines 14–15 – Num 7:2

(14) העדה לנשיאים לראשי בתי האבות לבני ישראל (15) ולשרי אלפים ולשרי המאיות. In Num 7:2 we read ויקריבו נשיאי ישראל ראשי בית אבתם הם נשיאי המטת הם העומדים על־הפקדים. We note that the context is different, i.e. the offering in Numbers and dedication of booths in the Scroll. On the other hand, it is likely that the terminology in 11QT concerning the party of the leaders, is dependent on the Bible. This is REWB.

Lines 16–17a – Lev 23:42, Neh 8:17

(16) ויושבים שמה עד {ע}הלות את עולת המועד אשר (17) לחג הסוכות שנה בשנה. (superscript ע above {ע}) In Lev 23:42 we have בסכות תשבו שבעת ימים כל־האזרח בישראל ישבו בסכות and Neh 8:17 reads ויעשו כל־הקהל השבים מן־השבי סכות וישבו בסכות כי לא־עשו מימי ישוע בן־נון כן בני ישראל עד היום ההוא ותהי שמחה גדולה מאד. Especially Leviticus is close to our passage. However, since the burnt-offering is mentioned on line 16 and not in Lev we understand this to be REWB.

4.4.11. Column 43

Line 5b – Ex 12:11a

ככה יהיו אוכלים אותו. In Ex 12:11a we read ככה תאכלו אותו, which is a parallel from a grammatical point of view. However, Exodus deals with the passover and line 43:5b relates to the feast of booths. Since the context is not the same, this is understood as REWB.

Lines 12–16a – Deut 14:24-26, Ex 3:18b

והיושבים במרחק מן המקדש דרך שלושת (13) ימים כול אשר יוכלו לבהיא יביאו ואם לא יוכלו (14) לשאתו ומכרוהו בכסף והביאו את הכסף ולקחו בו דגן (15) ויין ושמן ובקר וצאון ואכלוהו בימי המועדים ולוא (16) יואכלו ממנו. We can see that this extensive passage is influenced by Deut 14:24-26, (24) וכי־ירבה ממך הדרך כי לא תוכל שאתו כי־ירחק ממך המקום אשר יבחר יהוה אלהיך לשום שמו שם כי יברכך יהוה אלהיך (25) ונתתה בכסף וצרת בכסף בידך והלכת אל־המקום אשר יבחר יהוה אלהיך בו (26) ונתתה הכסף בכל אשר־תאוה נפשך בבקר ובצאן וביין ובשכר ובכל אשר תשאלך נפשך ואכלת שם לפני יהוה אלהיך ושמחת אתה וביתך. It is also possible that the limitation of three days may have some link to Ex 3:18b, that is ועתה נלכה־נא דרך שלשת ימים במדבר ונזבחה ליהוה אלהינו. The context in Exodus is, however, so different that we cannot treat שלשת ימים as a quotation. Hence, lines 12–16 are interpreted as REWB.

Lines 17b – Ezek 46:1a

בימי המעשה. An expression close to this is found only once in the biblical texts and that is in Ezek 46:1a, שער החצר הפנימית הפנה קדים יהיה סגור ששת ימי המעשה. The context is so different that we cannot understand it as BP. According to our definition it is REWB.

4.4.12. Column 44

Lines 5–7a – Ezek 40:46

(5) וכ֯[ו]ל֯ ימין שער לוי ושמאולו לבני אהרון אחיכה תח[לק] (6) שמונה ומאה נשכה וחדריהמה ושתי סוכותיהמה (7) אשר מעל הגג. In Ezek 40:46 we read והלשכה אשר פניה דרך הצפון לכהנים שמרי משמרת המזבח המה בני־צדוק הקרבים מבני־לוי אל־יהוה לשרתו. The design of the gates to the north and to the south of Levi's gate[14] is similar with Ezekiel's. We interpret lines 5-7a as REWB.

Line 14 – Jos 21:20

ומשער יוסף עד שער בנימין לבני קהת מ{ב}נ{י} הלויים. In Jos 21:20 we read ולמשפחות בני־קהת הלוים הנותרים מבני קהת ויהי ערי גורלם ממטה אפרים. The scribe first wrote מבני by mistake, and then afterwards corrected it to מנ by erasing the *beit* and *yod*. This could also be understood as IC. We have taken it as REWB because of בני־קהת that seems to be echoed in line 44:14.

4.4.13. Column 45

Lines 5b–6 – Neh 13:9a

ומטהרים את (6) הנשכות זואת אחרי זאות. In Neh 13:9a we read ואמרה ויטהרו הלשכות, which is not far from the reading in the Scroll. This is, therefore, REWB. It is also worth noting the peculiar spelling difference concerning the repeated זואת on the same line.

---

[14] See also Yadin 1983 vol. 1, 267.

Lines 8–9 – Ex 19:10-11

עד אשר [יש]לים שלושת ימים וכבס בגדיו (9) ביום הראישון וביום השלישי ורחץ
יכבֹּס בגדיו ובאה.

In Ex 19:10-11 we read (10) ויאמר יהוה אל־משה לך אל־העם וקדשתם היום ומחר וכבסו שמלתם (11) והיו נכנים ליום השלישי כי ביום השלישי ירד יהוה לעיני כל־העם על־הר סיני. Line 9 with יכבֹּס seems to be influenced by Ex 19. In any event the Scroll has the supralinear ורחץ. We note, however, that the contexts are quite different: the Scroll deals with a nocturnal emission, whereas Exodus tells about the preparations for receiving the Ten Commandments. Due to this and the addition of ורחץ we interpret the passage as REWB.

Lines 12b–13a – Lev 21:18, 2 Sam 5:8b

כול איש עור (13) לוא יבואו לה כול ימיהמה. In Lev 21:18 we read כי כל־איש אשר בו מום לא יקרב איש עור או פסח או חרום או שרוע and in 2 Sam 5:8b we have על־כן יאמרו עור ופסח לא יבוא אל־הבית. It is not unusual for the Scroll to be stricter in its halakhic rulings than the biblical texts. In this situation it is the other way around as Lev 21 contains more limitations on those who can enter the city. Furthermore, 2 Sam 5:8b shows that the ban is extended to all of Israel and not only to the priests. We understand this as REWB.

Line 14 – Ex 15:18

כי אני יהוה שוכן בתוך בני ישראל לעולם ועד. In Ex 15:18 we read יהוה ימלך לעלם ועד. The expression at the end of line 14, לעלם ועד, is a common phrase and can not really be taken as a quotation. We understand the whole passage as REWB.

Lines 15b–16a – Lev 15:13b: 11QT ≠ 𝔐 = 𝔊 ≈ ⅏

ויכבס ביום (16) השביעי בגדיו ורחץ את כול בשרו. In Lev 15:13b we read ורחץ בשרו במים חיים וטהר. The tense of the verb ויכבס in the Scroll – consecutive imperfect – is unlike וכבס – the consecutive perfect in 𝔐 and ⅏. The passage 45:15b-16a has an additional ביום השביעי in relation to the biblical traditions. At the end of this passage there is a minor difference between 𝔐 and ⅏, where ⅏ reads את. This word interestingly is included in line 16a. On the other hand, 11QT is stricter since it adds the word כול. In the light of the analysis above, we note that 11QT has additional details – perhaps in order to explain – and is, therefore, interpreted as REWB.

Lines 17–18a – Num 5:2

(17) המקדש וכול טמא ל נפש לוא יבואו לה עד אשר יטהרו וכול צרוע (18) ומנוגע לוא יבואו לה עד אשר יטהרוׄ[15]. In Num 5:2 we read צב את־בני ישראל וישלחו מן־המחנה כל־צרוע וכל־זב וכל טמא לנפש. The context in the Temple Scroll speaks about cleansing and Num deals with sending away the unclean.

Line 18b – Lev 14:10-12a

וכאשר יטהר והקריב את. In Lev 14:10-12a we read (10) וביום השמיני יקח שני־כבסים תמימים וכבסה אחת בת־שנתה תמימה ושלשה עשרנים סלת מנחה בלולה בשמן ולג אחד שמן (11) והעמיד הכהן המטהר את האיש המטהר ואתם לפני יהוה פתח אהל מועד (12) ולקח הכהן את־הכבס האחד והקרוב אתו לאשם ואת־לג השמן. The end of line 18 is a very short variety of Lev 14. On the other hand line 45:18b discusses cleansing and sacrifice. Therefore, we understand this as REWB.

4.4.14. Column 46

Line 4a – 1 Sam 20:31a, 2 Chr 6:31a

ועד כול הימים אשר אׄ[ני שוכ]ן בתוכׄםׄ. In 1 Sam 20:31a we read כי כל־הימים אשר בן־ישי חי and in 2 Chr 6:31a we have כל־הימים אשר־הם חיים על־פני האדמה. We note that the biblical expressions are not used in the same context as in line 46:4a and is, therefore, regarded as REWB.

Lines 9b–10a – Lev 16:33a

אשר יהיה (10) מבדיל בין מקדש הקודש לעיר. In Lev 16:33a we have וכפר־את מקדש הקדש ואת־אהל מועד. The context is different with desecration in the Temple Scroll and atonement in Lev 16. Therefore, we understand this as REWB.

---

[15] The dot above *waw* is a cancellation dot. See also the text-critical analysis.

Lines 10b–11a – Num 4:20

ולוא יהיו באים בלע אל תוך (11) מקדשי. In Num 4:20 we read ולא־יבאו לראות כבלע את־הקדש ומתו. The context is desecration in lines 46:10b–11a and death in Num 4:20. Therefore, we understand this as REWB.

Line 11b – 2 Chr 29:5b, Lev 19:30

וקדשו את מקדשי ויראו ממקדשי. In 2 Chr 29:5b we read וקדשו את־בית יהוה אלוהי אבתיכם והוציאו את־הנדה מן־הקדש. Lev 19:30 has את־שבתתי תשמרו ומקדשי תיראו אני יהוה. The passage, 46:11b, does not include the verb קדש. The context in 2 Chr is Hezekiah cleansing the temple. The passage of the Scroll deals, on the other hand, with the limitations to desecrate the temple during construction. Since the context is different we understand this as REWB.

Line 12a – Ex 24:16a

אשר אנוכי שוכן בתוכמה. In Ex 24:16a we read וישכן כבוד־יהוה על־הר סיני. This is interpreted as REWB.

Line 13–14 – Deut 23:13

(13) ועשיתה להמה מקום יד חוץ מן העיר אשר יהיו יוצאים שמה (14) לחוץ לצפון המערב לעיר בתים ומקורים. In Deut 23:13 we read ויד תהיה לך מחוץ למחנה ויצאת שמה חוץ. We are close to a BP in this passage. The Scroll deals with the עיר whereas Deuteronomy tells about the מחנה. The passage 46:13-14 has stricter commands than the biblical text: i.e. it is not enough to only take it outside the city / camp – the refuse should also not be noticeable to those who pass by. This is REWB.

Lines 16b–17 – Deut 19:2-4a

עשיתה (17) שלושה מקומות למזרח העיר מובדלים זה מזה. In Deut 19:2-4 we read (2) שלוש ערים תבדיל לך בתוך ארצך אשר יהוה אלהיך נתן לך לרשתה (3) תכין לך הדרך ושלשת את־גבול ארצך אשר ינחילך יהוה אלהיך והיה לנוס שמה כל־רצח (4) וזה דבר הרצח אשר־ינוס שמה וחי. Since the use of language is quite close in style we understand our passage as REWB instead of IC.

4.4.15. Column 47

Line 2a – Deut 28:13a

ל]מעלה ולוא למט[ה. In Deut 28:13a we read ונתנך יהוה לראש ולא לזנב והיית רק למעלה ולא תהיה למטה. Since we do not know the immediate context in the Temple Scroll we do not know how close the passages are to each other. Nevertheless, we interpret this as REWB.

Line 4a – Ex 24:16

אשר אקדיש לשכין שמי ומקד[שי בתוכה]. In Ex 24:16 we read וישכן כבוד־יהוה על־הר סיני. This is also understood as REWB.

4.4.16. Conclusion

In the examples of REWB, which have been presented above, we are able to make the following observations:

1) The feature occurring most often in the passages of REWB in the Temple Scroll is the change of the LORD speaking in third person to first person singular.[16]
2) The most common quality of REWB in this part of the Scroll seems, however, to be differences in context. A text may be very close to a BQ, but since the context is different compared to the Bible, it has been designated as REWB. An example of this, is Lev 10 with the context to present instructions for priests and line 37:5a with the context dealing with building of different structures.
3) Another example of REWB is when the Scroll uses specific vocabulary, for example פרור.

[16] Since this characteristic is repeated several times and systematically we understand it as REWB and not as BP.

4.5. Individual Composition

At the beginning of chapter four, the text of Cols. 29:3b–47:18 was classified into four categories: BQ, BP, REWB, and IC. IC is composed of the rest of the textual material that has not been categorised so far.[17] A comparison of this analysis with the other three groups will be presented in section 6.2.

As we go through the previous analysed material above we note that there are three columns that, according to our definitions, contain neither BQ, BP, nor REWB at all: these are Cols. 30, 38, and 41. They are, therefore, entirely interpreted as IC. In this study we are basically interested in the quantity of IC, since a detailed analysis of IC would add a lot of subjectivity to the results.

There are longer and shorter passages of IC in the other columns than the three columns interpreted as totally IC. We will now go, in order, through all the columns to get a qualified estimation[18] concerning the amount of IC in every column. We will do this by estimating the number of lines of IC.[19]

We will measure the length of the lines as the number of lines above does not give us sufficient information for a comparison. Hence we need an approximate average for the length of the lines in a column in order to obtain a meaningful result. The amount of the textual material in a category is obtained through multiplication of the average approximate length of a line (Ã) and the amount of lines, e.g. Col. 30: 11.5 x 5.7 (4.7 + 1 complete line) = 65.55. In conclusion, the IC material will be added together in order to get the total sum for the total amount of IC in our study. The results are presented in the table below:

---

[17] If the whole text is given the symbol T, we get the following formula for IC: IC = T – (BQ + BP + REWB).

[18] We are aware that the division of a text into groups always includes an element of subjectivity. Therefore, it would be problematic to speak with certainty in terms of the amount of e.g. BQ or REWB.

[19] The number for the lines is received in the following way: the unrestored textual material that does not belong to BQ, BP, or REWB, is measured in cm and divided by Ã (Ã is an average rounded to the nearest 0.5 cm measured from the text in section 3.1.) in order to get the result. To this number the amount of complete IC lines (with no restoration nor BQ / BP / REWB) is added: since we are interested in the amount of lines, it is reasonable to count a complete line as one line and not measure its length.

Column	29	30	31	32	33	34	35	36	37
Ã[20]	10.0	11.5	11.0	11.0	10.5	11.0	10.0	9.5	9.5
Lines	X[21]	5.7	5.4	6.5	6.0	6.5	5.9	9.1	8.3
IC	9.3	65.55	59.4	71.5	63.0	71.5	59.0	86.45	78.85

Column	38	39	40	41	42	43	44	45	46	47
Ã	11.5	10.5	11.5	8.5	8.0	8.5	8.5	11.0	10.5	10.0
Lines	7.7	X	8.5	12.5	11.5	7.2	10.0	5.4	7.4	13.8
IC	88.55	33.6	97.75	106.25	92.0	61.2	85.0	59.4	77.7	138.0

Sum of IC	1403.7 ≈ **1404**

TABLE 1. SUMMARY OF INDIVIDUAL COMPOSITION

As we take a look at the results we will not jump to conclusions too quickly. We are aware that a low amount of IC may depend on, for example, the small amount of survived lines. The textual quantity can easily be checked from section 3.1.

In any event it is interesting to have something for comparison. From the table above we note the following: 1) Col. 29 contains the lowest amount of IC. This is partly explained by the fact that the column both contains BP and REWB and that it is the shortest column. 2) Cols. 41 and 47 have a higher number than 100. This mostly resulted because these columns do not have as much textual material from the other categories. 3) Col. 47 has clearly the most IC of all the columns – that is 138 – because it has a reasonable amount of survived lines, which are quite long. Col. 41 mainly tells about the measurement between the different gates of the outer court and Col. 47 deals with purity issues in the temple city. Therefore, the high level of IC is not surprising.

The sum of IC of all the columns is 1404. This is a result of all the IC material in our study taken together. In the final chapter we will compare this number with the amount of the textual mass of the other categories.

[20] Average approximate length of lines in cm.

[21] The X-letter indicates that the column does not contain complete lines and the sum below is received by adding the length of the incomplete lines.

CHAPTER FIVE

The Courtyards

5.1. Aims

The material concerning the temple courtyards of 11QT is not in the biblical text-tradition. However, a comparison with the Bible could show us whether there has been any indirect influence on the temple courtyards in the Scroll. In this chapter only material from 11QT and the Bible will be considered. It is known, that Josephus has also written about Solomon's temple. However, his descriptions are not taken into account, because they at times seem to be dubious.[1]

In the following sections I will firstly describe the courtyards in the Temple Scroll. Then secondly, we will consider the biblical material concerning the courtyards in chronological order: the courtyards of the tabernacle and of the temple in the vision of Ezekiel.[2] In the conclusion these entities will be compared with each other.[3]

---

[1] Marcus mentions in footnote "c" the following before the section Ant. viii:95 begins: "The following unscriptural account of the temple courtyards etc. is probably based on Josephus' knowledge of the temple of Herod." Josephus 1977, 622. Yadin claims, that "in his description of Solomon's Temple Josephus drew upon the description in our scroll (that is 11QT), but also interpolated details from the Temple of his own day." Yadin 1983 vol 1, 194. As a consequence of what is written above the data provided by Josephus will be left out of this study.

[2] The tabernacle is presented here because of its function. It was the temple for the wandering Jewish people in the wilderness. The temple of Ezekiel will also be described even if it never was an actual building. This is actually the case with the temple in 11QT: it is only a theoretical building.

[3] Chyutin's publication "The New Jerusalem Scroll from Qumran" (1997) will not be referenced in this study apart from a few exceptional cases. This is due to the following reasons: 1) 11QT is here basically compared to biblical material. 2) It is hard to determine the number of courtyards. Chyutin states, "from the surviving fragments of the New Jerusalem Scroll it is difficult to reconstruct the number of courtyards and their description." Chyutin 1997, 37.

5.2. The Courtyards in the Temple Scroll

The commands to build the temple is given in the beginning of the Scroll, that is in line 3:4 יעשו לי בי]ת לשום שמי עליו. According to the Scroll, this seems to be an intermediate solution: the final sanctuary will be made by God himself on יום הבריה, as we read in lines 29:8b–9, אקדשה [את מ]קדשי בכבודי אשר אשׁכין (9) עליו את כבודי עד יום הבריה אשר אברא אני את מקדשי.

There is in fact little data concerning the temple.[4] As a consequence of that we will only give attention to what we know about the *courtyards* around the sanctuary. There are three courtyards to be built according to 11QT: the inner and the middle courtyard as described in line 38:12 ועשיתֹהֹ [ח]צר שנית סובבת אֹת הח]צר הפנ[ימית. In line 40:5 we read about the outer courtyard, that is the third courtyard: ועשיתה חצר שליש[י]ת.

5.2.1. The Inner Courtyard[5]

Since we want to describe the walls and be as exact as possible, it is worthwhile to note that פנה represents the outer corner of the wall and מקצוע describes the inner corner.[6]

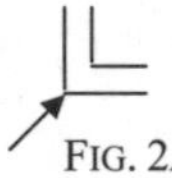

FIG. 2A OUTER CORNER

FIG. 2B INNER CORNER

Yadin points out, there is only one gate per sidewall of the inner courtyard. This is indicated from lines 36:12–13a: וּמפנת השער עד המקצוע השני לחצר עשרים (13) ומאה באמֹה. This states that the side in question only had one gate. From line 38:6 שער המערב it becomes clear that there also existed a gate to the west, with the result that the inner courtyard had four gates.[7] If these gates had names, they have not been preserved to us. In line 36:8 there

---

[4] Yadin has noted this and adds, that the author's "primary purpose was to describe the courtyards, since it was there that the main worship took place." Yadin 1983 vol. 1, 177.

[5] Yadin writes also about an additional inner wall, which is shown in his FIG. 5. This is due to line 37:9, בפרור הפנימי אצל קיר הֹחצֹר החיצון. Yadin 1983 vol. 1, 205-206. As there is no exact data concerning the measurements, the *locus* of this wall will not be developed.

[6] Yadin 1983 vol. 1, 204.

[7] Yadin 1983 vol. 1, 203.

is, however, information about their width: רוחב השער ארבע [עש]רה באמה.
On the other hand, Yadin shows convincingly, that this measurement could only concern the entrance of the gate, otherwise there would hardly be any space left when the walls and the chambers are brought into the picture.

We derive the total amount as 40 cubits[8] for the width of the gate with the help of the measurement of the chambers from lines 36:6-7a, ורוח]ב תא[יו] שש (7) ועשרים באמה and the thickness of the wall from line 36:5, ו[רו]חב קי[רו] שבע אמות.[9] As a result we get 26 + (2 x 7) = 40.

With the material above, we have the information for the Interior (ID) and Exterior (ED) Dimensions of the inner courtyard. These are for ID: (2 x 120) + 40 = 280 and for ED: thickness of wall, (2 x 7) in addition to (2 x 120) + 40 which equals 294.[10] Thus, the inner courtyard would appear as in FIG. 3:[11]

---

[8] All measurements from now on are presented in cubits (באמה or אמה), that is even if only the number is mentioned. The exception is the longer cubit that is designed with C.
[9] See detailed discussion in Yadin 1983 vol. 1, 201-202.
[10] Mink has 300 x 300 for the "inner forecourt": he seems to deduct the numbers with the help of the middle courtyard. Mink 1987, 40. Maier gives the following measurements of the ID: 280 x 280 and for ED: 300 x 300. Maier 1997, XLVI. He does not explain how he gets the result of 300 cubits for the external dimensions. These should correspond to 294 in Yadin's measurements.
[11] The temple and the buildings for the gates of the inner courtyard are here drawn with dotted lines, as they are not the objects of comparison. They are inserted only to give the reader a general picture of the dimensions. Concerning the gates belonging to the outer courtyard we know that they stood out from the wall itself. The reader should, however, note that Yadin in his Fig. 4 draws the gate to protrude by seven cubits. Yadin 1983 vol. 1, 202. This is based on his restoration of line 36:15, פנימה אל תוך החצר (15) [x אמות ויוצאים מקיר החצר y אמות]. Yadin, 156. To be able to do this, Yadin uses line 41:12 (the outer courtyard, see below) as a parallel. As we do not have any facts concerning the protruding gates of the inner courtyard, they will not be drawn. In addition to this, there is not any information about the 1600 cubits of the wall of the outer courtyard (see section 5.2.3) that would support a protruding gate on the inner wall.

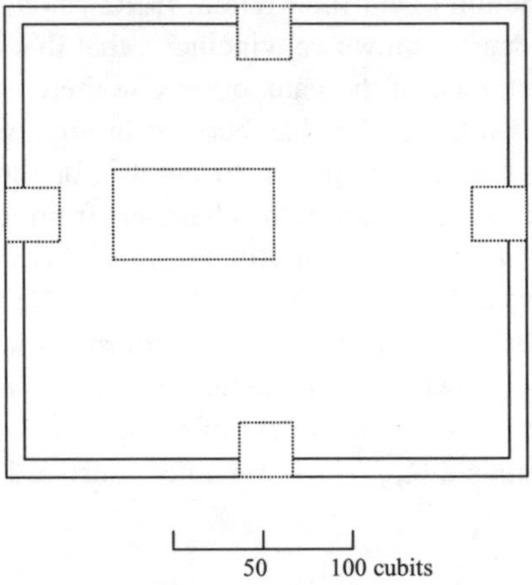

FIG. 3. THE INNER COURTYARD

5.2.2. The Middle Courtyard

In line 38:12 we have the command to build a "second courtyard." The location of the wall of this courtyard comes later on the same line, רחוב מאה באמה. This gives us a distance of 100 cubits between the walls of the inner and the middle courtyard.[12] From lines 38:13-14a we get the length of these walls, that is ואורך לרוח הקדם שמונים וארבע מאות באמה וככה רוחב ואורך לכול רוחותיה לנגב ולים ולצ צפון (14).[13] The thickness of this wall is written on line 38:14, that is ורוחב קירה [אר]בע אמות.[14]

The Gates. In Col. 39 it becomes evident that the middle courtyard is to have 12 gates.[15] In addition, we also get the names of the gates, which are from north-east (NE) clockwise as follows: Simeon, Levi and Judah; Reu-

[12] Yadin points out, that the scribe intended רוחב *pro* רחוב. This measurement marks the width between the walls of the inner and middle courtyard. Yadin, 163.

[13] Yadin explains ולצ צפון as a mistake, where the scribe tried to avoid a flaw in the Scroll by writing צפון once more. Yadin, 164.

[14] When we add the different measurements, we will notice that the width of the walls is included in the 480 cubits. As a consequence this number represents the external dimensions of the wall of the middle courtyard.

[15] Lines 39:11b–13: ושם [הש]ערים אשר ל[ח]צר הזואת על שמ[ות] (12) בני יש[ר]אל שמעון לוי ויהודה בקדם מזרח [ר]אובן יוסף ובנימין לנגב (13) דרום יש שכר זבולון וגד לים דן נפתלי ואשר לצפון.

ben, Joseph and Benjamin; Issachar, Zebulun and Gad; Dan, Naphtali and Asher.[16] The width of these gates is found in lines 39:14b-15a, והשער (15) שמונה ועשרים. Their location is described in line 39:14, מן פנה למזרח צפון עד שער שמעׄוׄן תשׄעׄ ותשעים באמה. The distance between the gates is 99 cubits from lines 39: 15-16a, ומשער הזה עד שער { }[17] לוי תשׄעׄ ותשעים (16) באמה.

As a result of the numbers above we finally get the following sum: 99 + 28 + 99 + 28 + 99 + 28 + 99 = 480. This seems to be the ED of the wall of the middle courtyard. If this is the case, the ID would be 472.[18] In FIG. 4[19] it looks like this, as the inner courtyard is located inside the middle courtyard for comparison:

---

16 The New Jerusalem Scroll shows a striking similarity concerning the names of the city-gates: only the gates heading to the south are located in a different order, that is from west to east, Reuben – Benjamin – Joseph. The measurements are however gigantic even compared to the temple city of Ezekiel: 18.5 x 26 km. Chyutin 1997, 76.

17 Erasure by a scribe. The erased part is very difficult to discern.

18 Maier arrives to slightly different numbers for both ED: 500 x 500 and ID: 480 x 480. Maier 1997, XLVI.

19 The gates as they are located by Yadin. Yadin 1983 vol. 1, 244.

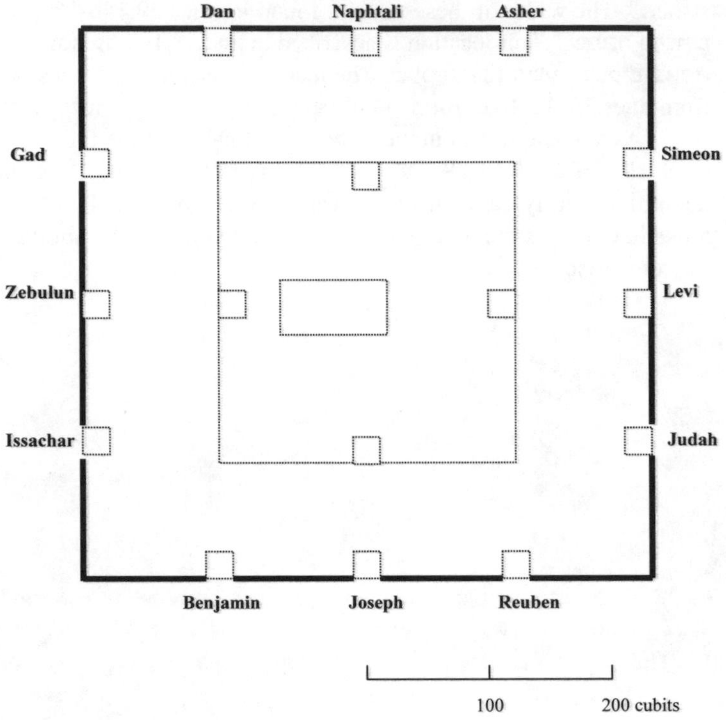

FIG. 4. THE INNER COURTYARD INSIDE THE MIDDLE COURTYARD

5.2.3. The Outer Courtyard

There is a command to build a third courtyard in line 40:5. According to line 40:7, רו]חב סביב לחצר התיכונה שׁ[ש] מׄאׄ[ות]אמה, this third wall should be located 600 cubits from the middle courtyard.[20] Concerning the measurements of this wall, the author firstly gives an approximate length of the wall in line 40:8, באורך כאלף̇ ושש [מאות ב]אמ̇ה̇ מפנה לפנה and adds, that all the sides are to be of the same length, לכול ר̇וח ורוח כמדה הזאו̇ת̇. On line

[20] We agree with Qimron, who has a similar restoration with ו]ר̊ו̊חב at the beginning. Qimron, 57. Yadin restores differently, ש[שים וחמש מאות באמה], based on an approximate measurement of the distance between the two walls. Yadin, 170.

40:8 we get the thickness of the wall, רוחב הקיר שבע אמות. Concerning the gates we have the following information: their thickness is written in line 40:12, ורוחב השערים חמשים באמה, and the distance between is written in line 40:13, ובין שער לשער [מדה] שלוש מאות וששים באמה. The same distance is recorded in lines 40:13–14a from the פנה to the first gate mentioned, that is שער שמעון.

From lines 40:14–15 and lines 41:1–11 it becomes evident that also the wall of the outer courtyard has 12 gates and that they are arranged in the same order as the gates on the wall of the middle courtyard.[21] When we make the following sum we get the length of the wall: 360 + 50 + 360 + 50 + 360 + 50 + 360 = 1590. As we noted, the dimensions were given from הפנה עד שער שמעון. From this we understand that the thickness of the wall is included in the 360 cubits[22] and that this gives an ID of the outer wall of 1576.

Before the outer courtyard can be shown in a figure, e.g. FIG. 5, there are still some measurements to be taken into account: the first is mentioned in line 41:12, ויוצאים השערים מקיר החצר לחוץ שבע אמות. Yadin notes, the approximate length of 1600 that was mentioned above actually is 1604 cubits.[23] This 1604 is the real ED for the wall of the outer courtyard.[24] In line 41:17 chambers are mentioned, נשכות, whose width inwards is 20 cubits. Their position will be shown with a thinner line inside the outer wall in FIG. 5.[25] The פרור, which are located 10 cubits[26] from the chambers inwards, are indicated by a dotted line.[27]

---

[21] There is no doubt about this, even if the beginning of Col. 41 needs a lot of restoration. The end of Col. 40, i.e. lines 40:14b–15, reads ומשער שמעון עד שער לוי (15) ומשער לוי עד שער יהודה כמדה הזואת ששים ושלוש.

[22] According to his Fig. 14 Yadin seems to suggest that 360 is counted to the inner corner (מקצוע) even if he claims that it should be the outer corner (פנה). Yadin 1983 vol. 1, 253.

[23] Yadin 1983 vol. 1, 251. The protruding seven cubits are exaggerated so that they could be observed in FIG. 5. This will slightly distort the dimensions of the gates. Concerning the steps leading up to the entrance: they are not indicated because they are unimportant for the present study and because they would confuse the dimensions even more.

[24] Maier gives rather inexact dimensions for ED: 1700 x 1700 and for ID: 1600 x 1600. Maier 1997, XLVII. We cannot even assume that he adds the width of the חיל to the outer wall, as this would give us 1800 x 1800 cubits.

[25] Line 41:17, ובין {ע}שער לשער תעשה פנימה נשכות.

[26] The פרור will, however, be drawn far away from the chambers. The width is half the width of the chambers, even if their width in FIG. 5 for practical reasons is the same.

[27] Line 42:4, ופרו[ריהמה כולמה יהיו רו]חב עשר אמות.

The last measurement in relation to the outer wall concerns the חיל, a kind of a trench,[28] whose function was to make a distinction between the holy place and the surroundings. This is mentioned in line 46:10, מבדיל בין מקדש הקודש לעיר. The command to build the surrounding חיל is found on the preceding line, 46:9, ועשיתה חיל סביב למקדש רחב מאה באמה. With these facts we may now illustrate the outer wall in FIG. 5:

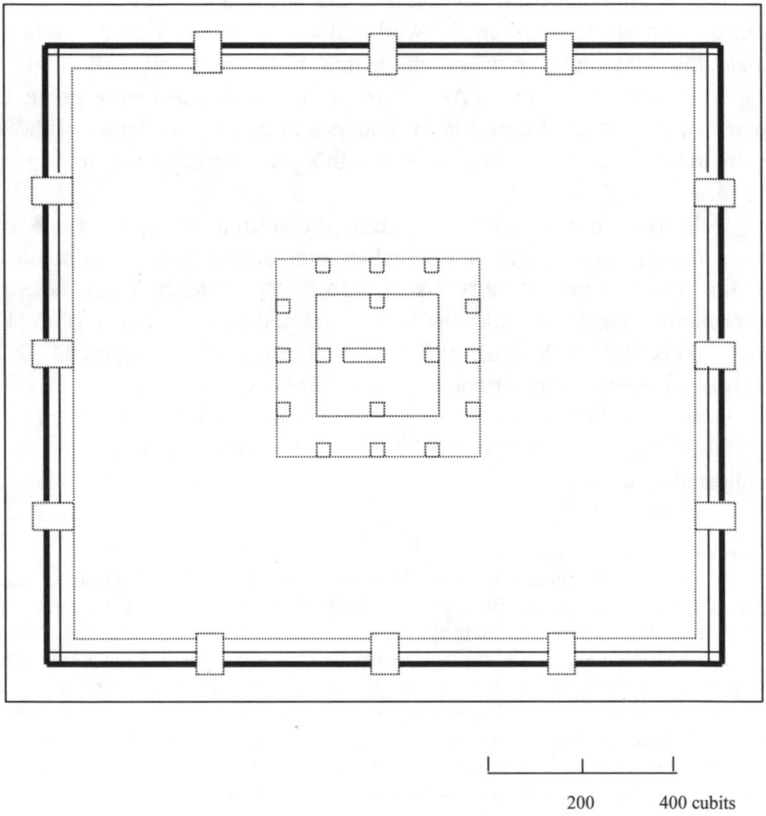

FIG. 5. THE OUTER WALL

[28] García Martínez uses this term in his translation. García Martínez 1994, 168.

5.3. The Courtyard of the Tabernacle

In Ex 27:9 we read the command to build a courtyard for the tabernacle. The measurements are according to Ex 27:18a, ארך החצר מאה באמה ורחב חמשים בחמשים. In the middle of the curtain eastwards an entrance was located,[29] that was 20 cubits wide. This is recorded in Ex. 27:16a, ולשער החצר מסך עשרים אמה. In FIG. 6 these measurements are described as follows:[30]

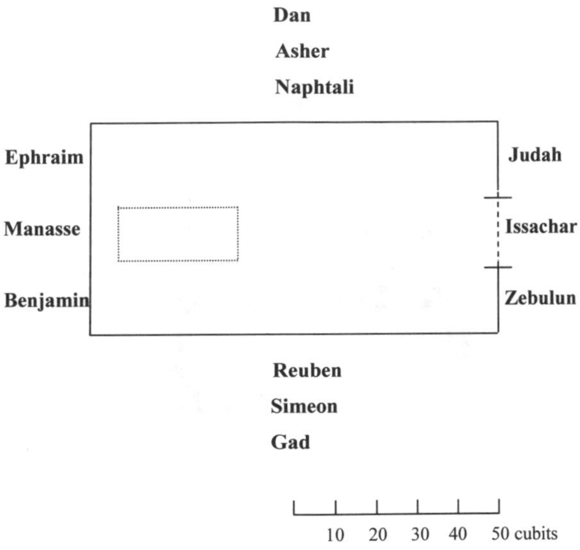

FIG. 6. THE COURTYARD OF THE TABERNACLE

[29] Ex 27:13-14, (13) ורחב החצר לפאת קדמה מזרחה חמשים אמה (14) וחמש עשרה אמה לכתף השנית חמש עשרה קלעים עמדיהם שלשה ואדניהם שלשה קלעים.

[30] The arrangement of the tribal camps (Num 2:3-31). These have been shown in FIG. 6.

5.4. The Courtyards of Ezekiel's temple

The book of Ezekiel uses a "longer cubit" and is mentioned in Ezek 40:5b, וביד האיש קנה המדה שש־אמות באמה וטפח. The standard Hebrew cubit was about 0.44 m and the cubit of Ezekiel could have been 0.52 m.[31] This would give us a ratio close to 17:20 between the two measurements.[32] The measurements in this section will be described according to the way the prophet has given them. However, in the next section, 5.5, Ezekiel's cubits will be transformed to the standard size of the measurement to enable a comparison.[33]

In Ezekiel's vision we get the length of the temple to be 100 C from Ezek 41:13a, ומדד את־הבית ארך מאה אמה. Also we calculate the width of the building from Ezek 41:4a ורחב עשרים אמה אל־פני ההיכל, 41:5 וימד קיר־הבית שש אמות ורחב הצלע ארבע אמות סביב סביב לבית סביב and from 41:9a רחב הקיר אשר־לצלע אל־החוץ חמש אמות. From these numbers we get a width of 50 C. The building roughly corresponded to FIG. 7:[34]

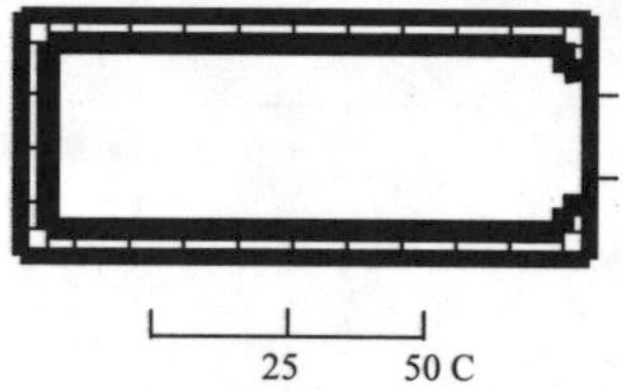

FIG. 7. EZEKIEL'S TEMPLE

---

[31] There are difficulties in transferring biblical measurements into the modern system. Concerning e.g. the longer cubit there are different opinions about its length. However, the absolute length of the cubit is not the most important question in this section. The numbers above relate to the table in Eerdmans Bible Dictionary 1987, 1053, the article "Weights and Measures."

[32] When the measurements of Ezekiel is discussed, C will be used as the symbol for the longer cubit. In addition to that, we will not have a distinction between ED and ID concerning the walls of Ezekiel's courtyards, because we the thickness of these walls is not known.

[33] We have no reason to doubt that the cubit in DSS would follow the standard size measurements (cubit).

[34] The cells in the wall in FIG. 7 are the side cells of the temple written about in Ezek 41:6a, והצלעות צלע אל־צלע שלוש ושלשים פעמים. Naturally they should each be of the same size, so the figure does not display this accurately. The width of 50 C is the sum of 20 + (2 x 6)[the temple walls] + (2 x 4) [the cells] + (2 x 5) [thickness of the outer wall].

In Ezek 40:47 we read about the temple courtyard: וימד את־החצר ארך מאה אמה ורחב מאה אמה מרבעת. This seems to be a square in front of the temple. This would give a courtyard, that is at least 200 C long,[35] as the temple was 100 C.[36] The size of the gateways are the same in the inner and the outer courtyards,[37] that is 50 C long and 25 C wide. The measurements for the outer courtyard, 500 C, are found in Ezek 42:20, לארבע רוחות מדדו חומה לו סביב סביב ארך חמש מאות ורחב חמש מאות להבדיל בין הקדש לחל. From Ezek 40:27, ושער לחצר הפנימי דרך הדרום וימד משער אל־השער דרך הדרום מאה אמות, we get the position of the outer wall in relation to the inner courtyard: 100 C from a gate in the wall of the outer courtyard to the protruding gate of the wall of the inner courtyard.[38]

There also seems to be an additional wall that surrounded the city. In Ezek 48:3 ff there is information about length of this wall and its gates, e.g. verse 32a: ואל־פאת קדימה חמש מאות וארבעת אלפים ושערים שלשה and verse 35a: סביב שמנה עשר אלף. Also these gates have names which are Reuben, Judah, Levi, Joseph, Benjamin, Dan, Simeon, Issachar, Zebulun, Gad, Asher, Naphtali.[39] In FIG. 8 the temple, the inner, and the outer courtyard alone are pictured.[40]

---

[35] This dimension of at least 200 cubits is derived from practical reasons. It is, henceforth, calculated as exactly 200 (in figures and tables).

[36] In the illustrations FIGS. 8 and 9 the square of 100 x 100 C is understood as חצר and the larger territory including the temple as החצר הפנימי.

[37] Ezek 40:25b, חמשים אמה ארך ורחב חמש ועשרים אמה. The same size of the gateways becomes evident in several places, for example in Ezek 40:32b, וימד את־השער כמדות האלה.

[38] If the gates did not stand out from the inner courtyard, there would be little room for anything else other than gateways in the inner courtyard.

[39] Ezek 48:31-34, (31) ושערי העיר על־שמות שבטי ישראל שערים שלשה צפונה שער ראובן אחד ושער יהודה אחד ושער לוי אחד (32) ואל־פאת קדימה חמש מאות וארבעת אלפים ושערים שלשה ושער יוסף אחד ושער בנימן אחד ושער דן אחד (33) ופאת־נגבה חמש מאות וארבעת אלפים מדה ושערים שלשה שער שמעון אחד שער יששכר אחד שער זבולן אחד (34) פאת־ימה חמש מאות וארבעת אלפים שעריהם שלשה שער גד אחד שער אשר אחד שער נפתלי אחד. There are, however, neither numbers for the width of the gates nor information about how they are located along the city-wall. As a consequence of this, they will only have an estimated size and position in FIG. 9.

[40] The rectangular object in dotted style behind the temple represents for example what is written in Ezek 41:12a, והבנין אשר אל־פני הגזרה פאת דרך־הים רחב שבעים אמה.

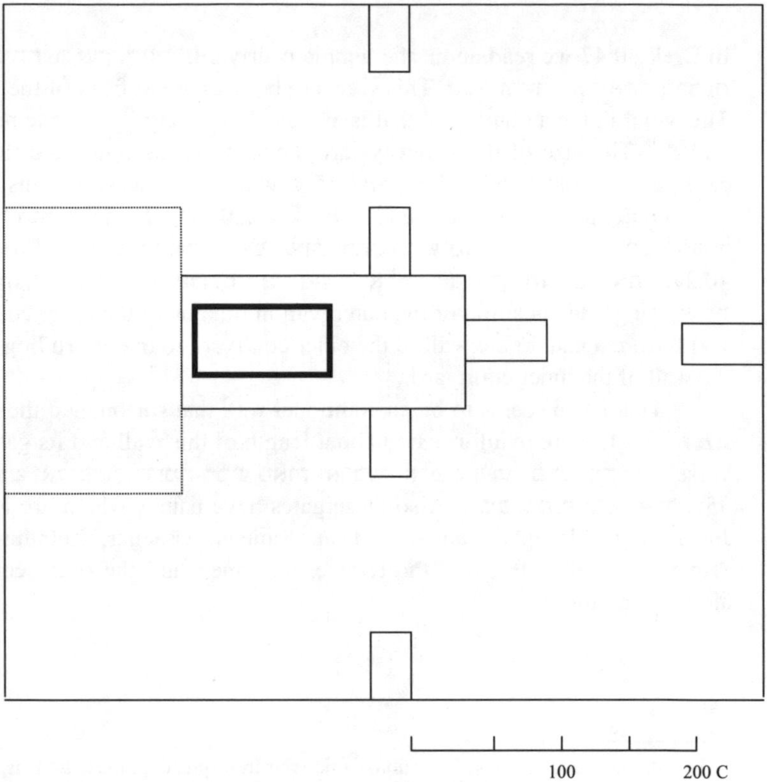

FIG. 8 THE TEMPLE, THE INNER, AND THE OUTER COURTYARD

Subsequently the city-wall is shown in FIG. 9 together with the elements in FIGS. 7 and 8, to get an impression about the general dimensions of Ezekiel's vision.

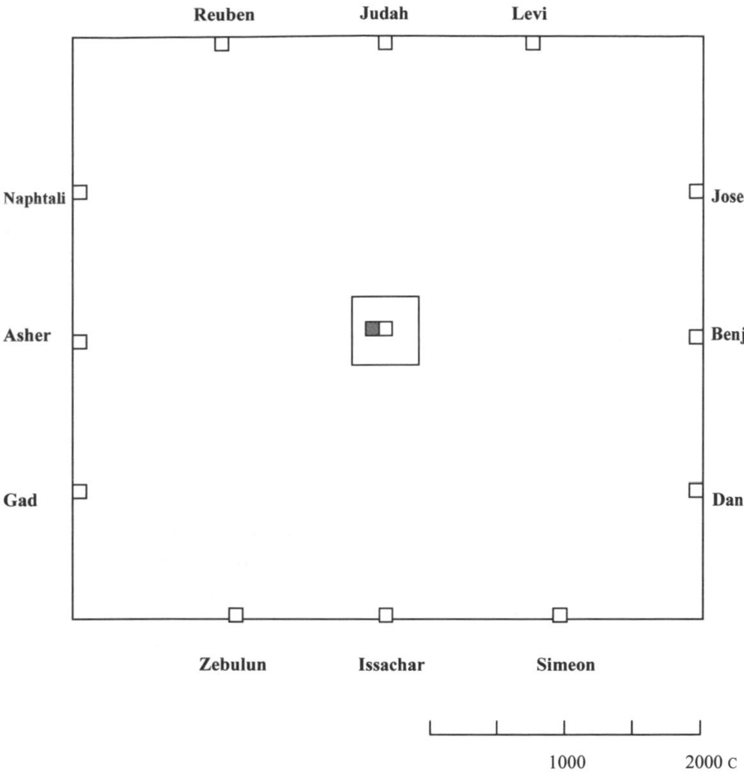

FIG. 9 EZEKIEL'S VISION: THE TEMPLE, THE INNER AND THE OUTER COURTYARD, AND THE CITY-WALL

5.5. A Comparison of the Figures in 5.2, 5.3, and 5.4

With the help of the material above we will now compare the size of the different courtyards.[41] The complex of the 11QT temple has three courtyards,

[41] When the measurements of Ezekiel were considered, it was evident that he does not distinguish between outer and inner dimensions of the courtyard walls. Therefore, the numbers for the courtyard dimensions in this comparison will relate to the outer dimen-

the inner courtyard (I), the middle courtyard (M) and the outer courtyard (O). The tabernacle had only one courtyard. The temple of Ezekiel[42] contained two courtyards. In addition to its inner and outer courtyards, Ezekiel's temple also has a wall around the city (TCW). The length of the walls is presented in TABLE 2 below (in cubits):

	Court-yards	I	M	O	TCW[43]
11QT temple	3	294 x 294	480 x 480	1604 x 1604	--
Tabernacle	1	50 x 100	--	--	--
Ezektemple[44]	2	118 x 236	--	591 x 591	*5319 x 5319[45]*

TABLE 2. THE LENGTH OF THE WALLS

From TABLE 2 we note that the measurements do not have much in common. However, the ratio between the O and I concerning 11QT temple and Ezekiel's temple are quite close to each other, i.e. for 11QT temple: 1604:294 ≈ 5.46 and for Ezekiel's temple: 591:118 = 5.0. In addition to this, we could suggest that Ezekiel's temple actually has three courtyards (city-walls included), as the case is with 11QT temple.

The Gates. The amount of the gates is presented in TABLE 3:[46]

Gates	IG	MG	OG	TCG
11QT temple	4	12	12	--
Tabernacle	1	--	--	--
Ezektemple	3	--	12	12

TABLE 3. THE AMOUNT OF THE GATES

sions only. In addition to that, Ezekiel's long cubit is transferred to the shorter cubit with the help of the following formula c = C:0.846.

[42] The temple of Ezekiel is shortened to Ezektemple in the tables.

[43] The Temple Scroll does not have information about walls or gates of the temple-city. It is possible that it had both.

[44] 100: 0.846 ≈118 and 200:0.846 ≈ 236 (I); 500:0.846 ≈ 591 (O); 4500:0.846 ≈ 5319 (TCW).

[45] The size of the temple-city is presented in this context as it is possible to interpret it as a very large courtyard, even if this was actually not the case.

[46] IG is the shortened form for the Inner courtyard Gates etc.

The correspondence between the amount of the gates is quite similar. If we take the outer gates of Ezekiel's temple as middle gates and his temple-city gates of as the outer gates we have a resemblance between the 11QT temple and the Ezektemple. We can, furthermore, write the names of the gates in a manner that makes the overview easier. These are presented in an order from east through south, west and north in TABLE 4 below:

11QT temple	**Tabernacle**[47]	**Ezektemple**
Simeon	*Judah*	Joseph
Levi	*Issachar*	Benjamin
Judah	*Zebulun*	Dan
Reuben	*Reuben*	Simeon
Joseph	*Simeon*	Issachar
Benjamin	*Gad*	Zebulun
Issachar	*Benjamin*	Gad
Zebulun	*Manasseh*	Asher
Gad	*Ephraim*	Naphtali
Dan	*Dan*	Reuben
Naphtali	*Asher*	Judah
Asher	*Naphtali*	Levi

TABLE 4. THE NAMES OF THE GATES

We agree with Yadin, who there does not seem to be a clear pattern in the order of the tribes.[48]

For a final comparison of the different courtyards we shall take a look at them all together in FIG. 10. Through this we will get an understanding about the different dimensions:[49]

---

[47] The names for the tribes in this column are written with italics in order to make a distinction from the two other columns: the names do not represent gates in the context of the tabernacle. In any event, it is interesting to see the names in the same table for comparison.

[48] However, he claims that the author's principles concerning the location of the gates may be understood, e.g., that the gate of Levi is placed in the middle of the eastern side and that the gates of Issachar, Zebulun and Gad are placed in the west. See a detailed discussion concerning these locations in Yadin 1983 vol. 1, 256. In this context we will not develop these thoughts further on, as the principles seems to be quite subtle.

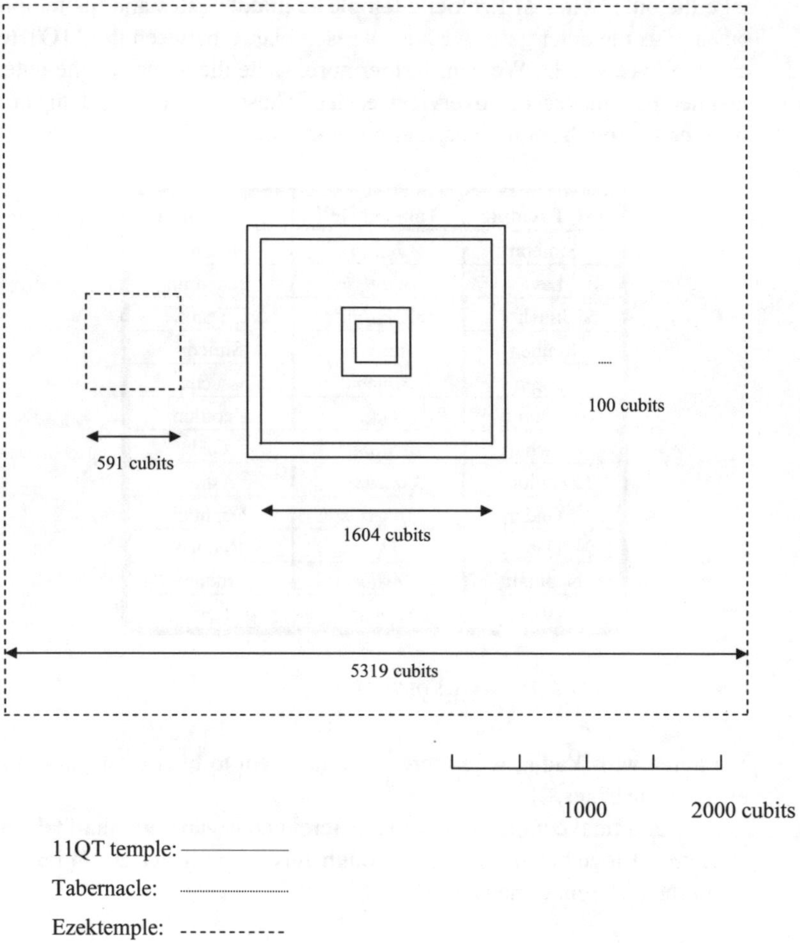

FIG. 10. AN OVERVIEW OF ALL THE COURTYARDS

---

49 The different courtyards have been drawn beside each other, inside the city of Ezekiel. Otherwise they could not have been distinguished in the same figure. In addition, the gateways have not been included in FIG. 10. This gives a clearer picture of the different sizes of the courtyards.

5.6. Conclusion

From the numerical results in the tables above, it is quite clear that there is no among the three different systems of courtyards. However, there seems to be some kind of relationship between the temple in 11QT and Ezekiel's temple. This is the case concerning the amount of courtyards. That is if we consider the temple-city as a large outer courtyard, then the temple of Ezekiel could be considered as surrounded by three courtyards as is the case with the 11QT temple. There is also a similar ratio between the inner and outer courtyards of these two, that is for 11QT temple: 1604 / 294 ≈ 5.46 and for Ezekiel: 591 / 118 = 5.0. Finally, there is a correspondence between the amount of gates between these two temples, if we consider the 12 outer gates of Ezekiel's temple as middle gates and his 12 temple-city gates as the outer gates.

It addition, it is worthwhile to point out a kind of an "ideal" structure principles that characterises the courtyards of the Temple Scroll. This may be seen in the fact, that the inner courtyard has gateways in all four directions. Also, in a larger context it is possible to distinguish a great deal of symmetry in the ground plan.

CHAPTER SIX

The Results of the Study

6.1. Biblical Quotations (BQ)

In the light of the analysis in chapters two and four, it has been shown that the amount of quotations in Cols. 29:3b-47:18 is low compared to the analysis of Cols. 2-13:9. In my dissertation[1] 27 quotations[2] of the Torah in the Temple Scroll were analysed in order to divide the quotations into primary or secondary readings to find out which biblical text-tradition they followed more closely. In the present study, Cols. 29:3b-47:18, the quotations are very few. There are only three passages: lines 34:11b-12a, line 45:15, and line 45:16b.[3]

Lines 34:11b–12a. 11QT = 𝔐 = ⅏ = 𝔊 (376) ≠ 𝔊 (BA). (12) על האש אשר על המזבח. The text-critical analysis revealed that this passage of 11QT probably is a primary reading, which also was found in 𝔐 and in ⅏ of Lev 1:8b. In addition, it was found in a minuscule manuscript of 𝔊, 376. We noted that the 𝔊-reading of B and A seemed to represent a secondary reading due to grammatical reasons: τὰ ὄντα referred to the wood τὰ ξύλα in Lev 1:8. In 𝔐 and ⅏ it is obvious that אשר refers to האש.

Line 45:15. 11QT = 𝔐 = ⅏ = 𝔊. מזובו וספר לו שבעת ימים לטהרתו. All the biblical text-traditions of Lev 15:13a known to us agree with this reading. Thus it is understood as a primary reading.

Line 45:16b. 11QT = 𝔐 = ⅏ = 𝔊 (*reliqui*) ≠ 𝔊 (BA). במים חיים. 11QT agrees with the 𝔐 and ⅏ versions of Lev 15:13b, and with some

[1] *The Temple Scroll and the Biblical Text Traditions. A Study of Columns 2–13:9.*
[2] Riska 2001, 156. The definition for a Biblical Quotation was identified in section 1.2: 1) The general biblical connection is established. 2) The quotation in 11QT, which has to be literal, is used in the same context as in the Bible.
[3] Since the quotations are so few, it is pointless to gather them together in order to present even a minor part of the Bible that the author was quoting from. This collection of Biblical Quotations was entitled 11QT*Vorlage* in my doctoral dissertation. Of course it is possible that the amount is low, because of careful limitations in terms of our definition of a BQ. On the other hand, we needed to formulate our definition as similar as possible to my first study of 11QT in order to be able to compare the present results with the previous ones.

manuscripts of 𝔊, which read ὕδατι ζωντὶ. B and A of 𝔊 read ὕδατι only. Therefore, it seems that the longer reading in the Scroll is secondary because we are aware that the shorter readings at times have a tendency to be closer to the original one.

Hence, we note that according to our definition of a secondary reading we only have one reading of that kind. The two other passages were interpreted as primary readings. Therefore, they are not as interesting in the context of this study because textual traditions often are known to overlap.

It is, however, interesting to note that even if the amount of quotations is so low, that all three of them were found from the book of Leviticus.

6.2. Biblical Paraphrase (BP)

In the columns of this study we classified 17 different passages as BP: Col. 29 has 2 incidences, Col. 34 has 4 incidences, Col. 43 has 2 incidences, Col. 45 has 4 incidences, Col. 46 has 3 incidences, and Col. 47 has 2 incidences. Of these 17 incidences, 3 Biblical Paraphrases were compared closer to the textual traditions in a similar way as we did with the BQ. This was done as the passages were similar to quotations. They are presented below:

Lines 34:13b–14a. 11QT ≈ 𝔊 ≠ 𝔐 ≈ ɯ. והקטירו הכוהנים בני אהרון את הכול (14) על המזבח אשה ריח ניחוח לפני יהוה. We observed that the 𝔊-reading of Lev 1:9b was very similar to the Scroll: although, the verbs והקטירו and ἐπιθήσουσιν are not equivalent. Moreover, we also noted that 𝔐 and ɯ were nearly identical.

Lines 45:13b–14a. 11QT ≠ (≈) 𝔐 = ɯ = 𝔊. ולוא יטמאו את העיר אשר אני שוכן (14) בתוכה. Since the corresponding passage in Num 5:3 has מחנה *pro* העיר in the Scroll, we interpret this as BP. These passages are, however, so close that we have designated their relationship with the rather cryptic symbol of "≠ (≈)."

Lines 47:10b–11. 11QT ≈ 𝔊 ≠ 𝔐. אשר (11) אנוכי משכן את שמי ומקדשי בתוכה. We noted that 𝔊 of Ezek 43:7b that has ἐν οἷς κατασκηνώσει τὸ ὄνομά μου ἐν μέσῳ οἴκου Ισραηλ τὸν αἰῶνα is slightly closer to the Scroll than the 𝔐-reading, אשר אשכן־שם בתוך בני־ישראל לעולם.

We have, furthermore, noted biblical references in section 4.3. There are is 20 allusions to the following biblical books: Exodus – 3 times; Leviticus – 10 times; Numbers – 2 times; Deuteronomy – 2 times; and Ezekiel – 3 times. From these results we observe the peak is Leviticus with 10 occurrences. It would appear that the subtle focus on Leviticus, which was discovered in section 6.1, has further support.

6.3. Rewritten Bible (REWB)

We have classified 52 different passages as REWB: Col. 29 has 4 incidences; Col. 31 has 3 incidences; Col. 32 has 1 incidence; Col. 33 has 3 incidences; Col. 35 has 7 incidences; Col. 36 has 1 incidence; Col. 37 has 2 incidences; Col. 39 has 4 incidences; Col. 40 has 2 incidences; Col. 42 has 4 incidences; Col. 43 has 3 incidences; Col. 44 has 2 incidences; Col. 45 has 7 incidences; Col. 46 has 7 incidences; and Col. 47 has 2 incidences. Of these 52 incidences, 6 incidences received a closer comparison with the textual traditions in a similar way as we did with the BQ. This was done since the passages were similar to their biblical sources. They are presented below:

Line 29:8b. 11QT ≈ 𝔊 ≠ 𝔐 = 𝔪. ואקדשה [את מ]קדשי בכבודי. This is an interesting passage because from a comparison with the 𝔊 it is BP of Ex 29:43b. 𝔊 has the same subject as the Scroll. In contrast, 𝔐 and 𝔪 do not include the subject because it uses the passive form, ונקדש. Therefore we interpreted this as REWB. Further as the studied text contains REWB, the whole passage is classified as REWB.[4]

Line 31:9b. 11QT ≈ 𝔐 = 𝔊. ועשה ככול אשר אנוכי מדבר אליכה. Since the context in Ezek 44:5a was different the passage in the Scroll was understood as REWB.

Line 33:11b. 11QT ≈ 𝔐 ≈ 𝔊. חלונים פנימה אטומים. Since the context was different, this was understood as REWB. Ezek 40:16a refers to the chambers, 11QT deals with the house of laver.

Line 35:7b. 11QT = 𝔊 (53*-129) ≠ 𝔐 = 𝔪 = 𝔊 (B). ולוא יׄחל[לו את מק]ד֯ש אלוהׄיׄהמה. We focused on the last word in this passage,[5] אלוהׄיׄהמה. It was matched with a 𝔊-reading from the *f*-group τοῦ θεοῦ

[4] It is logical – as an exception – to interpret BP as REWB. To do the opposite is more difficult. It would be odd to understand REWB as BP, since REWB is further from the biblical source than BP is.

[5] Due to difference in context it cannot be recognized as BP.

αὐτῶν, which furthermore appears to show that the reading in the Scroll is a secondary reading and a variant. Furthermore, we noted that 𝔐 and ⅏ are similar to 11QT, apart from the verb that needs to be restored in plural due to its grammatical context.

Line 36:8. 11QT ≈ 𝔊 ≠ 𝔐. וׄהׄ[יו]צאים במה רוחב השער ארבע [עש]רׄה באמה וגובהמׄה. In the text-critical analysis we noted that 𝔊 of Ezek 40:48b has the measurement of 14 cubits, which on the other hand is not included in the 𝔐-reading.

Lines 45:15b-16a. 11QT ≠ 𝔐 = 𝔊 ≈ ⅏. ויכבס ביום (16) השביעי בגדיו ורחץ את כול בשרו. The Scroll adds details to Lev. 15:13b and appears to have stricter commandments than the biblical traditions, e.g. by reading כול בשרו *pro* בשרו in 𝔐.

These biblical references in section 4.4 have been recorded, that is together 72 allusions to the following books: Genesis – two times; Exodus – 17 times; Leviticus – 17 times; Numbers – 5 times; Deuteronomy – 4 times; Joshua – one time; 1 Samuel – one time; 2 Samuel – one time; 1 Kings – 3 times, Ezekiel – 14 times; Zechariah – one time, Nehemiah – two times, 1 Chronicles – one time, and 2 Chronicles – two times. From these counts above we observe the highest occurrence is for Exodus, Leviticus, and Ezekiel. Thus, we note as a conclusion that the book of Leviticus occurs with most frequency when we take into consideration BQ, BP, and REWB.

6.4. A Comparison between the Ratio of Biblical Quotations (BQ), Biblical Paraphrase (BP), Rewritten Bible (REWB), and Individual Composition (IC)

In section 4.5 we presented the frequency of IC. We will now do a comparison between the categories. The Hebrew text in section 3.1 is used to assess frequency to each category.[6] The amount of textual mass will firstly be portrayed in appropriate tables below:

[6] The textual material will be measured with the same method as in section 4.5. The amount of lines is counted accordingly: the unrestored textual material that does not belong to IC (since this material is already counted), is measured in cm and divided with the average length of a line in order to get the result. To this number the amount of complete lines of BP / REWB are added if extant. This is not the case in BQ since there is so little textual material. Thus we are able to measure the BQ material without the multiplication.

Bible Quotations (BQ)

Column	34	45
BQ	4.1	8.1

Sum of BQ	12.2 ≈ 12

TABLE 5. SUMMARY OF BIBLE QUOTATIONS

Bible Paraphrase (BP)

Column	29	34	43	45	46	47
Ã	10.0	11.0	8.5	11.0	10.5	10.0
Lines	X[7]	3.4	2.4	X	X	X
BP	17.8	37.4	20.4	26.1	10.9	12.1

Sum of BP	124.7 ≈ 125

TABLE 6. SUMMARY OF BIBLE PARAPHRASES

[7] The X-letter indicates that the column does not contain complete lines and the sum below is received by adding the length of the incomplete lines.

Rewritten Bible (REWB):

Column	**29**	**31**	**32**	**33**	**35**	**36**	**37**
Ã	10.0	11.0	11.0	10.5	10.0	9.5	9.5
Lines	4.1	X	X	3.6	5.0	X	X
REWB	**41.0**	**27.3**	**16.4**	**37.8**	**50.0**	**6.9**	**8.7**
39	**40**	**42**	**43**	**44**	**45**	**46**	**47**
10.5	11.5	8.0	8.5	8.5	11.0	10.5	10.0
7.4	X	5.5	4.8	3.2	6.0	5.3	X
77.7	**13.6**	**44.0**	**40.8**	**27.2**	**66.0**	**55.65**	**8.0**

Sum of REWB	521.05 ≈ **521**

TABLE 7. SUMMARY OF REWRITTEN BIBLE

The numbers which we have gathered in the tables above shed light on the impression that we have got from chapter four: the smallest group is BQ and the largest category by far is IC. The results, which are also presented as percentages in order to show their quantitative relation to each other, are shown in TABLE 8 below:

BQ	**12**	**0.58 %**
BP	**125**	**6.06 %**
REWB	**521**	**25.27 %**
IC	**1404**	**68.09 %**
Sum	**2062**	**100 %**

TABLE 8. THE RATIO OF THE DIFFERENT CATEGORIES

6.5. A Comparison with the Study of Cols. 2–13:9

One of the main results from my study on Cols. 2–13:9 was that BQ from Exodus had an inclination towards textual traditions of 𝔊. Since our present study is comprised of so few quotations we are limited in explaining that connection. Further, due to the small amount of quotations, we will not make a collection of citations in order to highlight the biblical texts the author was using, which I did for my doctoral dissertation.[8]

Furthermore, we recall that Cols. 2–13:9 represented material where both the quantity of BP and REWB were significantly higher than IC. This is a definite difference, with our present study: the mid-part of the Scroll, Cols. 29:3b–47:18. This part is mainly built around IC.

Finally, the textual material belonging to this present study was better preserved than the previous part, and has therefore given us more reliable results.

6.6 Final Conclusions

The text-critical analysis has been foundational for forming the textual summary of Cols. 29:3–47:18. We do not propose this text as a new reconstruction. Work on this text has benefited from two main reasons: 1) Since the material is located in the middle of the Scroll, the text has survived the 2000 years much better than the beginning of the Scroll. 2) We were able to check the particularly difficult passages with the help of old transparencies.

The present study did not reveal as many details concerning the biblical text-traditions as my previous study. In any event, we can note that this part of the Temple Scroll is also well impregnated with biblical influence.

In chapter five, we noted that there seems to be some similarities between the temple in 11QT and Ezekiel's temple. It was, furthermore, possible to distinguish a great deal of symmetry in the ground plan of the temple in the Temple Scroll.

As the amount of biblical quotations was low, the emphasis in this study was concentrated on the other categories. Moreover, the ma-

---

[8] Riska 2001, 164.

jority of the text was revealed to be Individual Composition.[9] On the other hand, the method to calculate this was perhaps a bit unorthodox, i.e. to measure it in centimetres. It should be remembered, however, that all the measurements were done according to the Hebrew text presented in section 3.1. Thus, we should not focus on the amount of centimetres but rather on the textual mass belonging to one group in relation to the other one.

Further, we are aware of the fact that there may be some subjectivity in the classification into the categories of Biblical Quotation, Biblical Paraphrase, Rewritten Bible, and Individual Composition. We do claim, however, that the differences between these groups were so clear that another decision concerning e.g. Biblical Paraphrase or Rewritten Bible would probably not alter the ordering too much.

With regard to the content, we assume that a specific source – which some scholars call the "Temple Source" – probably existed. Hence, in the light of this work it seems probable that a significant part of the Individual Composition-material of Cols. 29:3–47:18 is based on this source. Furthermore, we suggest that in this kind of a study, less different categories give a more reliable and objective portrait of the composition Temple Scroll than would a higher amount of categories.[10]

One of the main targets with this study was to investigate this Scroll's connection to biblical text-traditions. Even if the outcome concerning citations was unexpectedly meagre, it has been clearly shown that the book of Leviticus was the biblical text that has had the broadest influence upon this text. That may indicate that behind this intriguing Scroll, from the Dead Sea vicinity, lies a priestly hand.

---

[9] Since this method of measuring is new, it is a bit difficult to compare our result with other studies.

[10] Kaufman has presented six and Wise has suggested 11 different categories.

Summary

In my doctoral dissertation that was published in 2001, the textual material of the columns 2–13:9 was analysed in order to study the biblical text-traditions, in particular where Hebrew Bible was quoted. In this study the rest of the Temple Scroll that contained the construction of the temple and its furnishings, has been examined. The basis for my second study of 11QT – columns 29:3b–47:18 – was a text-critical analysis that was carried out systematically, line by line.

Since the amount of biblical quotations was lower than initially expected, the focus has been on the three additional categories: Biblical Paraphrase, Rewritten Bible, and Individual Composition. The number of categories is low in order to minimize subjectivity.

One of the main results of my dissertation showed that Cols. 2–13:9 represented a higher amount of Biblical Paraphrase and Rewritten Bible than Individual Composition. This present study reveals that the second section, Cols. 29:3b–47:18, contains a significantly higher amount of Individual Composition than any of the other categories. This result was achieved by measuring the textual mass of the different groups and comparing them with each other.

Furthermore, the study shows that the book of Leviticus from biblical materials, has had the broadest influence on this section of the Scroll. That may indicate a priestly hand in the composition of the Scroll.

Another important result is the summary of the Hebrew text of Cols. 29:3b–47:18. This result is a balanced evaluation of the best readings. It includes a few alternative suggestions. Old transparencies have been used in order to decide on particularly difficult cases of reconstruction.

There is a plausible theory that among other material a source called the "Temple Source" was used in the composition of the Temple Scroll. Through this study the text of the Temple Source is analysed in its entirety.

Abbreviations and Sigla

A	Codex Alexandrinus
B	Codex Vaticanus
BDB	Brown-Driver-Briggs Lexicon
BP	Biblical Paraphrase
BQ	Biblical Quotation
DSS	Dead Sea Scrolls
ED	Exterior Dimension
I	Inner Courtyard
IC	Individual Composition
IG	Inner courtyard Gates
ID	Interior Dimension
M	Middle Courtyard
MS(S)	Manuscript(s)
𝔐	Masoretic Text
O	Outer Courtyard
OG	Outer courtyard Gates
σ	Symmachos' version of 𝔊
𝔪	Samaritan Pentateuch
𝔊	Septuagint
TCG	Temple City Gates
ℭ	Targum
𝔙	Biblia Sacra. Iuxta Vulgata Versionem
א̇	Damaged letter, reading certain
א̊	Damaged letter, reading uncertain
[אבגדהו]	Reconstruction
[אבג]	Only partly reconstructed
[ ]	At present too difficult to reconstruct
{ א }	Text erased from MS
…	Traces of letters, exact number uncertain
/ abc /	The textual material is written between the lines in the MS
®	Single clearly readable letter not translated

Sources and Literature

Allegro, John M. 1968. *Qumran Cave 4: Ordinances (4Q159)*. Discoveries in the Judaean Desert of Jordan V. Oxford: Clarendon.

Aristeas to Philocrates. 1973 (Letter of Aristeas). Edited and translated by Moses Hadas. New York: Ktav.

Attridge, Harold, Torleif Elgvin, Josef Milik, Saul Olyan, John Strugnell, Emanuel Tov, James VanderKam, and Sidney White. 1994. *Qumran Cave 4: VIII. Parabiblical Texts, Part 1*. Discoveries in the Judaean Desert XIII. Oxford: Clarendon.

Avigad, N. 1958. "The Palaeography of the Dead Sea Scrolls." *Scripta Hierosolymitana. Volume IV. Aspects of the Dead Sea Scrolls*. Jerusalem: Magnes Press, Hebrew University, 56–87.

Baillet, Maurice. 1962. *Les 'Petites Grottes' de Qumrân. Planches.* Discoveries of the Judaean Desert in Jordan III. Oxford: Clarendon.

– 1962. *Les 'Petites Grottes' de Qumrân. Textes.* Discoveries of the Judaean Desert of Jordan III. Oxford: Clarendon.

Ben-Hayyim, Zev. 1977. *The Literary and Oral Tradition of the Hebrew and Aramaic amongst the Samaritans. Vol. IV. The Words of the Pentateuch.* Jerusalem: The Academy of the Hebrew Language (Hebrew).

– 1977. *Vol. V. Grammar of the Pentateuch.*

Biblia Hebraica Stuttgartensia. 1984. Ed. K. Elliger and W. Rudolph. Stuttgart: Deutsche Bibelgesellschaft.

Biblia Sacra. 1969. *Iuxta Vulgatam Versionem.* Tomus I. Genesis–Psalmi. Stuttgart: Württembergische Bibelanstalt.

Bonani, G., M. Broshi, I. Carmi, S. Ivy, J. Strugnell, and W. Wölfli. 1991. "Radiocarbon Dating of the Dead Sea Scrolls." *'Atiqot* 20:27–32.

Brin, Gershon. 1987. "Concerning Some of the Uses of the Bible in the Temple Scroll." *RQ* 12:519–528.

Brooke, George J. 1992. "The Temple Scroll and LXX Exodus 35–40." *Septuagint, Scrolls and Cognate Writings. Papers Presented to the International Symposium on the Septuagint and Its Relations to the Dead Sea Scrolls and Other Writings (Manchester, 1990)*. Atlanta, Georgia: Scholars Press, 81–106.

– 2000. "Rewritten Bible." *Encyclopaedia of the Dead Sea Scrolls. Volume 2*. Ed. Lawrence H. Schiffman and James C. VanderKam. Oxford: Oxford University Press, 777–780.

Brown, Francis, S. R. Driver, and Charles A. Briggs. 1974 (reprint). *Hebrew and English Lexicon of the Old Testament. With an Appendix Containing the Biblical Aramaic.* Oxford: Clarendon.

Callaway, Philip. 1986. "Source Criticism of the Temple Scroll: The Purity Laws." *RQ* 12:213–222.

Cassuto, Umberto. 1967. *A Commentary on the Book of Exodus.* Jerusalem: Magnes Press, Hebrew University.

Charlesworth, James H. 1991. *Graphic Concordance to the Dead Sea Scrolls.* Tübingen: J. C. B. Mohr.

Cross, Frank Moore Jr. 1961. "The Development of the Jewish Scripts." *The Bible in the Ancient Near East.* London: Routledge & Kegan Paul, 133–202.

The Dead Sea Scrolls Concordance. Volume One. The Non-Biblical Texts from Qumran. 2003. Ed. Martin G. Abegg, Jr. with James E. Bowley and Edward M. Cook in Consultation with Emanuel Tov. Leiden: Brill.

The Dead Sea Scrolls Study Edition. Volume Two: 4Q274–11Q31. 1998. Ed. Florentino García Martínez and Eibert J. C. Tigchelaar. Leiden: Brill.

Driver, S. R. 1961. *An Introduction to the Literature of the Old Testament.* Edinburgh: T. & T. Clark.

Duncan, Julie Ann. 1995. *Qumran Cave 4: IX. Deuteronomy, Joshua, Judges, Kings: 4QDeut[e]*. Discoveries in the Judaean Desert XIV. Oxford: Clarendon.

The Eerdmans Bible Dictionary. 1987. Revised Edition. Ed. Allen C. Myers. Grand Rapids, Michigan: William B. Eerdmans.

Elledge, C. D. 2003. "Exegetical Styles at Qumran: A Cumulative Index and Commentary." *RQ* 82:165–208.

Freedman, D. N., and K. A. Mathews. 1985. *The Paleo-Hebrew Leviticus Scroll (11QpaleoLev).* Winona Lake, Indiana: American Schools of Oriental Research.

García Martínez, Florentino. 1992. "11QTemple[b]. A Preliminary Publication." *The Madrid Qumran Congress. Proceedings of the International Congress on the Dead Sea Scrolls, Madrid, 18–21 March, 1991. Volume Two.* Ed. Julio Trebolle Barrera and Luis Vegas Montaner. Leiden: Brill, 363–390.

– 1994. *The Dead Sea Scrolls Translated: The Qumran Texts in English.* Trans. Wilfred G. E. Watson. Leiden: Brill.

– 1999. *The Temple Scroll and the New Jerusalem. The Dead Sea Scrolls After Fifty Years. Volume Two.* Ed. W. Peter Flint and James C. VanderKam. Leiden: Brill.

Garcia Martinez, Florentino, Eibert Tigchelaar, and Adam S. van der Woude. 1998. *Qumran Cave 11. 11Q2–18, 11Q20–31.* Discoveries in the Judaean Desert XXIII. Oxford: Clarendon.

Gesenius, Wilhelm. 1987. *Hebräisches und Aramäisches Handwörterbuch über das Alte Testament.* Unter verantwortlicher Mitarbeit von Udo Rutersworden, bearbeitet und herausgegeben von Rudolf Meyer und Herbert Donner. 18. Auflage. 1. Lieferung: alef–gimel. Berlin: Springer-Verlag.

Gesenius' Hebrew Grammar. 1910. Second edition. Ed. E. Kautzsch and rev. A. E. Cowley. With a Facsimile of the Siloam Inscription by J. Euting and a Table of Alphabets by M. Lidzbarski. Oxford: Clarendon.

Gray, John. 1967. *Joshua, Judges, and Ruth.* The New Century Bible. London: Nelson.

Haran, M. 1968. "*מקדש יחזקאל*." *Encyclopaedia Biblica. Thesaurus Rerum Biblicarum Alphabetico Ordine Digestus. Tomus Quintus*. Jerusalem: Instituti Bialik, 346–359 (Hebrew).

Hatch, Edwin, and Henry Redpath. 1983 (reprint). *A Concordance to the Septuagint and the Other Greek Versions of the Old Testament (Including the Apocryphal Books). Volumes 1–2. Additional Words and Occurrences of Words in Hexaplaric Fragments. Volume 3.* Oxford: Clarendon.

Der Hebräische Pentateuch der Samaritaner. 1914. *Zweiter Teil. Exodus.* Ed. August von Gall. Giessen: Alfred Töpelmann.
– 1915. *Dritter Teil. Leviticus.*
– 1916. *Vierter Teil. Numeri.*
– 1918. *Fünfter Teil. Deuteronomium.*

Josephus, Flavius. 1943. *Josephus with an English Translation. In Nine Volumes. VII: Jewish Antiquities, Books XII–XIV.* Loeb Classical Library. Ed. and trans. Ralph Marcus. London: William Heinemann Ltd.
– 1977. *V: Jewish Antiquities. Books V–VIII.*

Joüon, Paul S. J., and T. Muraoka. 1996. *A Grammar of Biblical Hebrew. Volume II. Part Three: Syntax. Paradigms and Indices. Subsidia Biblica 14/II.* Roma: Editrice Pontificio Instituto Biblico.

Kantola, Asko. 1996. *Temppelikäärön (11QT) puhtaussäädökset.* M.Th. thesis. Univ. Helsinki (Finnish).

Kaufman, Stephen A. 1982. "The Temple Scroll and Higher Criticism." *HUCA* 53: 29–43.

Koehler, Ludwig, and Walter Baumgartner. 1953. *Lexicon in Veteris Testamenti Libros.* Leiden: Brill.

Kutscher, Eduard Yechezkel. 1984. *A History of the Hebrew Language.* Ed. Raphael Kutscher. Jerusalem: Magnes Press, Hebrew University.

Liddell, Henry George, and Robert Scott. 1968. *A Greek–English Lexicon.* Revised and augmented throughout by Henry Stuart Jones. With a Supplement. Oxford: Clarendon.

Maier, Johann. 1985. *The Temple Scroll. An Introduction, Translation, and Commentary.* Sheffield: JSOT.
– 1997. *Die Tempelrolle vom Toten Meer und das "Neue Jerusalem". 11Q19 und 11Q20; 1Q32, 2Q24, 4Q554–555, 5Q15 und 11Q18. Übersetzung und Erläuterung. Mit Grundrissen der Tempelhofanlage und Skizzen zur Stadtplanung.* 3., völlig neu bearbeitete und erweiterte Auflage. München – Basel: Ernst Reinhardt Verlag.

Milgrom, Jacob. 1980. "Further Studies in the Temple Scroll." JQR 71:1–17, 89–106.

Milik, J. T. 1955. *Qumran Cave 1: Livre des Mystères.* Discoveries in the Judean Desert I. Oxford: Clarendon.
– 1957. "Le Travail d'Édition des Manuscrits du Désert de Juda." *Supplements to Vetus Testamentum, vol. IV. Volume de Congres. Strasbourg 1956.* Leiden: Brill, 17–26.

Mink, Hans-Aage. 1987. "The Use of Scripture in the Temple Scroll and the Status of the Scroll as Law." *SJOT* 1:20–50.

The Old Testament in Syriac. 1977. *According to the Peschiṭta Version. Part 1, fascicle 1. Preface. Genesis–Exodus.* Leiden: Brill.
– 1991. *Part 1, fascicle 2; Part 2, fascicle 1b. Leviticus–Numeri–Deureronomium–Joshua.* Leiden: Brill.

Peters, Melvin K. H. 1992. "Septuagint." *The Anchor Bible Dictionary*. New York: Doubleday, 5:1093–1104.

Van der Plœg, J. P. M. 1985. "Les Manuscrits de la Grotte XI de Qumran." *RQ* 12: 3–15.

Pseudo-Jonathan. Nach der Londoner Handschrift. 1903. (Targum Jonathan ben Usiël for Pentateuch). Ed. M. Ginsburger. Berlin: S. Calvary.

Puech, Émile. 1998. "4QRouleau du Temple." *Qumrân Grotte 4: XVIII. Textes Hébreux (4Q521–4Q528, 4Q576–4Q579)*. Discoveries in the Judaean Desert XXV. Oxford: Clarendon, 85–114.

Qimron, Elisha. 1978a. "לשונה של מגילת המקדש". *Leshonenu* 42:83–98, 136–145 (Hebrew).

– 1978b. "New readings in the Temple Scroll". *IEJ* 28:161–172.

– 1980. "למילונה של מגילת המקד". *Shnaton* IV:239–262 (Hebrew).

– 1982. "כוננה = כלי מכלי המבח". *Tarbiz* 52:133 (Hebrew).

– 1986. *The Hebrew of the Dead Sea Scrolls.* Atlanta, Georgia: Scholars Press.

– 1987. "Further New Readings in the Temple Scroll." *IEJ* 37:31–35.

– 1992. "Observations on the History of Early Hebrew (1000 B.C.E.–200 C.E.) in the Light of the Dead Sea Documents." *The Dead Sea Scrolls: Forty Years of Research*. Ed. D. Dimant and U. Rappaport. Leiden: Brill, 349–361.

– 1996. *The Temple Scroll. A Critical Edition with Extensive Reconstructions.* Jerusalem: Israel Exploration Society.

Riekkinen, Vilho, and Timo Veijola. 1986. *Johdatus Eksegetiikkaan. Metodioppi.* SESJ 37. Helsinki: Suomen Eksegeettinen Seura.

Riska, Magnus. 2001. *The Temple Scroll and the Biblical Text Traditions. A Study of Columns 2–13:9.* Publications of the Finnish Exegetical Society 81. Helsinki: Finnish Exegetical Society.

Rosenthal, Franz. 1974. *A Grammar of Biblical Aramaic.* Wiesbaden: Otto Harrassowitz.

Saukkonen, Juhana. 2005. *The Story behind the Text. Scriptural Interpretation in 4Q252.* Doctoral Dissertation. Univ. Helsinki.

Scanlin, Harold. 1993. *The Dead Sea Scrolls & Modern Translations of the Old Testament.* Wheaton, Illinois: Tyndale.

Schiffman, Lawrence H. 1992a. "The Furnishings of the Temple According to the Temple Scroll." *The Madrid Qumran Congress: Proceedings of the International Congress on the Dead Sea Scrolls, Madrid, 18–21 March, 1991. Volume Two.* Ed. Julio Trebolle Barrera and Luis Vegas Montaner. Leiden: Brill, 621–634.

– 1992b. "The Deuteronomic Paraphrase of the Temple Scroll." *RQ* 15: 543–567.

– 1994. "The Community of the Renewed Covenant." *The Notre Dame Symposium on the Dead Sea Scrolls*. Ed. Eugene Ulrich and James C. VanderKam. Notre Dame, Indiana: University of Notre Dame Press, 37–55.

The Septuagint with Apocrypha: Greek and English. 1982 (reprint). Grand Rapids, Michigan: Zondervan.

Septuaginta. Vetus Testamentum Graecum. Vol. III, 2: Deuteronomium. 1977. Ed. John William Wevers. Auctoritate Academiae Scientiarum Gottingensis editum. Göttingen: Vandenhoeck & Ruprecht.
– 1977. *Vol. XVI, 1. Ezechiel.*
– 1982. *Vol. III,1. Numeri.*
– 1986. *Vol. II, 2. Leviticus.*
– 1991. *Vol. II, 1. Exodus.*
– 1993. *Vol. VIII, 2. Esdrae liber II.*

הספרים החיצונים. 1956. לתורה לנביאים לכתובים ושאר ספרים חיצונים. תל אביב: מסדה (Hebrew).

Skehan, Patrick W., Eugene Ulrich, and Judith E. Sanderson. 1992. *Qumran Cave 4: IV. Palaeo-Hebrew and Greek Biblical Manuscripts.* Discoveries in the Judaean Desert IX. Oxford: Clarendon.

Sollamo, Raija. 1979. *Renderings of Hebrew Semiprepositions in the Septuagint.* Annales Academiae Scientiarum Fennicae. Dissertationes Humanarum Litterarum 19. Helsinki: Suomalainen Tiedeakatemia.

Stegemann, Hartmut. 1989. "The Literary Composition of the Temple Scroll and Its Status at Qumran." *The Temple Scroll Studies.* Ed. George J. Brooke. Sheffield: JSOT Press, 123–148.

Swanson, Dwight D. 1995. *The Temple Scroll and the Bible. The Methodology of 11QT.* Leiden: Brill.

Tov, Emanuel. 1982. "The 'Temple Scroll' and Old Testament Criticism." *Eretz Israel* 16:100–111 (Hebrew).
– 1993 (ed.). *The Dead Sea Scrolls on Microfiche. A Comprehensive Facsimile Edition of the Texts from the Judean Desert.* Leiden: Brill.

Ulrich, Eugene. 1994. *Qumran Cave 4: VII. Genesis to Numbers. 4QLev*^{b}. Discoveries in the Judaean Desert XII. Oxford: Clarendon.
– 1999. *The Dead Sea Scroll and the Origins of the Bible.* Grand Rapids, Michigan/Cambridge, U.K.: William B. Eerdmans. Leiden: Brill.
– 2000. *Qumran Cave 4 XI. Psalms to Chronicle: 4QEzra.* Discoveries in the Judaean Desert XVI. Oxford: Clarendon.

Vermes, Geza. 1977. *The Dead Sea Scrolls. Qumran in Perspective.* London: Collins.
– 1995. *The Dead Sea Scrolls in English.* Revised and Extended Fourth Edition. Sheffield: Sheffield Academic Press.

Wacholder, Ben Zion. 1991. "The Fragmentary Remains of 11QTorah (Temple Scroll), 11QTorah^{b} and 11QTorah^{c} Plus 4QparaTorah Integrated with 11QTorah^{a}." HUCA 62: 1–116.

Wacholder, Ben Zion, and Martin G. Abegg. 1995. *A Preliminary Edition of the Unpublished Dead Sea Scrolls. The Hebrew and Aramaic Texts from Cave Four. Fascicle Three.* Washington, D.C.: Biblical Archaeology Society.

White Crawford, Sidnie. 1994. *Qumran Cave 4: VIII. Parabiblical Texts, Part 1. 365a. 4QTemple?* Discoveries in the Judean Desert. XIII. Oxford: Clarendon.
– 2000. *The Temple Scroll and Related Texts.* Sheffield: Sheffield Academic Press.

Williams, Ronald J. 1967. *Hebrew Syntax. An Outline.* University of Toronto Press.

Wilson, Andrew M., and Lawrence Wills. 1982. "Literary Sources of the Temple Scroll." Harvard Theological Review 75:275–288.

Wise, Michael Owen. 1990. *A Critical Study of the Temple Scroll from Qumran Cave 11.* Chicago: The Oriental Institute.

Wise, Michael, Martin Abegg, Jr., and Edward Cook. 1996. *The Dead Sea Scrolls. A New Translation.* San Francisco: HarperCollins Publishers.

Würthwein, Ernst. 1979. *The Text of the Old Testament. An Introduction to the Biblia Hebraica.* Grand Rapids, Michigan: William B. Eerdmans.

Yadin, Yigael. 1977a. *The Temple Scroll. Volume Three. Plates and Text.* Jerusalem: Israel Exploration Society.

– 1977b. *The Temple Scroll. Volume Three. Supplementary Plates.*

– 1983. *The Temple Scroll. Volume One. Introduction.*

– 1983. *The Temple Scroll. Volume Two. Text and Commentary.*